You Can't Just Say It Louder!

Differentiated Strategies for Comprehending Nonfiction

Author

Debby Murphy

Foreword by Cindy Strickland

SHELL EDUCATION

T73682

You Can't Just Say It Louder!
Differentiated Strategies for Comprehending Nonfiction

Editor
Joan Irwin, M.A.

Editoral Assistant
Jamey Acosta

Editorial Director
Lori Kamola, M.S.Ed.

Editor-in-Chief
Sharon Coan, M.S.Ed.

Creative Director/Cover Design
Lee Aucoin

Print Production Manager
Don Tran

**Interior Layout Designer/
Print Production**
Robin Erickson

Publisher
Corinne Burton, M.A.Ed.

Shell Education

5301 Oceanus Drive
Huntington Beach, CA 92649-1030
http://www.shelleducation.com
ISBN 978-1-4258-0519-7
© *2010 Shell Education*
Made in U.S.A.

Table of Contents

Foreword

As a former French teacher, I suppose it is inevitable that I be "into" *vocabulaire*. And so, when I think about the highest quality differentiation, I focus on key words and phrases that anchor this model of instruction: **teacher-student relationships, high-quality curriculum, respectful tasks, interests, learning profile, readiness**, and **ongoing assessment**. In this book, teachers have the opportunity to explore and refine their practice with regard to each of these concepts.

One of my favorite quotes is found in *The Big Picture: Education Is Everyone's Business*: "You cannot have a relationship with or make things relevant for or expect rigor from a kid you don't know" (Littkey and Grabelle 2004, 39). To me, this sums up differentiated instruction quite nicely. The quote reminds us that everything we do in the classroom revolves around the **relationship** we establish with each of our students. To form and nurture a healthy relationship, we must know the student. This includes developing an awareness of current student interests, preferred ways of learning (learning profile), and levels of readiness so that we can make the **high-quality curriculum** we aim to teach as accessible, intriguing, and relevant as possible. Because student interests, learning profiles, and readiness levels will vary, we cannot teach the same thing to all students in the same way and at the same speed.

Once we recognize student differences, the logical next step is to plan for differentiation. When we plan differentiated activities, we have a responsibility to design **respectful tasks** for all students involved so that everyone feels that they are working toward the same or very similar goals and standards, and that one student's work is not a lot more engaging than another's. In the differentiated classroom, our goal is to have the students not really care which version of a task they are given or choose because the version they get seems to fit them so well! We work to design tasks that, from the student's perspective, are appropriately challenging, engaging, and relevant.

That said, the teacher in a differentiated classroom has a balancing act to perform. First, we want to honor current student **interests** because we know that will motivate students to learn, but at the same time, we have a responsibility to introduce students to material that may spark new areas of interest. How can a student know if he or she is interested in something to which they have never been exposed?

Second, we want to encourage students to work in ways that are comfortable for them in terms of style, intelligence preference, and other aspects of their **learning profile** because when they do so, they are at their most efficient in learning (Tomlinson 2001). Yet we must also ask students to work in ways that are not so comfortable for them, because the reality is they will not always have a choice in how they work!

Finally, we want to be aware of student **readiness** with respect to the curriculum so that we can support rigorous work that is an appropriate starting point for the student and that increases in difficulty in increments that are "just right" for that student. When students are asked to work on tasks that are too difficult, they become frustrated. When asked to work on tasks that are too easy, they may become apathetic. This means we must pay careful attention to evidence of a student's current and ever-changing levels of readiness via **ongoing assessment** practices. Student readiness varies from skill to skill and often from day to day. Teachers in a differentiated classroom commit to formative assessment practices, *including pre-assessment,* so that they can group and regroup students for instruction.

This book will prove useful to all teachers whose curriculum depends at least in part on students' reading readiness. Teachers who were not trained in specific reading strategies will find explicit strategies for understanding where a student's difficulties may originate and a host of specific ways to address these issues. Teachers who do have training and experience in reading strategies will find new ideas and new twists on old ideas that will spice up their current work with students. Students who struggle with reading need access to the content of the written material in order to accomplish the learning. This may mean that the teacher provides access to this content via varied levels of text, annotated or scaffolded readings, or books on tape. Yet the reading deficits of these students must not be ignored or students may never catch up to their peers.

Because this book breaks down the skill of reading nonfiction into its component parts, it allows us to better determine exactly where students are having difficulty and then focus small-group instruction on those areas. Equally important, identification and assessment of specific skill areas allows teachers to recognize when students have mastered key skills and are ready to move on to more advanced work, again with appropriate small-group instruction. All students deserve the opportunity to grow, even if they are already working at or beyond grade-level expectations.

The strategies in this book will be of great help to teachers who are looking for a wide variety of ways to instill and reinforce key skills in ways that will appeal to students with very different learning styles, intelligence preferences, and interests. For example, when introducing text (see chapter 4), some students will find the Sketch the Scene strategy intriguing, while others might prefer Act it Out or Tiny Text. By becoming familiar with a wide range of techniques leading to the same goals, teachers increase the likelihood of matching students to a strategy that works well for them.

As you read this book, pay attention to the ways in which the philosophy and practices put forth reinforce respectful **teacher-student relationships**, support the teaching of **high-quality curriculum,** encourage **ongoing assessment** practices, and offer an array of **respectful tasks** that appeal to students' varied **interests, learning profiles,** and **readiness levels**. By doing so, your classroom experiences and, by extension those of your students, will truly be *magnifique!*

Cindy Strickland
Author of *Exploring Differentiated Instruction*

Acknowledgements

On a personal note, my mother used to say, "I am a part of all that I have met." In later years, I discovered that she borrowed this thought from Alfred Lord Tennyson (1842), but nowhere is this quote truer than for educators. We all rest on each other's shoulders to achieve the greatest task imaginable—teaching the students of today and tomorrow.

I am a part of all that I have met for over thirty years in this field. The memories of my own excellent teachers who instilled my personal love of learning and a faith in a calling to teach arising from my childhood continue to inspire me. Every student that came through my classroom door walks with me. My own children, the ultimate teacher's gift and challenge, taught me far more than I did them. My husband, another life-long educator, is my loving, special someone who shares my ideals and passion for teaching. I have avidly read multitudinous professional education books through the years, and I have collaborated with incredible colleagues and observed marvelous teachers in action. As a practitioner and a constructivist, I have adapted, changed, added to, and modified many ideas through the years, as well as come up with quite a few of my own original "creations." To the best of my ability in *You Can't Just Say It Louder!* I have credited the experts and authors who influenced my thinking and have gone before me into the published world.

I want to thank Lori Kamola, Editorial Director for *Shell Education*, for asking me to finally write down all the thoughts and ideas from my many presentations to teachers. Without her encouragement, this book would still only be in my head. I graciously acknowledge Rachelle Cracchiolo, Corinne Burton, Sharon Coan, Deanne Mendoza, Trish Garza, and all the wonderful people of *Shell Education*. I truly appreciate and admire my incredible editor, Joan Irwin, and thank her for all her suggestions and support. This is a better book because of her. For anyone else who has crossed my path—family, friends, students, teachers, colleagues—I thank you for all you have given me through your presence and your words. I appreciate your soft voice and clear example. I am glad that I met you and that you are now a part of me.

Introduction

Consider this scenario: A teacher asks a small group of students gathered at a table for a reading lesson, "Boys and girls, what is the main idea of the text you just read?" Dead silence ensues. The teacher rephrases the question in an attempt to clarify, "What is this text mostly about?" The silence continues as students assume the positions of deep thinkers. Finally, the teacher repeats the question for the third time in a slower, more deliberate, and much louder voice, **"What is this text mostly about?"**

Likely, these students hear quite well, and hopefully, this frustrated teacher does not really believe that naming this comprehension strategy again in a louder voice will actually support students in their efforts to problem solve a reading challenge. Many teachers are at a loss about how to deal with students who, year after year, struggle with comprehension strategies, such as identifying the main idea, summarizing, and understanding the meaning of words in a text. These strategies are assessed yearly on state exams, and too many students continually demonstrate that they are not yet skilled in the use of these strategies. Teachers attempt to reteach these strategies, but often repeat the same instruction that they used before an assessment. This is ineffective because in order for students to become truly proficient with a strategy, you can't just say "it" *(the identical instruction)* louder. These students fail to apply the strategies of proficient readers, and the teacher must isolate and address the point at which the confusion exists in order for these students to progress. A different approach for specific, assisted instruction for learning powerful comprehension strategies can provide the key to helping students become successful processors of text. Teachers search for an approach by considering the language that carefully articulates how to use a comprehension strategy. They then search for a concrete demonstration of the steps necessary to apply that strategy.

I wrote this book as a practitioner. This is a how-to book—a book about how to talk to students about what good readers do to understand text, especially nonfiction text. After many years in the classroom and then many more as a literacy coach and consultant, I, too, recognize that all students do not get it the first time, or even the second or third time. We recognize that we need to differentiate instruction in order to successfully meet the needs of all the many levels of readers in our classrooms. Yet as teachers, we struggle to frame the language and processes that explicitly describe what readers do to effectively create meaning from text. We search to identify the necessary steps to support students in their attempts to build meaning from text so they can become independent readers who deeply understand and enjoy what they read. At the same time, we want to provide advanced readers with succinct, powerful skills to flexibly apply in any reading experience.

Therefore, as teachers considering where our students are as learners, we need to be able to deconstruct and clearly articulate the explicit actions and procedures of a reading strategy at the point of use. By doing so, we can ensure that all readers develop deliberate processes to comprehend text. We want to provide carefully crafted, appropriate lessons with focused practice that challenge every student at the cusp of his or her learning potential. This book gives teachers a springboard for powerful decision making as they contemplate sound learning theory and multiple examples of targeted lessons designed to teach students how to use reading comprehension strategies in authentic reading contexts.

Overview of Chapters

You Can't Just Say It Louder! Differentiated Strategies for Comprehending Nonfiction consists of 10 chapters and a conclusion. The first three chapters are foundational; they provide the contexts within which strategy instruction has developed. Chapters 4–10 describe the metacognitive language—words that describe the thinking behind a comprehension process—necessary to actually teach comprehension-strategy use. The text explains how teachers can develop the incremental procedural language to describe a strategy's use while modeling the critical attributes of that comprehension strategy during reading—this is referred to as "talk the walk." The clearly defined procedures outlined in each model lesson engage students in active "meaning making" during reading as they move from learning and practicing the processes of a reading comprehension strategy in an instructional context to using the strategy automatically and fluently while reading independently.

Chapter 1: Constructing a Personal Theory About Learning explores some of the findings of education and psychology experts that inform reading comprehension strategy instruction. Three aspects of research and practice are reviewed: the critical nature of the social context and language in learning, the gradual release of responsibility model, and the impact of applied brain-based research.

Chapter 2: Moving from Strategies to Skills: You Can't Just Say It Louder! describes the essence of comprehension instruction— moving students from strategy to skill. This chapter considers the impact of effective, ongoing assessment that drives the focus for strategy teaching and how students evolve from intentional problem-solvers during reading to automatic, fluent processors of text through a gradual release of responsibility.

Chapter 3: Differentiation Rules addresses the concept of differentiating instruction based on students' reading strengths and learning needs by selecting a "just right" text while choosing from a variety of instructional processes that best address the students' readiness levels, learning preferences, and interests.

Chapter 4: Preparing Students to Read with Meaning— Activating Student Thinking Through Text Introductions presents multiple before-reading strategies to set students up to read with maximum meaning.

Chapter 5: Understanding Word Meaning in Texts focuses on the use of context and word structure to enable students to deal with the ever-increasing demands of vocabulary in nonfiction texts that they will encounter as they advance through school.

Chapter 6: Using Text Features to Determine Importance, Develop Main Ideas, and Create Text Summaries describes the characteristics of texts that are designed to support readers before, during, and after reading. These features take many forms in nonfiction text—headings, subheadings, graphics, and various design elements—and students need to be familiar with all of these as they move toward independence in reading.

Chapter 7: Visualizing the Text examines several visualization strategies that guide students in forming mental images—strategies that draw upon various learning modalities.

Chapter 8: Asking Questions and Making Inferences centers on the generative aspects of reading. Engaged readers become involved with text as they question the author and distinguish between ideas that are stated explicitly and those that must be inferred by connecting personal knowledge with the author's details.

Chapter 9: Recognizing Nonfiction Text Structures and Author's Purpose focuses on the various ways in which authors structure their texts and how readers can recognize these structures. The chapter includes a number of graphic organizers—visual representations of the text that support students in making meaning.

Chapter 10: Monitoring Comprehension: The Ongoing Orchestration of Meaning draws together concepts about metacognitive awareness that are presented in previous chapters.

STAR (Strategic Thinker and Reader) Model Lessons

STAR Model Lessons, built on the gradual release of responsibility model described in Chapter 1, are used in Chapters 5–10 to demonstrate the selected reading strategies. The lessons feature examples of teacher-student conversations that demonstrate how to use a focused "thinking plan" for processing text while employing such strategies as understanding word meaning, determining importance and main ideas, asking questions, making inferences, and visualizing. The STAR Model Lessons and accompanying STAR Points charts in each chapter articulate the thinking and procedures that support each strategy. Nonfiction texts used to model each strategy in the STAR lessons include a range of topics and reading levels from emergent through sixth grade. The reading levels are stated for each sample of nonfiction text. A listing of these materials is given in Instructional Resources at the end of the book.

I hope you will spend time examining and reflecting on the *STAR Model Lessons*—the modeled strategy use, the teacher-student discussions about the text, and the stated, explicit steps of the reading comprehension strategy instruction. The lessons demonstrate the careful progression of strategy implementation, and the possible student comments illustrate the application of the strategy in a real-life classroom context. In these lessons, you will find effective processes for teaching reading strategies that involve these deliberate instructional conversations and models. These models are designed to engage students in authentic, motivating interactions with text as they try out purposeful moves to truly comprehend their reading. Each lesson provides an excellent alternative to just saying "it" louder.

Features of this Book

As I wrote this book, I kept in mind that teachers are busy and their time is valuable—something I experienced daily in my own classroom. As you read this book, you will encounter features that invite you to take just a few minutes to reflect on the content before implementing it. Some suggestions may lead you into conversations with your colleagues.

- Each chapter opens with a quotation and "Considerations from Research." These features are presented to prompt explorations of your thought related to strategy instruction and emphasize that the instructional practices described in this book are evidence based.

- Additional quotations are interspersed throughout the chapters in order to provide succinct commentaries relevant to the ideas in the chapter and provide additional opportunities for you to reflect on your teaching practices.

- "Pause and Ponder" segments, which can be found within and at the end of each chapter, are just what the title states—places where you can take a breather and think about yourself as a teacher and a reader as well as some of the experiences that occur in your classroom.
- "Differentiation Notes" offer suggestions for adapting the strategy instruction for English language learners (ELLs), struggling students, and students who are able readers.

Chapter 1

Constructing a Personal Theory About Learning

> *"A personal vision for why one is teaching is a crucial part of expertise. Teachers with a vision possess both a thematic framework for their constructivist instruction and the passion that sustains them through the difficulties of daily teaching"* *(Duffy 2002, 229).*

Considerations from Research

- Effective teachers learn from teaching. They understand how to systematically organize useful learning activities and adapt instruction to the diverse needs and interests of their students.
- Improving classroom instruction is an important factor in improving student learning.
- Telling is not teaching.
- The power of the teacher's language in the classroom cannot be underestimated. Skillful language enhances students' learning, sustains their motivation, expands their interests, builds their confidence and self-awareness, and strengthens teacher-student and student-student rapport.

What is your personal vision for teaching? How does one develop a personal vision for teaching? More specifically, how important is a personal vision for teaching, and how does that vision affect what you do as you teach reading comprehension?

According to Duffy (2002), a personal vision drives the evolution of teaching expertise and fuels enough passion for teachers to continue to face sometimes seemingly impossible odds to connect with students and guide their successful acquisition of the strategies they need to deeply comprehend text. A powerful personal theory of learning sustains teachers as they seek to construct the best instructional context for their students. This theory guides teachers as they glean educational excellence through best practices set forth by those who have led the way with significant, sustainable research about learning and what works in reading instruction. A personal theory for how students learn to process text and internalize comprehension strategies provides a compass for teachers when making critical decisions as they create an effective community of learners, design reading instruction based on assessment of students' strengths and needs, and advocate for the students in their classrooms.

In this chapter, I present a brief overview of three significant contributions from experts in education and psychology whose work has influenced my personal theory and vision for framing effective, powerful instruction for students' success in reading comprehension. These contributions include:

- the critical role of language in teaching for comprehension
- the gradual release of responsibility model
- the significance of rich input in brain-compatible reading instruction

✦ Pause and Ponder ✦

What forms the foundation of your personal learning theory or vision for teaching? What are your beliefs about how students learn to comprehend text? What beliefs guide your teaching decisions?

Write a bulleted list of tenets that drive your reading instruction, especially in the area of comprehension. Consider the experts whose voices and ideas have become a part of who you are today as a teacher. What impact have they had on your evolving understanding of best practices in reading instruction?

When you have finished reading this chapter, return to your list of tenets. How do your tenets compare to those described in the chapter? In what ways have the ideas in the chapter affected your learning theory? ✎

The Critical Role of Language in Teaching for Comprehension

An essential premise of this book is that engaging, focused dialogue between the teacher and students is the bedrock for the mental development necessary for students to acquire strategies to effectively comprehend text. Targeted language allows teachers to demonstrate the ideas and procedures behind such cognitive processes as summarizing the important ideas of a text or creating an inference after reading. Carefully designed "teacher talk" and modeling assist students by allowing them to "see into" the mind of a reader. Intentional interactions and conversations with someone more experienced in using a reading strategy support students in creating meaning and developing a system for categorizing new learning or input. When the interactions between the students and the "expert" are active, stimulating, and engaging, the students build more complex systems for categorizing new information and increase their capacity to use the strategy in new contexts (Lyons 2003).

Vygotsky's insights on the personal construction of meaning through social interactions about cognition began to spread in the 1960s with the translation

> "A by-product of a teacher's skillful use of language is that students often begin using language more skillfully themselves. … Learning to use teacher language to its full potential means becoming aware of our habitual ways of speaking and the messages, positive or negative, that these may be sending to our students" (Denton 2007, 10).

of his 1934 work *Thought and Language*. Over the years, many researchers, psychologists, and educators have explored and expanded upon Vygotsky's theories about learning (Vygotsky 1962; Tharp and Gallimore 1988; Bodrova and Leong 1996; Lyons 2003). The next section provides a brief overview of some of this work and its implications for developing one's own personal theory or vision for teaching reading comprehension.

The social and cultural context for learners is a key component of the development of cognitive processing (Vygotsky 1962). Purposeful conversations with a student about new learning change over time as the student takes on more responsibility for strategic cognition. Social language moves to shared language through an inter-cognitive exchange that engages the learner in authentic talk with a more knowledgeable "other" about the learning objective (Lyons 2003). Eventually, the learner develops an inner control of the new learning, and a personal, unseen self-talk to process that learning in context develops and becomes both flexible and automatic.

The Zone of Proximal Development

Vygotsky best describes this learning development through his zone of proximal development (ZPD) concept. The zone represents a continuum of potential strategies or behaviors that are close to developing or emerging in the learner in the near future (proximal) with purposeful assistance and social interactions with one more capable than the learner. The ZPD is fluid, cyclic, and ever-changing as a student moves from what he or she can do with assistance to independent action and back to taking on new learning with assistance.

The ZPD represents the distance between what a student can do independently through personal processing and problem solving and what the student can achieve through collaboration with and assistance from a more knowledgeable adult or peer. Tharp and Gallimore (1988, 33–39) build upon Vygotsky's theories by articulating four distinct phases or stages of the zone of proximal development. These phases can be considered in the context of teaching a reading comprehension strategy.

In the first phase of the ZPD, a teacher/coach provides assistance to the student through specific cognitive language and demonstration of what the reading comprehension strategy is, how it looks and sounds when a reader uses it, and where and why to use it. During this phase, the teacher/coach attempts to "scaffold" the student into an understanding of the strategy and its application by making the role of the learner easier. This is done by providing assistance that gradually decreases as the learner takes on more responsibility for the strategy (Wood, Bruner, and Ross 1976). The expert models the strategy and explicitly explains the procedures of cognition through think alouds. The student begins to imitate the teacher/coach and apply the new strategy with assistance. In this phase, the expert engages the learner in meaningful dialogue and experiences with the strategy by helping the learner organize the cognitive structures or procedures for strategy use; asking questions that help the student rephrase the learning, make connections, and take action; offering specific feedback; and providing instruction through interactive use of the strategy (Pearson and Gallagher 1983; Tharp and Gallimore 1988; Bodrova and Leong 1996).

During the second phase of the ZPD, the control for the strategy's application during reading shifts to the student. The student starts to internalize the socially-constructed language of the strategy (developed in phase one with the support of the teacher/coach) to rehearse the strategy. The student employs "self-talk" to plan out and make purposeful moves to problem solve reading challenges. The teacher/coach supports the student's self-assistance by monitoring his or her thinking "moves" and providing targeted feedback. The expert continues to prompt or redirect the student as necessary to prevent the student from habituating errors in processing the strategy or the procedures that define its effective use.

Read the transcript that follows about a student named David. David's self-talk illustrates how he attempts to solve the problem he encountered while reading. His conversation with his reading teacher as he addresses this personal challenge exemplifies the evolution from phase one to phase two of the ZPD. David's comments also reveal how a student picks up on and uses the teacher's "strategy talk."

Example of Student Strategy Use

David: Hmmm, this is a tricky part. Now, don't help me.

Teacher: I won't. *(Teacher does not provide assistance.)*

David: *(Returns to his "tricky part" in the text and begins asking himself questions.)*

What can I do to help myself? This part does not make sense to me.

Let me see.

Does the picture help me? *(Carefully examines the picture.)*

If I reread the text, maybe it will make more sense. *(Rereads the problematic text section.)*

Now, can I make a movie in my mind of what I just read? *(Looks off and appears to be thinking.)*

Oh, I get it. I know what this part means now.

Here, let me tell you what I think. *(Tells teacher what he thinks the tricky part means.)*

Teacher: I saw you do several things to help yourself as you thought about the tricky part. *(Renames David's monitoring moves.)*

How did these strategies help you understand what you read?

David's use of self-talk as he searches and checks the text to re-establish meaning indicates that he is in the second phase of the ZPD. His teacher acknowledges his intention to help himself and gives him the opportunity to reflect on the effective moves he applied and the sources of information that he used to make sense of the text.

During phase two, students take on increasing control of their own learning and performance of the strategy. Processing of the strategy begins to move underground, becoming unseen as self-directed speech evolves into a purposeful internal conversation. The teacher in this example expects David to eventually shift from his audible, self-directed speech to private speech. The teacher also recognizes that more processing will occur in David's head as he becomes increasingly adept at using known strategies to maintain meaning as he reads. When a student's reading behaviors—searching, checking, monitoring, and self-correcting—become quick, effective, and covert, the student moves into phase three of the ZPD, demonstrating signs of inner control and independent strategy use (Clay 1991).

In the third phase of the ZPD, the learner self-regulates the strategy, maintaining control of and responsibility for the task. The student appears to have internalized the strategy and can use it with increasing flexibility and fluency. Private speech becomes abbreviated and efficient; it is literally transformed in the student's mind, becoming shortened and automatic as the student uses the strategy to process the text. Tharp and Gallimore (1988, 35) refer to this automatization of the strategy as "fossilized" performance, in which the student displays independence and control with the strategy. In this phase of the ZPD, the language and procedures of the strategy are in the head of the learner, who now "owns" the strategy. The student employs internal, personal cognition to plan and process learning.

A final phase of the ZPD occurs when a strategy becomes "de-automatized" through the introduction, purposefully or incidentally, of a more complex application of the strategy. This forces the student to revert to an earlier phase of the ZPD to solve the problem. The student may return to self-talk to work through the processing challenge or may require the direct assistance of the teacher to hone the strategy. The new task may add a different level of complexity to the student's cognitive and procedural patterns for the strategy, which is now being applied in a new context. Appropriately, the teacher adjusts the scaffold, providing as minimal support as possible to help the student deal with the challenge.

To foster new learning and the development of advanced reading strategies, the teacher creates intentional instructional conditions that continually move the student recursively through the ZPD in order to introduce, build, and solidify increasingly sophisticated neural networks to support reading comprehension. For example, the teacher incorporates a different level of complexity in strategy acquisition into instruction so that the student returns to a lower stage of the ZPD to gain needed assistance with the new dimensions of that strategy. When a student has inner control over a specific reading comprehension strategy but encounters a more difficult text or a less familiar genre of text (such as shifting from fiction to nonfiction), the student often returns to auditory self-talk to work through the challenge or seeks scaffolding assistance from an expert. Whenever the student encounters new concepts or the need for a deeper understanding and application of a reading comprehension strategy, the student recycles through the phases of the ZPD to build ever-increasing reservoirs of procedural processes and cognitive networks.

✦ *Pause and Ponder* ✦

Take a moment to sum up in your own words the zone of proximal development and how students move through the phases to gain independent, flexible, and automatic use of a reading comprehension strategy.

Now select a comprehension strategy that you are considering as an instructional reading target for a small group of students. Where are these students in relation to "owning" this strategy, or consistently and competently using it in their reading? What aspects of this strategy do these students currently control? Are all of the students in the group in the same phase of the ZPD? What scaffolds will you need to provide to help students move to the next phase of the ZPD? ✦

The Gradual Release of Responsibility Model

Focused, purposeful performance assistance supports students throughout the early phases of the ZPD through the use of thoughtful think alouds and explicit modeling, authentic conversations about the new learning, carefully considered questioning and teaching moves, powerful prompts and cues, and specific feedback. As the students try out the critical attributes of a reading strategy, they develop the self-talk and procedural processing that will eventually enable them to automatize and fossilize that strategy as they read. The intensity of support and assistance needed in the first phases of the ZPD varies from student to student. Teacher observation and informal assessment of where the students are in relationship to owning the reading comprehension strategy determine how the teacher structures lessons. The teacher moves from modeled demonstration of the strategy to shared, interactive practice to guided practice to independent practice and flexibility with the use of the strategy (Holdaway 1979; Pearson and Gallagher 1983; Tharp and Gallimore 1988). This instructional context moves students from the greatest level of teacher support to a minimal level of support as students take on an inner control of the strategy.

The gradual release of responsibility model (Pearson and Gallagher 1983) is a carefully structured instructional plan based on the concepts and stages of the ZPD. In this lesson design model, students develop critical-thinking and problem-solving strategies through initial support from the demonstration of strategic thinking and processing by the teacher.

The students then take on those strategic actions through a gradual release of responsibility from the teacher to the students. The teacher gradually decreases scaffolding support until the students independently incorporate the new patterns for learning into their own meaning-making processes. Four specific levels of teacher support represent this release of responsibility to the students: teacher control of the strategy through modeling and purposeful student-teacher conversations; shared, interactive engagement between the teacher and students through a collaborative use of the strategy; guided practice of the strategy in which the students take control of the strategy and the teacher provides prompts, clarification, feedback, and support as needed; and finally, independent use of the strategy by the students (Pearson and Fielding 1991; Wilhelm 2001; Duke and Pearson 2002). The design of the STAR (Strategic Thinker and Reader) Model Lessons for reading comprehension instruction in this book reflects this gradual release of responsibility from the teacher to the student. Although the levels of assistance within the lesson structure are described in a linear fashion, students often move recursively through the lesson with the teacher responding to their needs. The teacher chooses to return to a more supportive level in the model when the students experience confusion or need brief, additional scaffolding in order to continue to move toward independent processing of a reading comprehension strategy. Figure 1.1 below illustrates the recursive nature of activities in this instructional model.

Figure 1.1 The Gradual Release of Responsibility Model

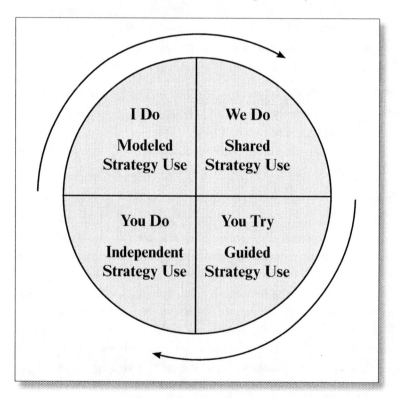

Phases of the Gradual Release of Responsibility Model

I Do—Modeled Strategy Use

At this level of instruction, the teacher introduces the strategy focus for the lesson and thinks aloud about the strategy:

- what it is
- why it is used
- how and when to use it

The teacher makes the implicit explicit by carefully breaking down and articulating the critical attributes of the strategy and mental pattern necessary to incorporate that strategy into an authentic meaning-making context (Pearson and Gallagher 1983; Jensen 2000). The teacher uses the metacognitive language of a reading expert, explaining short, comprehensible parts of the strategy while modeling how readers process text using this strategy. During the I Do phase, the teacher actively engages students in conversations about the work the strategy requires, providing concrete examples of the strategy's application and even visual models of the patterns of thinking employed by a reader when using the strategy.

We Do—Shared Strategy Use

In this part of the lesson, the teacher still controls the strategy use but invites the students to enter the learning, sharing the actions of a reader in utilizing the comprehension strategy to process text. Students sample the language and actions of a strategic reader engaged with text as the teacher gradually passes increasing control of the strategy to the students. The actions of the students occur in a risk-free context, allowing them to come in and out of the collaborative experience as they begin to understand the procedural processes of the strategy. The teacher discusses the critical attributes of the strategy; prompts students to problem solve through short, purposeful examples and shared practice of the strategy; asks questions to help students reflect on the hows and whys of the strategy's application; and reframes or redirects students' thinking when necessary. The teacher scaffolds and adjusts instruction through pacing, the increments of practice, the size of the text chunks, the reading level of the text, and the specificity of the language. The We Do portion of the lesson design is exactly that—a social experience shared between the expert and the novice during interactive engagement with targeted reading work.

You Try—Guided Strategy Use

Now the level of teacher talk fades as the responsibility of the strategy is handed over to the students. At this phase of the lesson, students are working individually with the strategy; however, the teacher still maintains an active role through a guided-practice context. As they define the strategy for themselves, the students control the reading of the text through self-talk and the targeted actions of strategic, active problem solvers. The teacher is right there to drop in on readers and monitor, prompt and cue, clarify, redirect student intentions or reteach, and provide specific feedback for students. The teacher supports students' reflection on the reading by asking such questions as:

- What are you thinking right here?
- How did you solve this tricky part?
- When you did this (name action/behavior), what did you discover?
- How did doing this (name action/behavior) help you as a reader?
- What would happen if you considered this (name action/ behavior)?

During this guided portion of the lesson, the teacher expects to see students making approximations and errors as they try out the strategy. The teacher specifically praises the students' attempts to problem solve and names what the students are doing as readers.

When necessary, the teacher intervenes to prevent the students from going too far astray and habituating procedural-processing (strategy) errors as they read. The teacher's interventions during guided practice reinforce the behaviors of effective readers: they self-monitor meaning and try different "fix-up" strategies to reestablish understanding as they work through the text. Although the students focus on the featured strategy during the guided practice, the teacher recognizes or prompts the orchestration and integration of students' known comprehension-monitoring strategies as they read.

You Do—Independent Strategy Use

During guided practice, the teacher uses observation and informal assessment to determine whether the students are ready to take on a reading comprehension strategy with minimal support. This means the students are ready to move into purposeful independent practice of the strategy. At this point, the students develop an inner control of the strategy's language and procedural processing, and the students' use of the strategy as they read becomes more fluid and automatic. The teacher is still available to monitor and assist when necessary, but the teacher's role changes significantly from side-by-side guidance to affirming and celebrating students' efforts. The goal for the You Do portion of the gradual release of responsibility model is to provide the students with real opportunities to practice the reading comprehension strategy with text at their instructional or independent level. The students develop flexibility and automaticity with the strategy through this independent practice, signaling the evolution of the strategy to a skill. (See Chapter 2 for more details about the development of a skill.) In the classroom, independent practice takes place in a variety of settings, including self-selected reading, reading in the content areas, literacy centers/workstations, and other comparable literacy engagements. Students become vital members of a reading community as they have conversations about their reading using the strategic language of *comprehenders* of text.

↬ *Pause and Ponder* ↫

Design an introduction to a reading comprehension strategy for students using the first step of the gradual release of responsibility model presented on p. 29—I Do. Select an instructional text that you can use to illustrate the strategy for students.

Consider how you will model the use of your strategy. What specific language will you use to describe the procedures of the strategy? How will you scaffold the students into the strategy through a think aloud and demonstration that will prepare them to practice the strategy in a shared, interactive context? ∾

The Importance of Rich Input in Brain-Compatible Instruction

Through the lens of applied-brain research, Jensen (2000) identifies certain stages of learning that set up the learner to develop powerful neural networks through creating, developing, and strengthening connections in the brain. Jensen's approach consists of five stages:

- Preparation
- Acquisition
- Elaboration
- Memory formation
- Functional integration stage

In the preparation stage, the teacher creates a meaningful context for the students' learning by activating their prior knowledge or building their background knowledge in order to support the students' ability to process the new information. The acquisition stage actively engages the students in a variety of experiences through rich sensory input to help them make powerful connections between what they know and the new information. Learning by doing solidifies the acquisition of new procedural processes and the development of cognitive patterns. The elaboration stage continues to place the students in authentic contexts to actively experiment with and practice a strategy. Specific teacher-peer feedback helps students adjust their learning, strengthen their motivation, and deepen their neural connections. In the final two stages—memory formation and functional integration—the students' learning continues to be solidified and reinforced so they can expand upon and flexibly apply the strategy (Jensen 2000, 31–38).

Aligning Jensen's stages of learning with the gradual release of responsibility model demonstrates the correlation between understanding how the brain incorporates new learning and how instruction can be structured to support the internalization of that learning. For example, Jensen's preparation and acquisition stages represent the powerful input provided by the teacher in the I Do and We Do phases of the gradual release of responsibility model. The link between the elaboration stage and the You Try phase of the gradual release model is evident as students engage in guided practice of the new strategy, receiving specific feedback to help them effectively hone the reading strategy, and adjust their thinking to develop essential meaning-making processes.

The impact of rich, active engagement in motivating learners and activating cognitive connections to learning is another significant correlation between Jensen's stages and the gradual release of responsibility model. When students engage in sensory-rich interactions with the teacher, other students, the content/text, and the reading comprehension strategy, they construct more complex and authentic connections between what they already know and the new learning (Lyons 2003).

During the We Do phase of scaffolded reading instruction, lively discussions and targeted conversations about the act of thinking strategically increase students' learning potential. Becoming active participants in purposeful dialogue helps students take control of their learning by encouraging them to express that learning in their own words. Eventually students translate their socially-constructed language into an internal, personal conversation about their reading cognition (Tharp and Gallimore 1988). Because up to 90 percent of students' sensory input comes from visual sources (Jensen and

Johnson 1994), the addition of concrete visual images—photographs, illustrations, sketches, diagrams, graphic organizers, STAR Points strategy charts—to discussions about the critical attributes and procedural processes of a reading strategy further strengthens the students' neural connections. Graphic organizers in particular blend together the learners' verbal input and a visual model of the connections and patterns of students' thinking.

Adding a variety of multisensory experiences and considering students' learning modalities during lesson design improves students' recall, strengthens neural pathways, and increases the students' energy levels for learning (Lyons 2003; Jensen 2000). In addition, providing novelty and rich input before and during new learning enhances students' attention and creates relevance (Jensen 2000).

Gardner (1983) identifies multiple student intelligences for teachers to target in their instruction. Understanding these learning attributes is helpful to teachers as they create rich learning environments that address a variety of sensory-input venues that different students employ to learn and process information. According to Gardner, these intelligences include:

- verbal/linguistic (thinking through words)
- logical/mathematical (thinking through reasoning)
- visual/spatial (thinking through pictures and images)
- bodily/kinesthetic (thinking by using the body and movement)
- rhythmic/musical (thinking through melodies and rhythm)
- naturalist (thinking through classifying)
- interpersonal (thinking by talking ideas through with others)
- intrapersonal (thinking within the self)

Gardner believes that people possess all of the intelligences, with different intelligences more developed in certain individuals than others. When considering Gardner's theory of multiple intelligences, teachers incorporate opportunities for students to draw upon their preferred intelligences to effectively develop, practice, and retain new information and thereby cement neural connections.

Summary

The idea "I am a part of all that I have met" (Tennyson 1842), which I shared in the acknowledgements, implies the impact of various influences from theory and research that have helped me build my vision of teaching. In my instructional practice, I strive to incorporate the three tenets that characterize the nature of effective reading comprehension instruction: the critical role of language in teaching for comprehension, the gradual release of responsibility model, and the significance of rich input in brain-compatible instruction. These concepts form the framework of my personal vision for teaching and learning and serve as the foundation for the practices I describe in this book.

The contributions of many other experts add to an ever-evolving personal framework for best practices in instruction. Day-to-day experiences in real teaching with real students strongly influence teachers' personal theories about learning and effective reading instruction. Educators continue to read and learn, apply and study, and adjust and strengthen their personal theories in order to maximize true learning success for their students. Teachers are a part of all that they meet and continue to encounter, so a personal theory for learning is never static or complete.

✦ *Pause and Ponder* ✦

When presented with new information and concepts, what type of input best helps you learn and retain that learning? How do you plan for rich, sensory input before and during your reading comprehension instruction? How does that input influence your students' engagement, learning, and retention of new concepts and processes? ✖

Chapter 2

Moving from Strategies to Skills: You Can't Just Say It Louder!

"Strategies have wrongly become synonymous with comprehension, when, at best, they are a tool for facilitating and extending comprehension. Students are spending massive amounts of time learning and practicing these strategies, often without knowing how to apply them and not understanding how they fit into the big picture of reading ... remember when we read, we use all these strategies at the same time and that our comprehension process is largely unconscious" (Routman 2003, 119).

Considerations from Research

- A strategic approach to teaching reading comprehension involves providing specific comprehension lessons to build students' knowledge and use of strategies.

- The ultimate goal of reading instruction is to enable students to become self-sufficient in using strategies—reading for enjoyment and reading to build knowledge.

- Becoming skilled in comprehending a variety of texts for a variety of purposes is a long-term developmental process.

- Strategy instruction cannot be isolated from extensive reading experiences and must provide students with opportunities to share those experiences through talking and writing.

How to make visible the unseen processes of creating meaning from text is the greatest challenge of teaching strategies for reading comprehension. Personal theories on how real learning evolves drive teachers' stance on instruction and thoughtful interactions with their students. In the previous chapter, three tenets were described for powerful reading comprehension instruction: the critical role of language in teaching for comprehension, the gradual release of responsibility model, and the significance of rich input in brain-compatible reading instruction. In this chapter, I examine the critical nature of the specific language used to introduce and describe a reading comprehension strategy. I also explore how the responsibility for taking on that strategy gradually shifts from the teacher to the student, eventually resulting in the strategy becoming a fluent, automatic skill for the reader.

Strategies occur simultaneously as skilled readers process text and as students demonstrate increasing reading comprehension expertise through multiple engagements with a wide genre of texts, including all forms of nonfiction. Often, when students are not given sufficient time before applying the strategy to the text, they can only partially explain the strategy, and they do not demonstrate an active application of the strategy as they read. These students have not been given the necessary assistance through guided practice and specific feedback to integrate the new strategy into their procedural processes for reading. They also have not been given enough time to integrate the strategy into their repertoire of intentional meaning-making moves to create and maintain their comprehension.

Procedural knowledge develops as students learn new steps for comprehending text and take on the essential elements of a reading strategy. With time and targeted practice, the students modify and change their strategic moves while constantly monitoring their reading by asking themselves, "Does this make sense?" As readers take on new learning, they begin to integrate all their reading comprehension strategies and use them less consciously and with increasingly automatic control. With continued practice, the students become fluent in the meaning-making processes of a skilled reader (Marzano 2007).

Reread the quote from Regie Routman provided at the beginning of the chapter. Identify four or five words or short phrases that catch your attention. What do you think Routman wants a teacher to understand about reading comprehension strategy instruction? What does she tell us about a skilled reader?

Do you think that strategy instruction has the potential to be overemphasized? What do you think are the advantages of emphasis on strategy instruction? Talk with your colleagues about their views on strategy instruction in reading and other curriculum areas.

What do you think is the difference between a *strategy* and a *skill?* How important do you think it is for teachers to have clear definitions for these terms? ✧

Teaching for a Strategy

Through effective assessment and observation of students as they read and respond to text, teachers seek to understand where students are as learners and what they can do unassisted as *comprehenders* of text. Based on that assessment and observation, the teacher targets a comprehension strategy focus and selects a text to use to illustrate the strategy in action for the students. The teacher recognizes that there is little value in practicing a comprehension strategy without teaching what the strategy is and how to apply it in an authentic reading context. Through a gradual release of responsibility model, the teacher engages students in a close examination of the strategy and the cognitive processes that shape its application in reading.

At the outset, the teacher articulates the essential attributes of the strategy:

- what it is
- how it looks when a reader uses it
- when to use it
- the specific steps needed to use it

As experienced readers, teachers often struggle to break down a strategy, which for them is an automatic skill, into the essential attributes that will illustrate the strategy's procedural process for novice readers. Teachers reflect on the metacognition—thinking about thinking (Flavell 1977)—that defines the comprehension strategy and how to apply it during reading. Pressley (2002b) describes this process of describing the intentions and actions of the reader during strategy use as *transactional strategies instruction*. This instruction focuses on the actions and reactions of the students, the teacher, and their peers as they work together to employ the comprehension strategy and build a shared interpretation of the execution of the strategy.

Reading comprehension strategy instruction begins with the demonstration phase of I Do, a structured plan to actively engage students in the language and processes of the strategy. During this stage, conversational talk fosters social interactions that help students hear and adopt the specific language that describes the strategy's components. These activities help students create a conceptual framework for use of the strategy. By breaking the strategy down into small, manageable chunks, the teacher presents a concrete model of what the students will be doing as strategic readers. The teacher intentionally employs the language of the strategy throughout the model portion of the lesson, planting the words of the strategy procedures through teacher-student discussion. The STAR Model Lessons in the following chapters provide a guide for teachers to engage students through demonstrations of a variety of reading comprehension strategies. These instructional practices include using think alouds with specific step-by-step, metacognitive language that describes the procedural processes of the strategies in action.

"Reading strategies are deliberate, goal-directed attempts to control and modify the reader's efforts to decode text, understand words, and construct meanings of texts" (Afflerbach, Pearson, and Paris 2008, 368).

Next, the students move into interactive practice (We Do) to "try on" the strategy, sharing the language and modeled procedures of the strategy along with the teacher and other students. At this juncture, *if the students experience confusion with the strategy and the critical processing increments, teachers cannot simply say "it," meaning the previous instruction, louder.* Teachers must address the challenges students encounter with the strategy and provide a scaffold to assist them in reestablishing understanding. This scaffold often requires teachers to return to the initial level of assistance (I Do) and pursue another way to approach the learning. This can be accomplished in many ways, such as by breaking down the strategy into even smaller parts or re-engaging students through more descriptive metacognitive language and providing additional modeled examples. Ongoing assessment of the students' processing and mediation of the level of assistance that they need is key.

Teachers maintain vigilance throughout the You Try guided level of the gradual release of responsibility model, intervening when readers encounter difficulties by thinking aloud with students and providing feedback through prompts, cues, and questions (Duffy and Roehler 1989). During this period, in order to clarify students' confusion and prevent the habituation of errors, teachers may need to further explore how to structure or simplify the language of the strategy's use to support particular students. Guided practice builds a real understanding of the strategy and sets students up to internalize that strategy and use it as they read; guided practice is not just a mechanical practice of the steps of a strategy (Marzano 2007). Following each guided-practice session, the teacher and students discuss their reading and continue to clarify and refine the strategy and how to use it to comprehend text.

The I Do, We Do, and You Try phases of the gradual release model provide the context for students to learn a reading comprehension strategy and enact a plan for using that strategy at a point of difficulty during reading. A strategy represents a reader's deliberate attempts to problem-solve a tricky part for meaning. Strategic readers begin with a specific intention, using their repertoire of known strategic moves to apply a plan of action to successfully negotiate text (Afflerbach,

Pearson, and Paris 2008). Although not all of the attempts students make are successful, the extent of their control of the strategy is demonstrated in the ways they monitor, revise, or adjust their responses when confusions persist.

Teachers support this evolution of strategy development, especially during guided practice by providing students with an authentic context to practice being strategic readers. Teachers pause frequently to debrief with the students about what they are doing, step-by-step, and to discuss the effectiveness of their intentions to process the meaning of the text (Duke and Pearson 2002). With time, the responsibility of owning a reading comprehension strategy is passed to the students to apply outside of guided instruction to a variety of independent reading experiences.

✦ *Pause and Ponder* ✦

Considering the ideas presented in the preceding section about strategy instruction, analyze a reading comprehension lesson from your current reading program that you plan on using with one group of students.

Does the selected lesson set forth a clear learning objective or focus for developing and practicing the reading comprehension strategy? What kind of instructional language and teacher modeling is incorporated into the lesson? How is the lesson structured to provide scaffolded assistance as students "try on" the strategy? Does this lesson provide ample shared-and guided-practice opportunities for students to develop and apply specific procedural processes as they read? ✖

Moving from a Strategy to a Skill

As students' self-talk about the procedural processes of the strategy evolves into private speech and their reading work appears to happen in their heads, students seem to control the strategy with less effort and with increasing flexibility. Thus, students progress into the You Do phase of the gradual release of responsibility model. At this level, with frequent independent practice of the strategy to increase automaticity and flexibility, the reading comprehension strategy evolves into a reading comprehension skill. The reader's inner control of the strategy becomes effective and fluent, and the reader uses the strategy, now a new skill, without any apparent conscious awareness. The reader incorporates the strategy into a neural network of skills for comprehending text in an efficient, orchestrated manner (Afflerbach, Pearson, and Paris 2008; Routman 2003).

"Reading skills are automatic actions that result in decoding and comprehension with speed, efficiency, and fluency and usually occur without awareness of the components or control involved" (Afflerbach, Pearson, and Paris 2008, 368).

Summary

The teacher continues to use targeted assessment and informal observation, especially during the We Do and You Try phases of instruction, to note the deliberate attempts of students to process the meaning of text (strategies) and their use of known skills to monitor and maintain comprehension. The teacher stays alert to where the students are as readers and makes decisions about which strategies to introduce next or how to extend students' competency with a known strategy. Additionally, the teacher notes times when skilled readers revert back to the strategic level of problem solving—for example, when students attempt a more difficult level or a text with more complex concepts. The teacher provides as minimal assistance as necessary to scaffold the challenges for the readers so they take on new problem-solving strategies that will, in turn, develop into new or more sophisticated skills (Afflerbach, Pearson, and Paris 2008). By reframing the language of learning and having more than one way to describe the procedural processes of a reading comprehension strategy, teachers are not just saying "it" louder, but rather tailoring powerful instruction to support their many diverse learners as they build reading strategies into reading skills.

✦ *Pause and Ponder* ✦

Select a reading comprehension strategy, such as determining word meaning during reading. Choose a few students in your classroom. Are these students controlling the strategy of determining word meaning when reading at an independent text level (95 percent accuracy or above)?

To what extent do these students exhibit characteristics of an evolving skilled reader who effectively determines the meaning of words "on the run" as he or she reads? How well can students explain how they deal with challenges they encounter as they read?

- These students seem to have a repertoire of choices for problem solving a tricky word, such as looking for a meaningful part or chunk that they know, thinking about another time they have seen the word or a word like it, or searching the text for contextual clues to the word's meaning.

- The students apply these monitoring strategies quickly and almost seamlessly as they check any cue sources from the text, determine a probable meaning for a word, and move on. This processing of word meaning appears to happen in their heads almost automatically, and they negotiate the text as they read in a fluent manner with good understanding.

In the initial "Pause and Ponder" of this chapter, I invited you to define the terms *strategy* and *skill*. Compare your definitions with those provided in the quotations presented in the sidebars (p. 40 and p. 43). In what ways do you think distinguishing between a *strategy* and a *skill* informs your teaching of reading comprehension strategies? ✦

Chapter 3

Differentiation Rules

"Differentiation is making sure that the right students get the right learning tasks at the right time. Once you have a sense of what each student holds as 'given' or 'known' and what he or she needs in order to learn, differentiation is no longer an option; it is an obvious response" (Earl 2003, 86–87).

Considerations from Research

- The capacity of individuals to succeed in school is affected by many factors, including readiness for learning, interests, motivation, learning styles, school experiences, personal experiences, and social/cultural expectations.
- Differentiation demands vigilance on the part of the teacher to monitor student achievement in acquiring knowledge of content and learning processes.
- Differentiated instruction leads students toward ownership of their learning.

Differentiation is the rule for effective instruction. Through ongoing observation and assessment of students before, during, and after instruction, teachers acquire information that enables them to make decisions about how to differentiate instruction to meet the needs of all their students. Teachers look for clues to establish students' known strategies—what they can do unassisted to comprehend the text as they read. Then teachers explore where those students need to go next as effective processors of text meaning—what they can do with assistance from someone more knowledgeable than themselves.

Teachers lead the way: by first identifying how various students attempt to process information and then by providing targeted, scaffolded assistance that builds on students' strengths. These teachers recognize that students have different paths to travel to achieve the instructional goals for reading comprehension. Because individual experiences and learning contexts are processed differently in students' brains, no one single approach exists to teach or develop new learning (Lyons 2003). When teachers focus on the essential concepts and procedures of reading comprehension strategies and where their students are as learners taking on those strategies, they make a conscious choice to differentiate the "pace, level, or kind of instruction in response to learners' needs, styles, or interests" (Heacox 2002, 5).

Content—What Students Learn

As teachers observe students through the lens of the gradual release model of instruction, they attend to how individual students interact with new content/concepts and how they make connections between the current information and what they already know as readers. Students' conversations reveal the thinking behind their intentions and actions during reading. Along with input from formative and ongoing informal assessments, the teacher uses the students' responses to drive instruction and organize students in the best way possible to meet their readiness for learning. Because students often progress at different rates through the zone of proximal development (ZPD), instructional groups formed from assessment data are flexible, with membership changing as students advance or demonstrate the need for continued support. Thus, the complexity of the learning for the targeted reading comprehension strategy for any small group matches the participants' readiness levels (Tomlinson 2001). Teachers constantly adjust groups to scaffold students from dependence to independence with a comprehension strategy.

After assessing where students are as learners—their current strengths in reading comprehension and where they need to go next—teachers can differentiate instructional content to meet the needs of their learners.

When differentiating content for instruction, teachers maintain high expectations for all learners, but also recognize that not all students successfully read and create meaning from the same level of text. One of the great challenges many teachers face today is the inability of some students to read at grade level. Teachers with below-level readers have to consider how to accelerate the students' learning. They start with the students' current text level so students can use their existing strengths and knowledge to get to where they need to go tomorrow. Teachers support these students through planned, assisted instruction using texts suited to the students' reading level. Gradually, new texts at increased levels of difficulty are introduced, enabling the students to effectively tackle new reading strategies. The jump from where students are as readers and meaning-makers to where they need to be is negotiated through small, incremental steps that ensure continuing student success and increasing achievement toward grade-level goals. In addition, when these students are faced with learning content that is embedded in text that is too difficult for them to read and understand, the teacher provides other ways for students to access the concepts in order to achieve the targeted learning objectives (Tomlinson 2001).

Varying the text level of reading materials is one way to differentiate content to ensure that all students glean essential understandings from selected texts. Other options include:

- reading the text aloud to the students and discussing the main ideas
- highlighting the text's critical information and directing students to read those portions only
- providing technology-assisted reading of the text, such as listening to a book on tape or listening to an interactive reading of a text on a computer
- presenting graphic organizers that incorporate the salient points of the text's content using comprehensible language for the learners
- enlisting the support of a peer/mentor to assist the students in reading the text.

In the chapters that follow, the STAR Model Lessons and the text examples used in those lessons refer to reading levels as tools to support differentiation by considering the readiness of learners. Teachers reflect on data from a variety of assessments, both formal and informal (such as listening to a student read a particular level of text and noting his or her processing of that text through the student's errors and self-corrections), to determine an independent and instructional reading level for their students (Allington 2001, 44–69; Clay 1993; Fountas and Pinnell 1996). An independent-level text— used for practice of the comprehension strategy presented in the You Do section of the STAR lessons—is a text that a student can read at a 95 percent level of accuracy or above with good comprehension. At the independent level of reading, the student meets minimal decoding challenges and is freed up to direct attention to comprehending what is read. Through repeated independent-reading practice with this easier level of text, the student integrates the strategy from the lesson into his or her neural networks for processing text and develops the fluency, flexibility, and automaticity necessary to transform the strategy into a skill.

An instructional-level text used in the I Do, We Do, and You Try portions of the STAR Model Lesson represents text that a student can read with 90-94 percent accuracy. This level of text poses a few challenges for a reader, usually two to three new tricky parts to problem solve, yet still leaves that student sufficient "energy reserves" to actively process meaning. This text level provides the perfect venue for engaging a student in thinking about reading at a level slightly more difficult than what he or she can probably achieve without assistance. With the additional support of modeling/demonstration, shared/interactive practice, and then guided practice, the student can successfully read the text and learn, process, and apply the targeted comprehension strategy. Text levels are carefully monitored during guided-practice instruction in order to keep challenging the reader. This is accomplished by continually increasing the level of the text (and/or the complexity of the comprehension-strategy instruction) as soon as the student demonstrates the ability to take on new challenges. Frustration-level texts—below 90 percent accuracy—

should be avoided for instruction, as the student will encounter far too many difficulties in decoding the text to effectively determine the meaning of text. Students operating at the frustration level focus on "word calling" rather than comprehending text.

✦ *Pause and Ponder* ✦

What types of assessments do you use to determine the reading readiness levels of the students in your classroom? How do these assessments inform your instruction? How does the data from your formal and informal assessments help you group students for instruction and select "just right" texts for strategy introduction and practice?

How can you differentiate the content for below-level or high-achieving readers? What do you do to differentiate the content for English language learners? ✧

Leveled Text Example

The text examples that follow demonstrate how the same text can be differentiated to address various reading levels in a classroom. Using leveled texts during instruction, whether it's the same text at different levels or multiple texts about the same content at different levels, provides all students access to the content while allowing them to fully attend to constructing meaning by ensuring that the text corresponds to each student's instructional (or independent) reading level.

An example of a leveled text, "The Rock Cycle" from *Leveled Text for Science: Earth and Space Science* (Rice 2009), is shown on the following pages. In examining the examples, note that the symbol in the bottom corner of the text indicates the level of each text—the star level: 1.6; the circle level: 3.0; the square level: 4.9; and the triangle level: 6.8. For example, reading level = grade level and month, so 1.6 = first grade, sixth month of school year.

Figure 3.1 Sample Text—1.6 Reading Level

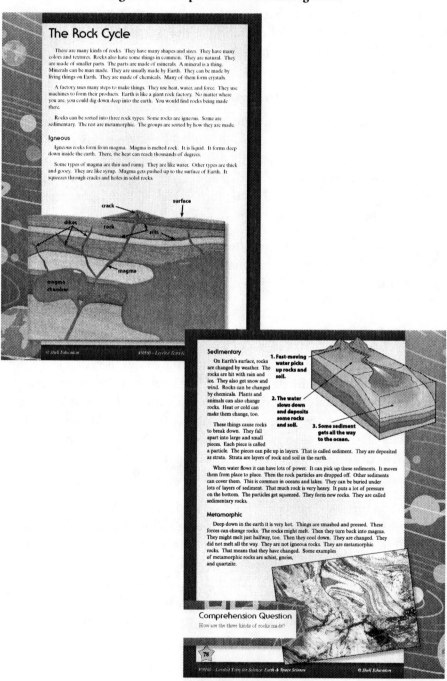

The Rock Cycle

There are many kinds of rocks. They have many shapes and sizes. They have many colors and textures. Rocks also have some things in common. They are natural. They are made of smaller parts. The parts are made of minerals. A mineral is a thing. Minerals can be man made. They are usually made by Earth. They can be made by living things on Earth. They are made of chemicals. Many of them form crystals.

A factory uses many steps to make things. They use heat, water, and force. They use machines to form their products. Earth is like a giant rock factory. No matter where you are, you could dig down deep into the earth. You would find rocks being made there.

Rocks can be sorted into three rock types. Some rocks are igneous. Some are sedimentary. The rest are metamorphic. The groups are sorted by how they are made.

Igneous

Igneous rocks form from magma. Magma is melted rock. It is liquid. It forms deep down inside the earth. There, the heat can reach thousands of degrees.

Some types of magma are thin and runny. They are like water. Other types are thick and gooey. They are like syrup. Magma gets pushed up to the surface of Earth. It squeezes through cracks and holes in solid rocks.

Sedimentary

On Earth's surface, rocks are changed by weather. The rocks are hit with rain and ice. They also get snow and wind. Rocks can be changed by chemicals. Plants and animals can also change rocks. Heat or cold can make them change, too.

These things cause rocks to break down. They fall apart into large and small pieces. Each piece is called a particle. The pieces can pile up in layers. That is called sediment. They are deposited as strata. Strata are layers of rock and soil in the earth.

When water flows it can have lots of power. It can pick up these sediments. It moves them from place to place. Then the rock particles are dropped off. Other sediments can cover them. This is common in oceans and lakes. They can be buried under lots of layers of sediment. That much rock is very heavy. It puts a lot of pressure on the bottom. The particles get squeezed. They form new rocks. They are called sedimentary rocks.

Metamorphic

Deep down in the earth it is very hot. Things are smashed and pressed. These forces can change rocks. The rocks might melt. Then they turn back into magma. They might melt just halfway, too. Then they cool down. They are changed. They did not melt all the way. They are not igneous rocks. They are metamorphic rocks. That means that they have changed. Some examples of metamorphic rocks are schist, gneiss, and quartzite.

Comprehension Question

How are the three kinds of rocks made?

Source: Shell Education 2009

Figure 3.2 Sample Text—3.0 Reading Level

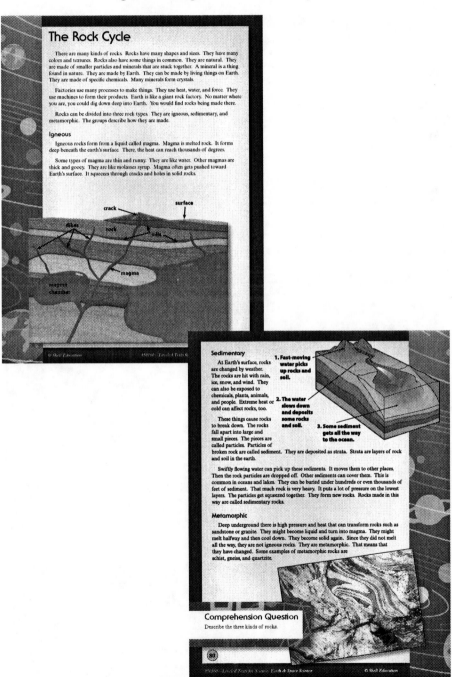

The Rock Cycle

There are many kinds of rocks. Rocks have many shapes and sizes. They have many colors and textures. Rocks also have some things in common. They are natural. They are made of smaller particles and minerals that are stuck together. A mineral is a thing found in nature. They are made by Earth. They can be made by living things on Earth. They are made of specific chemicals. Many minerals form crystals.

Factories use many processes to make things. They use heat, water, and force. They use machines to form their products. Earth is like a giant rock factory. No matter where you are, you could dig down deep into Earth. You would find rocks being made there.

Rocks can be divided into three rock types. They are igneous, sedimentary, and metamorphic. The groups describe how they are made.

Igneous

Igneous rocks form from a liquid called magma. Magma is melted rock. It forms deep beneath the earth's surface. There, the heat can reach thousands of degrees.

Some types of magma are thin and runny. They are like water. Other magmas are thick and gooey. They are like molasses syrup. Magma often gets pushed toward Earth's surface. It squeezes through cracks and holes in solid rocks.

Sedimentary

At Earth's surface, rocks are changed by weather. The rocks are hit with rain, ice, snow, and wind. They can also be exposed to chemicals, plants, animals, and people. Extreme heat or cold can affect rocks, too.

These things cause rocks to break down. The rocks fall apart into large and small pieces. The pieces are called particles. Particles of broken rock are called sediment. They are deposited as strata. Strata are layers of rock and soil in the earth.

Swiftly flowing water can pick up these sediments. It moves them to other places. Then the rock particles are dropped off. Other sediments can cover them. This is common in oceans and lakes. They can be buried under hundreds or even thousands of feet of sediment. That much rock is very heavy. It puts a lot of pressure on the lowest layers. The particles get squeezed together. They form new rocks. Rocks made in this way are called sedimentary rocks.

Metamorphic

Deep underground there is high pressure and heat that can transform rocks such as sandstone or granite. They might become liquid and turn into magma. They might melt halfway and then cool down. They become solid again. Since they did not melt all the way, they are not igneous rocks. They are metamorphic. That means that they have changed. Some examples of metamorphic rocks are schist, gneiss, and quartzite.

Comprehension Question

Describe the three kinds of rocks.

Source: Shell Education 2009

51

Figure 3.3 Sample Text—4.9 Reading Level

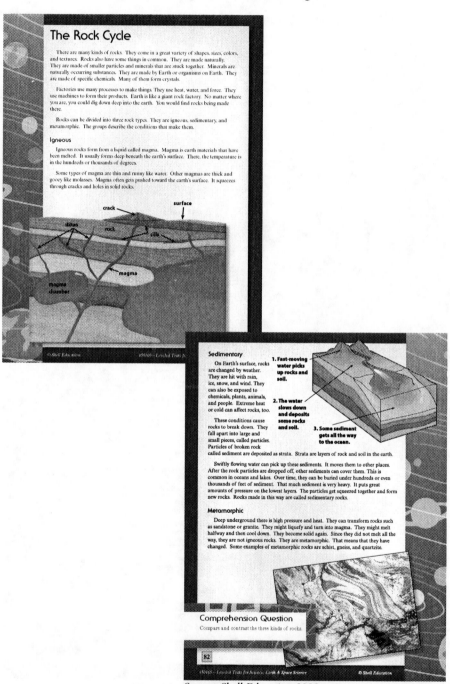

The Rock Cycle

There are many kinds of rocks. They come in a great variety of shapes, sizes, colors, and textures. Rocks also have some things in common. They are made naturally. They are made of smaller particles and minerals that are stuck together. Minerals are naturally occurring substances. They are made by Earth or organisms on Earth. They are made of specific chemicals. Many of them form crystals.

Factories use many processes to make things. They use heat, water, and force. They use machines to form their products. Earth is like a giant rock factory. No matter where you are, you could dig down deep into the earth. You would find rocks being made there.

Rocks can be divided into three rock types. They are igneous, sedimentary, and metamorphic. The groups describe the conditions that make them.

Igneous

Igneous rocks form from a liquid called magma. Magma is earth materials that have been melted. It usually forms deep beneath the earth's surface. There, the temperature is in the hundreds or thousands of degrees.

Some types of magma are thin and runny like water. Other magmas are thick and gooey like molasses. Magma often gets pushed toward the earth's surface. It squeezes through cracks and holes in solid rocks.

Sedimentary

On Earth's surface, rocks are changed by weather. They are hit with rain, ice, snow, and wind. They can also be exposed to chemicals, plants, animals, and people. Extreme heat or cold can affect rocks, too.

These conditions cause rocks to break down. They fall apart into large and small pieces, called particles. Particles of broken rock called sediment are deposited as strata. Strata are layers of rock and soil in the earth.

1. Fast-moving water picks up rocks and soil.

2. The water slows down and deposits some rocks and soil.

3. Some sediment gets all the way to the ocean.

Swiftly flowing water can pick up these sediments. It moves them to other places. After the rock particles are dropped off, other sediments can cover them. This is common in oceans and lakes. Over time, they can be buried under hundreds or even thousands of feet of sediment. That much sediment is very heavy. It puts great amounts of pressure on the lowest layers. The particles get squeezed together and form new rocks. Rocks made in this way are called sedimentary rocks.

Metamorphic

Deep underground there is high pressure and heat. They can transform rocks such as sandstone or granite. They might liquefy and turn into magma. They might melt halfway and then cool down. They become solid again. Since they did not melt all the way, they are not igneous rocks. They are metamorphic. That means that they have changed. Some examples of metamorphic rocks are schist, gneiss, and quartzite.

Comprehension Question

Compare and contrast the three kinds of rocks.

82

Source: Shell Education 2009

Figure 3.4 Sample Text—6.8 Reading Level

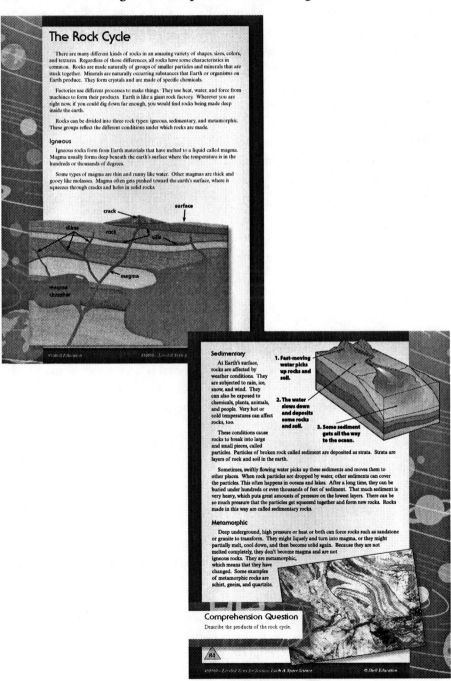

The Rock Cycle

There are many different kinds of rocks in an amazing variety of shapes, sizes, colors, and textures. Regardless of those differences, all rocks have some characteristics in common. Rocks are made naturally of groups of smaller particles and minerals that are stuck together. Minerals are naturally occurring substances that Earth or organisms on Earth produce. They form crystals and are made of specific chemicals.

Factories use different processes to make things. They use heat, water, and force from machines to form their products. Earth is like a giant rock factory. Wherever you are right now, if you could dig down far enough, you would find rocks being made deep inside the earth.

Rocks can be divided into three rock types: igneous, sedimentary, and metamorphic. These groups reflect the different conditions under which rocks are made.

Igneous

Igneous rocks form from Earth materials that have melted to a liquid called magma. Magma usually forms deep beneath the earth's surface where the temperature is in the hundreds or thousands of degrees.

Some types of magma are thin and runny like water. Other magmas are thick and gooey like molasses. Magma often gets pushed toward the earth's surface, where it squeezes through cracks and holes in solid rocks.

Sedimentary

At Earth's surface, rocks are affected by weather conditions. They are subjected to rain, ice, snow, and wind. They can also be exposed to chemicals, plants, animals, and people. Very hot or cold temperatures can affect rocks, too.

1. **Fast-moving water picks up rocks and soil.**
2. **The water slows down and deposits some rocks and soil.**
3. **Some sediment gets all the way to the ocean.**

These conditions cause rocks to break into large and small pieces, called particles. Particles of broken rock called sediment are deposited as strata. Strata are layers of rock and soil in the earth.

Sometimes, swiftly flowing water picks up these sediments and moves them to other places. When rock particles are dropped by water, other sediments can cover the particles. This often happens in oceans and lakes. After a long time, they can be buried under hundreds or even thousands of feet of sediment. That much sediment is very heavy, which puts great amounts of pressure on the lowest layers. There can be so much pressure that the particles get squeezed together and form new rocks. Rocks made in this way are called sedimentary rocks.

Metamorphic

Deep underground, high pressure or heat or both can force rocks such as sandstone or granite to transform. They might liquefy and turn into magma, or they might partially melt, cool down, and then become solid again. Because they are not melted completely, they don't become magma and are not igneous rocks. They are metamorphic, which means that they have changed. Some examples of metamorphic rocks are schist, gneiss, and quartzite.

Comprehension Question

Describe the products of the rock cycle.

Source: Shell Education 2009

Using the leveled text, "The Rock Cycle," the teacher can select from four possible texts, matching the level of the text to the students' reading strengths and their instructional goals. Although each text utilizes the same images and fonts, the readability levels varies from grade level 1.6 to grade level 6.8. Text level is determined by such factors as vocabulary, sentence structure and length, and other considerations such as the use of pronouns. The essential academic content-area vocabulary is preserved across all the texts and is introduced before the text is read. The teacher can then select a "just right" text for guided reading instruction and thereby make the social studies content of the text available to all students. In the sample texts shown on pages 50–53, I have indicated the reading level for each example.

✦ *Pause and Ponder* ✦

The readability level of the text examples shown on pages 50–53 varies widely. What do you think are the critical features of each text that enable students to read the material successfully?

Reflect on your experience using leveled texts with students. How have students responded to these texts? In what ways has the use of these resources contributed to the effectiveness of strategy instruction with students? How would you adapt your instruction if you didn't have access to leveled texts? ✺

Process—How Students Learn

When teachers differentiate the process during instruction, they first consider how their students effectively learn new information. On that basis, they can provide a variety of venues through which students can access the content, construct the key concepts, and apply critical procedural steps to comprehend text. Teachers recognize that "you can't just say *it* louder" to ensure that all students get *it*, but instead they must attend to the learning styles that predispose learners to various ways of interacting with new content and concepts (Jensen

2000; Tomlinson 2001).   Since the students in a classroom do not share a single learning style, teachers draw students into the learning by offering them flexible options for engaging in the lesson and creating meaningful connections.   Lessons based on the gradual release of responsibility model provide the teacher with the opportunity to select how the learning can be optimally scaffolded to ensure student success. Therefore, how a teacher brings students into the learning through specific language and direct experiences with the comprehension strategy during reading differs depending on the learning dispositions of the group members.   Expert teachers strive to create a just-right fit between the content, teaching materials, and focused instructional moves to match the way their students learn best (Allington 2001).

> "The key to effective differentiation is the accuracy and relevance of the information that we use to decide appropriate learning tasks for pupils, and our willingness to challenge these decisions from time to time by allowing students to surprise us" (Sutton 1995, 26).

As teachers plan instruction with the "how" in mind, they focus on process. By learning more about students' learning styles, intelligence preferences, applied-brain research, and cognitive styles, teachers bring additional insight into how to develop powerful learning profiles for their students (Tomlinson 2001; Heacox 2002; Dodge 2005). Based on these learning profiles, teachers can develop responsive, goal-focused lessons (see examples in Chapter 1). Teachers also respond to students' learning preferences when they allow students to choose how they interact with or demonstrate new learning. This invites students to enter the instructional context through their personal strengths. Because students do not have a single learning style, teachers cannot employ a single teaching move to ensure that all students achieve their maximum potential.

Summary

When teachers differentiate the content and process of reading instruction by attending to students' readiness levels, learning preferences, and even interests, students accept ownership of their learning. As members of an instructional environment in which they encounter appropriate yet challenging expectations for their own achievement in reading and comprehending text, students recognize a constant potential for individual success as readers. Students develop strong interpersonal relationships with the teacher and their peers when, during instruction, their individuality is respected and supported through a classroom community that responds to students' strengths and needs while motivating them to stay engaged in learning.

The next chapter presents multiple engagements and process choices to set students up for reading with meaning by attending to their varying learning profiles along with their readiness for learning. The before-reading support can also be differentiated, allowing teachers to select from more supportive to less supportive brain-compatible activities to "frontload" (Hoyt 2002) concepts and vocabulary during the I Do stage of a reading lesson. The STAR Model Lessons focus on the language of assistance and teacher modeling to scaffold the learning process for students as they take on a reading comprehension strategy. The *how to* of the lesson describes in detail the gradual release of the responsibility for meaning-making during reading to the students.

✦ *Pause and Ponder* ✦

Reread the section in Chapter 1 titled "The Importance of Rich Input in Brain-Compatible Instruction" (p. 32). Now think about differentiating the process to address the learning profiles of your students. How can you incorporate ideas from Chapter 1, or those presented above, to actively engage your students through their learning styles or preferences? What teaching moves do you make when you consider the "how" of a reading comprehension strategy lesson?

As noted in this chapter, what students learn (content) and how they learn (processes) are two important aspects of planning for differentiated instruction. In addition, the classroom climate—physical environment, teacher behaviors, and student engagement—contributes to effective differentiation (Chapman and King 2005). Think about the impact of each of these aspects on how you implement differentiated instruction. What changes would you like to make in any of these areas? ✎

Preparing Students to Read with Meaning—Activating Student Thinking Through Text Introductions

"In the context of reading comprehension, prior knowledge is built up and changed over time as readers engage with text ... Their active participation in using and modifying their prior knowledge means that there is a very strong reciprocal relationship between prior knowledge and comprehension" (Davis 2007, 17).

Considerations from Research

- Effective readers draw upon previous experience and knowledge to prepare for reading a new text.
- Transactional strategy instruction enables students to develop procedures that help them make connections between their prior knowledge and content in a text.
- Teacher-led activities before reading provide explicit instruction in strategies that enhance students' understanding of concepts and vocabulary in a text.

Teachers recognize that students approach reading with a wide variety of prior experiences with and background knowledge of the concepts presented in texts, especially nonfiction texts. Knowing this, teachers plan instruction that prepare students to read with maximum meaning. Prior knowledge underpins the reader's ability to reasonably predict information that might be presented in a text or to hypothesize about possible outcomes. Students often unconsciously make inferences that are based on their background experiences. However, students need to know that sometimes their prior knowledge is at odds with the information in the text. Consequently, they have to recognize that sometimes it is necessary to reinterpret their personal schema, or mental representations, in light of what they encounter in the text.

✦ *Pause and Ponder* ✦

How do you set yourself up to read a new text? What actions do you take before you read? What do you do if the text's topic is unfamiliar to you—perhaps an instruction manual for a new piece of technology?

Now consider how you approach a text that complements your prior knowledge, such as a book about teaching. In what ways does your approach to a text with a familiar topic differ from your approach to an unfamiliar text? How will your background knowledge affect your comprehension as you read? ✦

One positive step that readers can take to help themselves establish meaning before reading is to preview the text organizers to determine a tentative main idea about the selection. This type of preview— Text Walk—is discussed in detail in Chapter 6. There are many circumstances when students must read a text without any teacher support before reading; for example, during independent reading or testing. In these situations, students can set themselves up to read with more understanding by previewing the text organizers to develop a sense of the text structure, the main idea, and some of the significant details presented.

Yet, in an instructional setting, how do teachers support students who do not have the background knowledge necessary to read a particular nonfiction text with meaning even after doing a text preview? Without sufficient background knowledge, students may not be prepared to read with deep understanding. A powerful, rich introduction that establishes critical concepts and essential vocabulary before students read enables them to enter and process the text with greater comprehension (Christen and Murphy 1991).

Teachers support readers in associating any current schema they possess with the new information presented in a text. That way, students can assimilate or restructure this new information in order to add to or adjust their schema (Dechant 1991). Teachers engage students in understanding the text concepts and vocabulary and relate these to their current schema in order to activate their interest and connection to the topic. Teachers should note that the levels of support needed before reading vary from student to student. Therefore, the strategies the teacher selects to support students in navigating a particular text's challenges are differentiated based on students' readiness levels, learning styles, interests, and prior experience. Hoyt (2002, 104) uses the expression *frontloading* for comprehension—prereading tasks that activate and build on prior knowledge, engage students in rich experiences with unknown text vocabulary, and help students understand how to organize the new information into their schema for learning.

This chapter describes teacher-initiated before-reading activities. These activities create a meaningful context for students as they follow the teacher's lead in thinking about a text before they dive in. The strategies employ varying levels of teacher support to activate students' prior knowledge or frontload text concepts and vocabulary. Some of the before-reading activities engage students in activating their prior knowledge on a familiar topic in order to establish or review the vocabulary and concepts they currently control on a topic. This approach allows the teacher's instruction to focus on any gaps in understanding or misconceptions students may have on the topic. Other before-reading strategies are designed to be more supportive and provide sufficient frontloading for students

> "A good reader does not just dive into a text, proceeding from beginning to end. First, the good reader is clear about her or his goal in reading the text ... Second, the reader often skims the text in advance of reading or at least looks through it ... Third, before reading, good readers often activate prior knowledge, which can then be related to the ideas in the text" (Pressley 2002a, 294).

with little background knowledge of the concepts and vocabulary of the selected nonfiction text.

In Chapter 1, I described the various features of students' learning styles that teachers can draw upon as they plan instruction. Students' learning styles can be used to determine appropriate frontloading strategies for helping students build connections as they approach a new nonfiction text. The strategies outlined in this chapter include a variety of multimodal activities—visual, auditory, and kinesthetic. The suggestions align with such powerful brain-compatible strategies as sketching/visualizing; writing; exploring artifacts, visuals, or primary sources; manipulating objects; storytelling; dramatizing; moving; and utilizing graphic organizers (Tate 2003; Jensen 2001; Wolfe 2001).

A Structure for Planning Before-Reading Activities

To plan a targeted introduction to nonfiction text, begin by considering three Bs—Book, Brain, and Build. These factors are integral to effective planning for prereading activities:

- **Book**: Examine the text to identify critical concepts, vocabulary, and text structure that will affect students' reading performance.
- **Brain**: Consider the students' capabilities, including reading performance, familiarity with the topic, and learning-style preferences.
- **Build**: Select the instructional activities that will provide the most appropriate experiences and enable students to enter the text successfully.

Book

The teacher reads the selected nonfiction text before the lesson and reflects on the potential supports and challenges of that text. The questions that follow provide insight into the nature of the text and the potential supports and challenges it may offer your students.

- What is the depth of background knowledge readers need to successfully understand the text concepts? Consider the background knowledge that students need to control before reading the selected text in order to comprehend the content. What does the author assume readers understand before reading the text? What support does the author provide for readers on the concepts presented? What are the possible challenges readers will face if they do not understand certain concepts?

- Is the text structure familiar to students, or have they yet to encounter this structure in nonfiction? A chronological nonfiction text structure, such as in a biography, is probably familiar to readers since it resembles a narrative chaining or sequential structure of a story. On the other hand, a position-support text structure may be more of a challenge since students may have little experience with persuasive text, such as an editorial. Another challenge of nonfiction text structure is that two or more text structures can run simultaneously through a text (for example, a combination of chronological structure with cause-effect structure).

- Does the author provide rich text organizers to support the main ideas of the text, or is there a paucity of text organizers? Are the text organizers easy for students to interpret? Photographs, charts, subtitles, headings, captions, diagrams, bullets, stylized font—these and other examples of text organizers can support students' comprehension both before and during reading. How effectively do the text organizers convey meaning to readers? Are there any text organizers that students have not yet encountered?

- What is the level of elaboration or detail in the text? Does it provide support or pose a challenge for readers? Examine the words used by the author to explain the content and illustrate the main ideas of the text. Does the depth of development support readers' understanding and visualization of the text's concepts, or is the language used too difficult for readers to process? Consider sentence structure patterns and their frequency of use throughout the text. The sentence-structure affects the reading level of the text. Consider the length of the sentences and compare the number of simple sentences to the number of complex sentences. Are the sentences mostly simple and compound, or are they mainly complex or compound? Is sentence length and fluency a support or a challenge for readers?

- What is the essential content vocabulary in the text? Which vocabulary is critical for students to know before reading in order to successfully navigate the text with meaning? Which vocabulary is supported by context or meaningful roots/word parts that readers can draw upon to figure out the meaning of the words during reading?

Example of Nonfiction Text at Emergent Reading Level

Water, the text that follows, is an example of a book that can be used with students reading at an emergent level, or approximately a 1.3 grade level. Here the teacher looks for a text with significant supports and just a few challenges. Students at this reading level have an increasing repertoire of known high-frequency words, and they are consistently looking at beginning sounds to support their decoding. These students are starting to look at multiple sources of information as they read. The photographs and text features support their meaning making as they process the words of a nonfiction text. Students at this level are ready to be prompted to study unknown words, paying special attention to word endings, and check the visual information from words with what makes sense from the context and text organizers (in this case, the photographs). In addition, the teacher considers the content and structure of the selected text and the background knowledge needed to successfully comprehend the nonfiction text concepts. These factors of support or challenge are illustrated in Figure 4.2 on page 67.

Figure 4.1 Nonfiction Text at an Emergent Level

Water

Dona Herweck Rice

Water is all around you.

Where can you find it?

2

You can find water in streams.

3

You can find water in rivers.

4

Figure 4.1 Nonfiction Text at an Emergent Level *(cont.)*

You can find water in ponds.

You can find water in lakes.

You can find water in tide pools.

You can find water in oceans.

Water is all around you.

Source: Rice 2003

**Figure 4.2 Analysis of Text Supports and Challenges,
Emergent-Level Nonfiction Text**

Title: *Water*	Supports	Challenges
Background Knowledge	Students are familiar with water in many places in their environment.	Students may not be familiar with all the water sources named in the text.
Text Structure	Descriptive with examples. Students are likely familiar with the structure from read-aloud experiences with similar nonfiction texts.	
Text Features	Photographs explicitly support meaning.	
Level of Elaboration/Detail	Simple sentences with repetitive structure.	
Vocabulary	Known high-frequency vocabulary for most students at this level; *rivers, lakes, oceans* are most likely known words.	The high-frequency word, *find*, may need to be taught. *Streams, ponds, tide pools* may need to be frontloaded for meaning.

Example of Nonfiction Text at Third-Grade Level

In the third-grade-level text on page 69, "A Big Chunk of Ice," the teacher recognizes that students actively read for meaning and therefore considers the text supports for helping students sustain comprehension as they read. Before introducing a new text, the teacher also carefully notes any reading challenges. Prior knowledge of a topic provides students with a schema to use to enter a text. When students lack relevant prior knowledge, the teacher takes the time to build appropriate background. In third grade, students encounter an increasing variety of nonfiction text structures, but they may not understand how focusing on text structure can help them locate information and determine the main ideas of the text. At this level, students have had more experience with a variety of text features that they can use to support their meaning making before and during reading. As students move up through text levels, they need to process increasingly more complex sentence structures, as well as effectively read longer, multisyllable words. Depending on the context, vocabulary can be a support to readers' processing or a challenge to understanding what they read. Figure 4.4 on page 70 analyzes the text supports and challenges in this example of a third-grade-level nonfiction text.

Figure 4.3 Example of Third-Grade-Level Nonfiction Text

A Big Chunk of Ice

A new space mission heads for Pluto

By Nellie Gonzalez Cutler

On January 19, 2006, a rocket was launched. It took off from Cape Canaveral, Florida. At the top of the rocket sat the New Horizons **space probe**. It had taken more than 15 years to plan. Now, the probe was on its way into space. Its next stop: Pluto.

Pluto is made of rock and ice. Space scientists thought the small ball of rock was not like any of the other planets. But new discoveries have shown that Pluto is not an **oddball**.

It turns out that Pluto is just one of thousands of icy chunks of rock. They are in an area on the edge of our **solar system**. These objects circle the sun just like planets. But they are more than three billion miles away. And at least one of them is bigger than Pluto.

That is one reason why scientists have decided that Pluto is not a planet. Eight months after New Horizons took off, 2,500 scientists met. They set rules for what makes a planet. They said that a planet must orbit, or go around, the sun. It must be nearly round. Its orbit cannot cross the path of another planet. Pluto's orbit crosses another one's path. It crosses Neptune's path.

So poor Pluto now belongs to a new group. They are called "dwarf planets." But, that is good news for planet hunters. "Many more Plutos wait to be discovered," says Richard Binzel, a space scientist.

New Horizons sits atop a rocket at Cape Canaveral, shortly before taking off for Pluto.

Prepare to Be Surprised

Planet or not, scientists want to know more about Pluto. New Horizons should reach Pluto and its three moons in 2015. The probe has cameras. It has other tools as well. It will snap pictures of the surface. The probe will study Pluto's thin **atmosphere**. It will take its temperature.

What will the probe find? Pluto and its corner of space have been full of surprises. Scientists think the New Horizons mission will find more surprises.

Did You Know?

On Pluto time
A day on Pluto would last 6.4 Earth days. It takes Pluto 248 Earth years to circle the sun.

Weighty matters
Pluto's gravity is weak. A person weighing 300 pounds on Earth would weigh just 20 pounds there.

All in the family
Pluto has three moons. Two were found in 2005. They are hard to see from 3.5 billion miles away!

Sign our guestbook
The probe carries a CD with a list of 430,000 people who wanted their names to fly through space.

10773 (11965) Exploring Nonfiction • Second Edition—Level 3 © TIME For Kids

Source: Teacher Created Materials 2008

Figure 4.4 Analysis of Supports and Challenges, Third-Grade-Level Nonfiction Text

Title: "A Big Chunk of Ice"	Supports	Challenges
Background Knowledge	Students have knowledge of planets and space missions.	Students may not be familiar with new findings about Pluto and what defines a planet.
Text Structure	Problem and solution (Problem: Pluto was an oddball. Solution of scientists: Rethink Pluto's status). Cause and effect (Effect: Pluto is redefined as a dwarf planet. What are the causes for this?)	Although text structures or organizational patterns may be familiar, more than one structure exists in the article.
Text Features	Title, subtitle, photographs, captions, and headings supportive of meaning.	Students may not follow layout of article and recognize importance of inset boxes.
Level of Elaboration/ Detail	Mostly simple sentences with effective transitions between paragraphs; details help reader picture text ideas.	
Vocabulary	Known vocabulary for most students at this level: *planet, gravity, Pluto, Neptune, scientist; orbit* is contextually supported in paragraph four.	*Space probe, oddball, solar system, astronomers, New Horizons, Cape Canaveral, atmosphere* may need to be frontloaded for meaning.

Brain

Brain is the second B to consider when planning a targeted text introduction. What do you know about this group of students and where they are as learners as they prepare to read the text selected for them? Assessment is a critical ingredient of a teacher's understanding of what students currently control in their comprehension strategies and where they need to go next as readers. Day-to-day observation and evaluation as students talk about and respond to text inform the teacher's instruction and influence the design of new lessons. Revisit the Book questions on page 63, reflecting on what you know about your own particular students. How does what these students control in such areas as vocabulary and background knowledge, awareness of text structure, use of text organizers, and other processing strategies affect the level of support they will need before reading the text?

No two students approach a text in the same way. After assessing students' background knowledge and the text supports and challenges, teachers need to focus the before-reading activities and comprehension instruction on the strengths and needs of those students.

Build

Building the instructional plan for introducing students to the selected text is the third B in this process. The level of support necessary for students as they get ready to read the chosen instructional text varies based on their readiness levels, learning styles, and even interests. In the activities that follow, teachers can use the Build step to select the best one or two frontloading strategies for different groups of students in order to differentiate support as the text is introduced.

Prior to using any before-reading strategy, select an appropriate instructional-level text for students, determine a teaching focus based on assessment of students' strengths and instructional needs, and consider the supports and challenges of the text in relationship to the readiness levels and learning styles of students. Teachers will find that many of the before-reading strategies, once modeled and used by students several times, can also be used as after-reading strategies. This is when students respond to the text and create products to demonstrate their comprehension of the text, concepts, and vocabulary.

✦ *Pause and Ponder* ✦

Select an instructional-level nonfiction text for a specific group of students. Use the first two Bs—Book and Brain—to initiate a plan for a targeted introduction to the text.

First, consider the supports and challenges of the text. Then reflect on what you know about the students and the level of support they need before reading in order to master the text challenges and read with understanding. Finally, determine the best activity from the next section to use to scaffold comprehension for students before they read the text. ✦

Before-Reading Strategies

The before-reading strategies that follow highlight multiple venues for building powerful text introductions that scaffold students into a new text so they can read with maximum meaning. These strategies include Sketch the Scene; Act It Out; Models, Artifacts, Primary Sources, Demonstrations/Experiments, and Other Visuals; Tiny Texts; Concept Chorals; Packing Up Word Bags; Making "Sense" of It; and Brain Boxes. This wide variety of strategies allows teachers to choose an activity that provides the appropriate level of support based on students' strengths and current learning needs.

For each strategy, background is provided that explains the rationale for the strategy. The Materials section describes the resources for the frontloading strategy, and the Procedures section gives a step-by-step explanation of the strategy. I have also included examples and some possible variations of these strategies.

Sketch the Scene

Background

Sketch the Scene, a variation of a visualizing activity described by Short, Harste, and Burke (1996, 258), is an instructor-initiated frontloading strategy in which the teacher places unknown or partially known nonfiction vocabulary into a narrative context while sketching simple pictures in order to illustrate the meaning of the new words and their relationship to the text topic.

This supportive before-reading strategy combines storytelling with a nonlinguistic representation of the meaning of the vocabulary through sketching and visualization. This narrative chaining—creating links between the text vocabulary and a storylike format—engages students in the content and helps them recall the meaning of the new vocabulary (McGee and Wilson 1984). The sketching reframes the context and vocabulary into a different sign system other than words, which helps create meaning (Short, Harste, and Burke 1996).

In selecting vocabulary to use with Sketch the Scene, decide which words are essential for the reader to know in order to understand the content presented in the nonfiction text. Ask yourself the following questions when selecting vocabulary for the activity:

- How are those words used in the text?
- If the words have more than one meaning, which meaning applies in the context of the text?
- Which words can just be "planted" or worked into the narrative for Sketch the Scene, rather than directly taught (for example, names of people or places or words that students know but haven't seen frequently in print)?
- Are any of the words contextually supported in the text so students can figure out the meaning when they encounter them?

Materials

- Chart paper or whiteboard, markers

Procedure

- Identify the essential academic/concept vocabulary of the text to introduce to students through Sketch the Scene.

- Plan a short narrative think aloud that incorporates the selected vocabulary. Develop a simple sketch ("mind picture") and label to represent each word.

- Introduce the vocabulary to students by presenting a narrative that incorporates descriptions, definitions, and examples of the vocabulary. Be sure to sketch the "scene" or vocabulary mind pictures as the narrative unfolds. From time to time, stop and review the vocabulary thus far or include a dramatization of a word to build a concrete understanding of that word for students.

- At the end of the Sketch the Scene activity, have students retell the narrative in their own words and explain the vocabulary and the relationship of the words to the text topic. Students may also frame questions about the new words for a partner to answer by referencing the Sketch the Scene chart. Students can share personal connections to the vocabulary, provide additional examples or synonyms for the vocabulary, or use paper or whiteboards to sketch their own mind pictures for the vocabulary, creating a personal Sketch the Scene.

Two examples of Sketch the Scene are shown in Figure 4.5 and Figure 4.6 on the following pages. The teacher sketches the illustrations one at a time as students watch. The numbered statements provide the teacher-dialogue to accompany each sketch as it is drawn. The text does not appear on the Sketch the Scene chart.

Figure 4.5 Sketch the Scene for _Water_

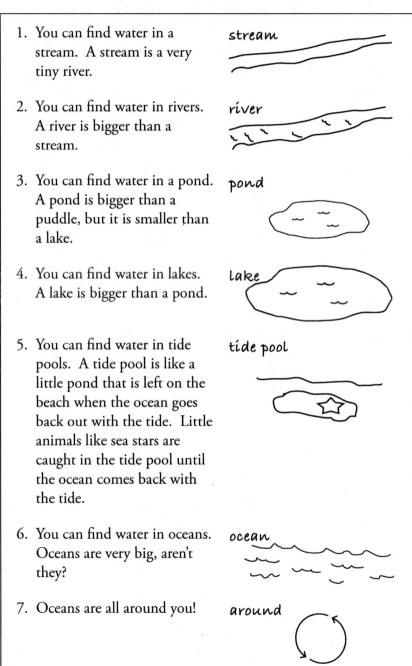

1. You can find water in a stream. A stream is a very tiny river.

   stream

2. You can find water in rivers. A river is bigger than a stream.

   river

3. You can find water in a pond. A pond is bigger than a puddle, but it is smaller than a lake.

   pond

4. You can find water in lakes. A lake is bigger than a pond.

   lake

5. You can find water in tide pools. A tide pool is like a little pond that is left on the beach when the ocean goes back out with the tide. Little animals like sea stars are caught in the tide pool until the ocean comes back with the tide.

   tide pool

6. You can find water in oceans. Oceans are very big, aren't they?

   ocean

7. Oceans are all around you!

   around

Figure 4.6 Sketch the Scene for "A Big Chunk of Ice"

1. Cape Canaveral, Florida, is where many United States rockets take off for outer space.

   Cape Canaveral, Florida

2. The New Horizons space probe sits atop a rocket ready to blast into space. A probe is a device sent into space to send back information to Earth.

   USA

   New Horizons space probe

3. Astronomers are people who study the stars and outer space. I know the meaning of two chunks of this word. *Astro* is a base that means "star." *-Er* is a suffix that can mean, "one who." Therefore, an astronomer is "one who studies the stars."

   astro|nom|ers
   "star"   "one who"

4. A mission is a special job or trip to get something done. The New Horizons space probe has a mission in space.

   mission

Figure 4.6 Sketch the Scene for "A Big Chunk of Ice" *(cont.)*

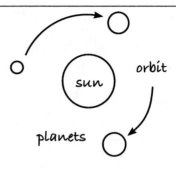

5. Our solar system is made up of the sun and things such as planets that circle, or orbit, around our sun.

6. Pluto, once thought to be an icy, rocky planet, orbits around the sun.

Pluto

7. Pluto has a thin atmosphere, or layer, of gases that wrap around it. I know the meaning of two chunks in this word. *Atmo/atmos* is a base that means "air." *Sphere* is a base that means "circle." Therefore, an atmosphere is "a circle of air."

"air"
atmo|sphere
"circle"

8. Scientists have long thought that Pluto was an unusual, strange planet—an oddball.

oddball?

Act It Out

Background

Act It Out provides strong cognitive links for students through movement, dramatization, and interpersonal interactions. In this strategy, students participate in a short, narrative role-playing activity that presents critical concepts and vocabulary selected by the teacher to establish the big ideas of a nonfiction text. Students move through a dramatic interpretation of the essential vocabulary and concepts that represent the meaningful relationships of the text. A dramatization format can activate students' prior knowledge, link it to new learning, and engage many portions of students' brains (Jensen 2001). Act It Out is definitely a more brain-compatible activity than having learners passively listen to a list of definitions before reading!

Materials

- teacher-written narrative script for introducing the text
- 8 ½-by-11 inch cards with the selected vocabulary words written on them in marker and large enough for the group to see during the dramatization
- any props selected by the teacher to use with the script (optional)

Procedure

- Identify the essential academic vocabulary of the text.
- Write a short, narrative script that incorporates descriptions, definitions, and examples of the vocabulary.
- Write each featured vocabulary word or concept on a card in large letters. Each card represents a student's "role" in the Act It Out script, or a word to be displayed as the script is read. If desired, props can also be provided to accompany the roles.
- Introduce the vocabulary and concepts by assigning students the various roles. Students stand and display the word cards or props at the appropriate times as the script is read by the teacher. Students may also choose to act out their words.

- At the conclusion of Act It Out, students review the word cards presented and explain the vocabulary in their own words. Students can share personal connections to the vocabulary or provide additional examples of the vocabulary and concepts presented.

Text

The script presented in Figure 4.8 on page 81 is based on the selection "Adaptation in Living Things" on page 80. Below the teacher can find a list of the necessary materials, a procedure for students, and a script for the teacher to read.

Materials

- word cards—*organisms, adaptations, genetic codes, traits, submerged, prey, predators, camouflage, mimic*
- bag labeled "Genetic Codes for Adaptations"

Materials for the Roles

- hummingbird—name card on yarn to wear, cone beak made from rolled paper to hold up to student's nose
- frog—name card on yarn to wear, paper headband with paper eyes glued on top for student to wear
- tiger—name card on yarn to wear, two brown paper strips to hold up like stripes
- gray butterfly—name card on yarn to wear, gray paper wings with a black spot in a white circle on each wing to look like large eyes

Procedure

Four students are assigned to the four roles. Students wear their name cards and stand backward, facing away from the audience. Place the props into the bag labeled "Genetic Codes for Adaptations." The teacher reads the script, and as each animal role is introduced, the student portraying that role turns around to face the audience and receives his or her prop from the bag. The teacher holds up the other word cards for the audience, one word at a time, as the italicized words are presented in the script.

Figure 4.7 Sample Fifth-Grade-Level Text: "Adaptation in Living Things"

8

Chapter 2 • Adaptation in Living Things

What Is Adaptation?

Why does a giraffe have a long neck? Why does a polar bear have white fur? Why do some seeds float on the wind?

The giraffe's neck, the polar bear's fur, and the seed that floats are all *adaptations* (ad-ap-TAY-shuns). An adaptation is a feature or trait that helps an **organism** to survive.

All living things have adaptations. A hummingbird has a long beak to help it drink nectar from a flower. A finch has a short, strong beak to help it eat nuts. A frog's eyes are near the top of its head. That lets it look above the water line while its body stays **submerged**.

Adaptations are part of the process of evolution. They get passed down in an organism's **genetic code**. Most organisms have many adaptations. They have developed over time.

The hummingbird has a long beak to reach the nectar.

Think

Can you think of an animal or plant that has an adaptation?

Words to Know

adaptation

camouflage

mimicry

Adapting to Survive

One common type of adaptation is *camouflage* (KAM-uh-flahzh). Camouflage allows an organism to blend in with its environment. Some animals use camouflage to hide from predators. On the other hand, a predator might use camouflage to help it hunt its **prey**.

Deer are born with white and brown markings that help them blend in with leaves in the forest. Tigers, leopards, and cheetahs all have markings to help them blend in with their surroundings.

Another form of adaptation is *mimicry* (MIM-ick-ree). Mimicry is when one organism looks like, or mimics, something else. For example, stick insects look just like sticks. A snake-mimicking caterpillar looks like a snake. This causes birds and other animals that might eat caterpillars to leave the snake mimic alone. The grey butterfly has spots on its wings. They look like the eyes of an owl. Those eye spots scare away predators. Mimicry helps keep animals alive.

The tiger is a predator. It has a camouflage adaptation.

You can see this butterfly. But predators see the big owl eyes. They stay away.

Use Your Imagination

Can you make up an animal that uses camouflage or mimicry as an adaptation?

Visualize / Determine Importance

Science

10775 (i1989) Exploring Nonfiction • Second Edition—Level 5   © TIME For Kids

Source: Teacher Created Materials 2008

Figure 4.8 Sample Act It Out Script for "Adaptation in Living Things"

Welcome to the world of *organisms* (*hold up word card*)—all living things! Today we are going to explore the *adaptations* that animals have to help them live. Let me look into my bag of *genetic codes*—genetic codes that have all the patterns of chemicals that animals have in their cells. These genetic codes help animals adapt with special features, or *traits*, so they can survive in their environment.

Here is a **hummingbird**. (*Hummingbird turns and faces audience.*) Hmm, let me see. What adaptation or trait shall we give this hummingbird so it can survive? (*Look in bag and take out paper cone beak.*) How about a long beak to help it drink nectar from flowers? (*Hummingbird takes the beak and pretends to drink from a flower.*) Now the hummingbird has one of these special *traits* in its *genetic code* so it can stay alive.

Ahhh, here's a **frog**. (*Frog turns and faces audience.*) Let's help him adapt by putting his eyes on top of his head (*look in bag and take out the headband with eyes*). He can survive by staying almost completely under the water, or *submerged*, so his *prey*—his food—won't see him and neither will his enemies, or *predators*. (*Frog puts on the headband and pretends to be submerged and catch prey.*)

Watch out! Here is a **tiger**. (*Tiger turns and faces audience.*) Why would he need to adapt? Since he is a predator, he doesn't want his food, his prey, to see him until it is too late. We can help him blend in with his environment—the grass and the shadows. Let's *camouflage* him with stripes. (*Look in bag and take out the paper strips. Tiger holds up stripes and pretends to hunt while blending in.*)

Shhh! Here is a **gray butterfly**! (*Gray butterfly turns and faces audience.*) It will need a special kind of adaptation. This butterfly does not want to become a bird's prey and be eaten for dinner! (*Look in bag and take out the paper wings.*) Let's put great big spots on his wings. These spots will *mimic*—copy or look like—the eyes of a big owl. That will scare away the gray butterfly's predators. (*Gray butterfly holds up wings and flutters them.*)

What other adaptations can I put in this bag? What other traits or features do different organisms have that help them survive? Can you think of an animal that uses camouflage or mimicry as an adaptation? (*Audience participates through discussion.*)

Models, Artifacts, Primary Sources, Demonstrations and Experiments, and Other Visuals

Background

Creating authentic engagements with the text content before reading is an effective way to introduce text concepts and vocabulary. Experiences with models, artifacts, demonstrations and experiments, and such primary sources such as documents, photographs, illustrations, posters, cartoons, maps, and film recordings tap into the visual strength of learners. Because almost 70 percent of a person's sensory receptors are in the eyes, students acquire more information visually than through any other sense (Wolfe 2001). When students can touch and manipulate the visual materials, learning is increased through the addition of kinesthetic input to the brain. Add in a lively discussion about those models, artifacts, demonstrations, or primary sources and students are going to be ready to read with meaning. And what students have not loved reading about volcanic eruptions after creating an eruption of their own with baking soda and vinegar?

Teachers can provide students with multiple hands-on experiences before reading to illustrate nonfiction text vocabulary and concepts. I still have collections of rocks, insects, shells, birds' nests, pinecones, bones, various measuring containers and gadgets, war medals and uniform buttons, foreign coins, postcards, and postage stamps in boxes in my garage that students have touched, sorted, and talked about before reading. One time to frontload vocabulary and concepts for the book *A Visit to an Automobile Factory* (*Nonfiction Readers, Early Fluent Level*), a student's father, who was a mechanic, brought in a car engine and let the students help him take it apart. Needless to say, the text was then a big hit with those students.

Another time, prior to reading a section of a text about President Abraham Lincoln's assassination and the beginning of Reconstruction from *Abraham Lincoln* (*Primary Source Readers: Expanding and Preserving the Union*), a family-owned copy of the *New York Times* extra that came out the morning after Lincoln's death was shown to students. Students were also shown a primary-source photograph from the Library of Congress found on the Teacher's Resource CD (*Primary Source Readers: Expanding and Preserving the Union*) that revealed the contents of Lincoln's pockets at the time of his assassination. The students used their background knowledge of Lincoln's life and the events surrounding the end of the Civil War to draw powerful conclusions about Lincoln's character before they even read the text section.

In addition to artifacts, models, and demonstrations, teachers can find a plethora of websites available for educators to obtain free downloads and primary-source documents to use to introduce a text's concepts and vocabulary. The Library of Congress website (http://www.loc.gov/index.html) is an excellent source for American history documents, photographs, recordings, and other primary sources. There are also multiple sites for virtual field trips for students on a variety of topics.

Tiny Texts

Background

One way to scaffold students into reading for meaning is to have them read and discuss a short summary of a selected nonfiction text that includes the critical concepts and vocabulary before they read. The teacher writes a Tiny Text—a succinct paragraph that extracts the main ideas and significant details and presents the essential vocabulary in a context that helps students understand the meaning of the words. The Tiny Text also serves as an effective model of a well-constructed summary for students after they read. Students can analyze the Tiny Text to note how it contains the elements of a summary—the main ideas and the significant supporting details—as well as some of the specific conceptual vocabulary. Figure 4.9 below presents an example of a Tiny Text.

Figure 4.9 Tiny Text Based on "Adaptation in Living Things"

An *adaptation* is a feature, or *trait*, that helps a living thing—an organism—live. In order to *survive*, animals have made changes in their *genetic codes* over time. A genetic code is the pattern of chemicals in the cells of organisms that makes those living things special. Some animals have adaptations that help them hide and avoid becoming *prey* (eaten by other animals). Some animals are *camouflaged* by colors or markings that help them blend and hide from *predators* that hunt them. Some animals copy, or *mimic*, how another organism looks so a predator will stay away.

Concept Chorals

Background

Gardner (1983) notes that the engagement of students through the musical intelligence can enhance students' ability to access academic content and serve as an entry point for learning that content. Music adds a multimodal dimension to frontloading before reading and aids the memory and recall of important concepts and vocabulary (Sprenger 1999). Teachers who use published songs and recordings on featured topics or write their own innovations to familiar tunes to introduce a nonfiction text boost their students' enthusiasm and understanding of the concepts of nonfiction text.

Materials

- published song/rap/chant on the nonfiction text topic or teacher-written lyrics for a familiar tune/rap/chant (teacher creates new words on the text topic)
- chart with words to song/rap/chant for all students to see or printed song sheets for each student
- recording of song (optional)

Procedure

- Identify the essential academic vocabulary and concepts of the nonfiction text.
- Select a published song on the text concepts or write original lyrics for a familiar tune that incorporates the concepts and vocabulary.
- Teach the song to students as they read the words on the song chart or their individual song sheets. Sing the song several times to build fluency and familiarity with the content and tune.
- Have students discuss the vocabulary and concepts presented in the song. Students can sketch their mind pictures of the ideas presented in the song and write labels or captions for their sketches. Students can also identify the big ideas and specific vocabulary in the song text.
- Variation: Before reading, students use what they already know about the text topic to create verses for a familiar tune. The teacher adds additional verses to introduce concepts and words students need to know before they read.
- Optional: After reading, students add new information from the text to the Concept Choral by composing another verse.

Figure 4.10 Concept Choral for "Adaptation in Living Things"

Adaptation

Tune: "Head, Shoulders, Knees, and Toes"

Text by Debby Murphy

What to do to live?
Adapt!
What to do to survive?
Adapt …
Long necks, long beaks,
Even quills.
Organisms can adapt, can adapt.

What to do to hide?
Camouflage.
What to do to survive?
Camouflage …
Brown grass, brown fur.
Blend right in,
Organisms can adapt, can adapt.

Sometimes looking just like you,
Mimicry!
Predators won't want me,
Mimicry…
Your spots, my spots,
We could be twins,
Organisms can adapt, can adapt.

Written in genetic code,
Adapt!
Passed down in this mode,
Adapt …
Features, traits,
Develop over time,
Adaptations to survive, to survive.

Packing Up Word Bags

Background

List-Group-Label (Taba 1967) is a strategy that builds on students' prior knowledge of a text topic and provides students with the opportunity to brainstorm words that they associate with the topic. Students then classify their words into categories, justifying their categories by creating associations and relationships among concept words. When students engage in Packing Up Word Bags, they use their prior experience and any background knowledge to generate words and short phrases about a nonfiction topic. Teachers add several key words that focus on the text being introduced. Each word or phrase is written on a paper slip, one word per slip. Then students "pack" the words and phrases into "bags" and label each bag with a "bag tag" that names the group of words/phrases they packed into the bag. After reading, students can "unpack" their bags to evaluate which words/phrases to keep or leave behind based on their text reading, as well as add any new words/phrases from their reading to their bags—"souvenirs" of their "trip" through the text.

Materials

- 25–30 paper strips and pencils for each pair or group of students
- four to six lunch-size paper bags with the tops cut off to make the bags about five inches tall; punch a hole in the top of each bag to tie on the bag tag
- four to six paper bag tags hole-punched with a piece of string or yarn attached

Procedure

- The teacher asks students to think of words or short phrases that relate to a specific topic. Students work together in pairs or small groups to brainstorm at least 20 words and short phrases on the topic. Students write these words and phrases on paper slips—one per slip.
- At this time, if there are several words critical to the concepts

from the text, the teacher introduces these vocabulary words and their meanings to students. Students also put these words on strips, one per strip.

- Students read all the words and phrases that they wrote on their strips and manipulate the strips to sort the words into groups or categories that make sense to them. The number of groups depends on how students sort the strips. Students may sort and re-sort their words as they discuss how best to classify the strips.

- Students pack each group of words and phrases into a word bag, one bag for each category. Depending on the number of groups they come up with, students may not use all of their bags.

- Students write a bag tag to label the category in the bag. Then they tie the appropriate bag tag on each bag.

- Students share their word bags with other students and discuss the rationale behind how they packed their bags with other student groups.

- Variation: For less-experienced readers and writers, the teacher can serve as the recorder and write students' responses on the paper strips. Then students work together to sort the strips as the teacher helps them read the words and phrases and think about possible groups before packing the word bags.

- Before reading the text, have students take the slips from one of the bags and compose several sentences utilizing some of the words and phrases. By creating sentences using some of the targeted words, students demonstrate their current understanding of the conceptual relationships among words and predict how those relationships and the vocabulary might relate to the new text (Moore and Moore 1986). Have students share their sentences before they read the text.

- Optional: After reading, have students unpack any words or phrases from their word bags that were not confirmed or supported by their reading. Then have students add new critical words and phrases from the text to their bags as souvenirs from their trip through the text.

Figure 4.11 Packing Up Word Bags Activity:
The Road to the American Revolution

Examples of Some Words and Short Phrases Written on Paper Slips by Students

colonists	England	Paul Revere
government	George Washington	Boston Tea Party
colonies	taxes	Thomas Jefferson
King George	monarchy	redcoats
soldiers	freedom	independence

Declaration of Independence   "the shot heard round the world"

French and Indian War

Examples of Students' Word Bags and Tags and the Words and Phrases in Each

colonists
King George
George Washington
Thomas Jefferson
soldiers
Paul Revere
redcoats

freedom
independence
government
monarchy
Declaration of Independence
taxes

England
colonies

"the shot heard round the world"
French and Indian War
Boston Tea Party

Making "Sense" of It

Background

Sensory language helps readers form pictures in their minds as they read. Giving students the opportunity to visualize and describe their mental sensory images of concepts and content before reading helps them anticipate the text they are about to read and also activates their prior knowledge. In Making "Sense" of It, students brainstorm words and phrases about the topic of the text they will be reading. Students then classify those words under the five senses—*seeing, hearing, smelling, tasting, and touching* (or only use the senses that are applicable to the topic). If students do not have much background knowledge about the text topic, this strategy can be initiated after introducing the topic with artifacts, models, or such primary sources as a film clip, or a class trip.

Materials

- a chart divided into five columns with each column labeled with one of the five senses *or* a large star with each point labeled with one of the five senses (see Figures 4.12 and 4.13 on the following pages)
- markers

Procedure

- Ask students to picture a tornado, one of the topics of the nonfiction text, *Tornadoes and Hurricanes* (*Nonfiction Readers, Early Fluent Level*), in their minds. Have students suggest words or phrases that describe what they see when they think about tornadoes. Write those words on the chart under "Things I See" (or by the point of the star labeled *See* in Figure 4.13 on page 92) as illustrated in Figure 4.12 on the following page. Support students in painting vivid word pictures with their words.
- Repeat the above process with each of the other senses as students discuss the images that each sense sparks on the topic.
- Review the chart with students before reading the text.

Students can use the chart to sketch some of their mental pictures of the topic before reading.

- Variation: After the Making "Sense" of It strategy has been modeled for students, have them work with partners or in small groups to perform this frontloading activity with a new text and topic.

- Optional: After reading, have students add new sensory details from the text to the Making "Sense" of It chart. Then ask students to write a short descriptive paragraph on the topic using ideas from the chart.

Figure 4.12 A Making "Sense" of It Chart
Based on *Tornadoes and Hurricanes*

Things I See	Things I Hear	Things I Touch	Things I Smell	Things I Taste
A twisting funnel cloud Blowing trash and debris Trees overturning Dark thunderheads gathering People running for safety Rain pouring Flashing skies	Whooshing wind Roaring like a train coming Cracking branches and lightning Rain pouring on the house Things crashing around outside A screaming tornado siren Something crashing on the roof	A stiff mattress pulled over my head The hard radio knob to turn up the weather report A cold flashlight for when the lights go out The smooth bathtub where I am hiding	Rain washing the other smells away Blowing dust going up my nose Fear My sister's bare feet as she hides next to me	My salty sweat Buttery popcorn that we eat while we are hiding and waiting The grit and sand that blows in my mouth from the storm

Figure 4.13 A Making "Sense" of It Chart

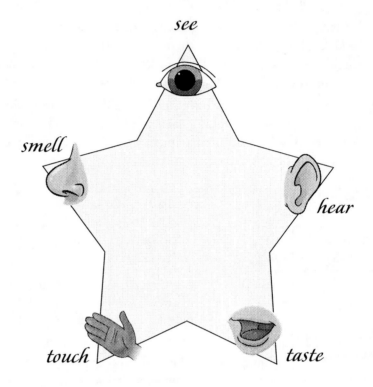

see

smell

hear

touch

taste

Brain Boxes

Background

A K-W-L chart focuses students on the personal experiences they bring to their reading. Using a K-W-L chart also frames students' reading with their own questions about the topic in order to improve students' comprehension (Ogle 1986). Brain Boxes are another concrete teaching tool designed to capture students' prior knowledge on a topic before reading a nonfiction text. This strategy brings to light both the accurate information students already know about a topic as well as what they partially know and any confusions or misconceptions they have. Brain Boxes focus students' attention during reading as they carefully search the text for additional facts to add to their Brain Boxes, note which Brain Box facts need to be revised based on text information, and after reading, determine which facts are inaccurate and need to be removed from their Brain Boxes. Using Brain Boxes before reading places students in control of identifying their own prior knowledge about a nonfiction text topic and considering their purpose for reading. This activity sets students up to be active readers. While reading, students search for and verify the information in their Brain Boxes, ask questions, modify the content of their Brain Boxes based on what they read, and use them to summarize what they have learned.

Materials

- Brain Boxes can be made from empty shoeboxes, cereal or pizza boxes, or plastic index-card boxes. Label the Brain Boxes and decorate appropriately with clip art or students' illustrations. The whole group can work with one Brain Box, or each student group, pair, or individual student can have a Brain Box.
- index cards and markers

Procedure

- Introduce Brain Boxes to students. Have students work together with one Brain Box prepared by the teacher, or give the students time to label and decorate their own Brain Boxes with their small groups or partners.
- Ask students to think about what they already know about a particular topic (i.e., the topic of the new text that students will be reading). It is critical to focus the topic of the Brain Boxes and not use a broad concept. Rather than using the topic of the entire nonfiction text, feature a portion of the text to frame the students' discussion and keep the activity succinct and doable in a short time period. For example, when reading a book about spiders, rather than asking students to describe everything they know about spiders, focus the conversation for the Brain Boxes on one section of the text, such as spiders' habitats, and ask, "What do you know about where spiders live?" A different section of the text can be used for the Brain Boxes at another time.
- The teacher or the students write one known fact about

the topic on an index card, phrasing that fact in a complete sentence. For less-experienced readers, a sketch may be added to the card to illustrate the sentence. If the fact provided by students is incorrect or incomplete, write it on a card anyway. Tell students that part of the process of the Brain Boxes strategy is to use the text to prove or disprove the initial facts placed into their Brain Boxes.

- Review all the facts collected for the Brain Boxes. Ask students if they have any questions about the topic or cards they placed in their Brain Boxes or if they have any facts that they would like to check in the text when they read. Tell students to consider the following three questions as they read the text:

  - Are the facts they wrote on their cards proved or disproved by the text?

  - Are there any new important facts or details from the reading that they want to add to their Brain Boxes?

  - Are there any facts on their original cards that were neither proved nor disproved by the text and will take further reading to verify?

- During and after reading: During reading, have students note text portions that support or disprove their current fact cards and mark their examples with sticky notes. Have students discuss new big ideas or supporting details that are important enough to add to their Brain Boxes. After reading, students make any necessary revisions to their original cards using information from the text. Students delete any fact cards from their boxes that were disproved by the text. Then students add any new significant fact cards based on the text concepts. Finally, students pull out any original cards from the Brain Boxes that the text did not confirm or deny and set them aside to verify with further reading. The teacher demonstrates how to group the final set of cards into meaningful categories and use the categories to make decisions on the most important ideas from the text. Model how to use the cards to summarize the text either orally or in a written paragraph.

- Optional: After reading several nonfiction books on the same concept, one Brain Box can be compiled for the whole class to use for that topic and placed in a literacy center/workstation. Students can use the fact cards in the Brain Box, to show the relationships among the pieces of information, by constructing graphic organizers using the cards. Students can write their own nonfiction compositions about the topic and select from a variety of ways to publish their writings: a paginated book, a news article, a big book for younger readers, a cartoon, or an illustrated mural.

Differentiation Notes

The before-reading strategies presented in this chapter offer teachers a variety of ways to introduce students to a text based on their reading level and their background knowledge of the text concepts. If the reading level of the selected text matches the strengths and needs of the readers, then frontloading decisions depend more on students' prior experiences with and background knowledge of the concepts and vocabulary of the nonfiction text.

Brain Boxes and Packing Up Word Bags are before-reading strategies that work well as assessment tools to inform instruction. The teacher can use this information to differentiate instruction based on where students are in processing important understandings and where they need to go next. That way, teachers don't waste any precious moments teaching students what they already know and can instead create a focused plan for how best to scaffold students into new content and concepts.

When working with English language learners and below-level readers on before-reading activities that involve writing, teachers can choose to control the pen and record students' thinking on a group chart. This frees students to focus on comprehension. Sketches can be added to writing for clarification. Introduce smaller text chunks one at a time, stopping to set up text meaning before reading and then reading and discussing each short portion of text.

Advanced readers also need a text introduction, especially if the text's concepts and vocabulary are unfamiliar to them. Before-reading activities may be less supportive for these readers, and they may be more independent in their explorations before reading (for example, working with Brain Boxes).

Summary

This chapter presents just a few of the many avenues that teachers can take to set their students up to enter a nonfiction text with meaning. Text previews, anticipation guides, concept or thinking maps, picture predictions, and introductions to a topic with a related read-aloud book or a guest speaker are other effective ways to introduce students to a new text. Teachers are encouraged to explore the ideas in this chapter and make them their own, varying and adapting the strategies to scaffold students into effective, positive reading experiences.

✥ Pause and Ponder ✥

Over the period of one or two weeks, examine your lessons to identify the various activities you use to activate student thinking before reading. What patterns do you observe? Are students relying on one or two familiar activities or are they employing a wide variety of strategies? To what extent are students actively engaged in the activities? Are they talking to one another, asking questions, responding to your questions, or jotting down ideas?

Think also about how you involve your students in talking about the ways in which these activities are helping them learn what good readers do. What can you do to help students who continue to dive into a selection and read nonstop from beginning to end? ✍

Chapter 5

Understanding Word Meaning in Texts

"Word learning is a complicated process. It requires giving students a variety of opportunities to connect new words to related words, analyze word structure, understand multiple meanings, and use words actively in authentic ways" (Bromley 2007, 536).

Considerations from Research

- Teachers need to know which words to teach and various ways to teach them; instruction should focus on terms that have a high probability of enhancing academic success.
- Effective vocabulary instruction does not rely on definitions; instruction needs to focus on helping students develop descriptions to represent their word knowledge in both linguistic and nonlinguistic ways.
- Incidental experiences in which students have opportunities to read, hear, use, and talk about new vocabulary complement explicit vocabulary-development activities.

Decoding words is critical to the reading process. Younger students try to sound out the letters and then blend those sounds together to make the words. More proficient students learn to take apart longer, multisyllable words as they read more challenging text. Yet decoding and just saying the words are not the total reading picture.

How many of us have encountered students in our classrooms who look and sound like readers? These students read the words, often fluently, but when asked to discuss what they read, they do not seem to have comprehended the text. These students are "word callers," not "word comprehenders." As teachers, we want to develop learners who understand the essence of words as they read, setting themselves up for creating meaning from text.

Because of the powerful link between understanding word meaning and reading comprehension (Baumann, Kame'enui, and Ash 2003), teachers invest instructional time both before and during reading to build essential background knowledge with conceptual vocabulary. Before reading nonfiction text, teachers introduce critical vocabulary so students can enter the text ready to ascertain the big ideas and important details (see Chapter 4). During reading, teachers model and prompt students to use word-meaning strategies to figure out the meaning of unknown words.

The Role of Context

Even as adults, we encounter partially known or unfamiliar words in text. For example, take a look at this word—*capacious*. What does this word mean? What strategies can readers apply to figure out the meaning of this word? Readers may look for a chunk or part that they know the meaning of—a prefix, suffix, or base word. If readers took four years of Latin in high school as I did, they could look for the Latin base. Perhaps readers may try to think of a time when they have come across this word before in text. Maybe they know another word that looks like this word, such as *capable* or *capacity*?

What other clues can readers use to help them figure out the meaning of *capacious*? Perhaps if they could hear or see this word in context, they could determine or verify a hypothesis about its meaning. Consider this sentence and see if it contains clues that would help readers determine the meaning of *capacious*: *The capacious closet easily held the 12 new pairs of shoes that Miranda purchased for herself when she went to New York.*

The Latin base *cap* means "hold, take, or get." Using this word base and considering the context of the sentence and clues such as "closet," "easily held," and "12 new pairs of shoes," readers can deduce that *capacious* means "able to hold something"; in this case, a *capacious* closet is roomy enough to easily hold Miranda's large shoe collection.

✦ *Pause and Ponder* ✦

What is the role of context in understanding word meaning? To understand the possible impact of context, try this exercise:

Cover the sentences below and then uncover the first sentence. Jot down a word that would make sense based on the context. Then uncover and read the next sentence. If your first answer still makes sense in the context of the new sentence, keep that answer. If not, change your response to fit the new sentence based on the new information provided. Repeat this process each time a sentence is uncovered, keeping your current answer or changing it to more correctly fit the context clues.

1. I like to play _____.

2. I like to play _____ outside.

3. I like to play _____ outside and score a point.

4. I like to play _____ outside and score a point when I hit the ball over the net.

At last, the entire sentence and context are revealed. Taking into account the new contextual information, your response might now be *tennis*, *badminton*, or even *volleyball*. ✦

Many words have multiple meanings, which makes figuring out the appropriate meaning even more challenging. Such situations require the reader to determine which meaning best fits the context. Many times, students may only be familiar with one meaning of a word, and they struggle when they come across this word in a new context. Multiple-meaning words may be especially confusing for English language learners.

Authors can support the reader by incorporating examples, descriptions, or explanations that serve to define or clarify the meaning. Perhaps the text contains a synonym or antonym of the featured vocabulary word. Using these and other text clues, the reader can sometimes infer the meaning of the featured word. However, the challenge for a student in using context to determine word meaning is locating specific proof to figure out the vocabulary. Many times, students want to identify or underline whole chunks of text rather than find words or short phrases that clarify the word's meaning. Since context is usually broader than just the sentence in which the word appears, students must be taught to reread and peruse the surrounding text to find proof for a word's meaning. However, even with the aid of context clues, determining the actual definition of a word may sometimes be difficult. Yet with practice, students can become more proficient in identifying and using available text clues, and combining those clues with relevant prior knowledge of the word, to support comprehension.

So what is the role of context? When vocabulary is supported by a contextually rich text, students can use context clues to help figure out a word's meaning. But some texts are contextually sparse, in which case not all meanings can be determined from text details. A paucity of context is one of the challenges that make understanding vocabulary during reading a tricky process, especially when readers do not have background knowledge of the text concepts, as is often the case when reading nonfiction text. By examining texts and assessing the relationship

Multiple Meanings
Consider the various meanings of the word *trunk* in the example below. What clues to the meanings could a reader draw upon from the context of each sentence?

As Josh arrived at the zoo, he was surprised to see an elephant's *trunk* waving over the wall of the zoo. He sprang from his car to get his camera from the *trunk* of his car. He took out the small brown *trunk* where he keeps his camera equipment. Leaning against a tree *trunk* to steady his arm, he snapped the perfect shot of the gray *trunk* as it reached over the wall.

between the students' prior experience with the vocabulary and the concepts of the text, teachers can determine where they need to focus their instruction on context support. When evaluating which vocabulary is critical for readers to understand, teachers determine which terms must be explicitly taught before reading. Furthermore, teachers can decide which vocabulary can be treated incidentally—word meaning that students can interpret through inference from the context.

The Role of Word Structure

But what if readers have another support for determining word meaning? What if readers also know the meaning of certain word parts or roots? A root is any part of a word that holds meaning. Then, readers have an additional path to take when determining the meaning of the word. Instruction in the meaning of word roots, including prefixes, suffixes, and base words, is a valuable tool for solving the meaning of unknown words. Since 90 percent of English words with two or more syllables have a Latin-based root and many of the remaining 10 percent have a Greek derivation, the teacher who actively teaches these Latin and Greek bases, along with the meaning of prefixes and suffixes, equips students with yet another powerful strategy for unlocking vocabulary's meaning (Rasinski, Padak, Newton, and Newton 2008). See the Appendix (page 277) for a list of possible roots for instruction.

Activities with Word Parts

Students enjoy collecting words from their reading that are derived from various Latin and Greek bases or include known prefixes and suffixes and writing the words on a "word wheel." These words can then be referenced in reading or writing experiences. A word wheel for the base *spec/spect* is shown in Figure 5.1 on the following page.

Examining Word Parts and Context

Example sentence: The *biologist* will study the plants and animals of the rainforest. Consider the parts of the word *biologist*:

- the root *bio-* means "life, live."
- the suffix *-ologist* means "one who studies or is an expert in."

Putting these two parts together, the meaning of *biologist* is "one who studies life." The context clue "study the plants and animals" deepens the readers' grasp of the word *biologist* so they more completely and fully comprehend the vocabulary.

Figure 5.1 Word Wheel

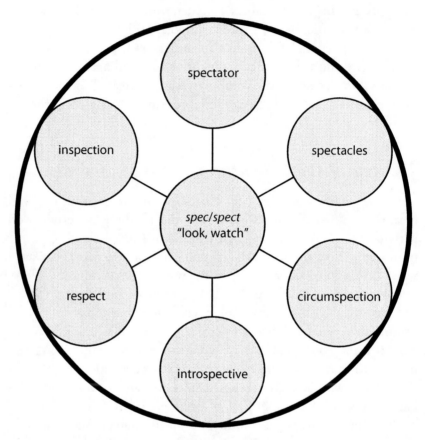

Word games and activities provide students with opportunities to study and play with word roots. There are many published word games that students can use, but simple activities allow students to practice using and internalizing meaningful word parts. Here are a few activities for you to try with students.

1. Write known prefixes, suffixes, and bases on index cards—one root per card—and let students create words using the cards. For example, one set of cards could be *un, able, like, happy, comfort, believe, deliver.* Note that with some of these examples, students would need to cover up the final *e* on *like* and *believe* to add the *-able* card.

2. Other activities include writing riddles with three to four clues featuring words that contain a particular Latin or Greek root.

- I am a noun.
- You wear me on your face.
- I help you see. *(spectacles)*

3. Students also enjoy writing their own riddles. Students can try to solve another kind of word riddle by filling in a missing word in a cloze-type sentence riddle (Rasinski and Padak 2004). A rich context supports the meaning of the word along with using the meaning of the base. Once again, after students have participated in this activity, they can write their own sentences with effective context clues so their classmates can guess the missing word with the featured word. Here are two examples of cloze-like sentence riddles:

- The woman carefully _____ the apples to make sure they did not have any brown spots or holes. *(inspected)*
- When the soldiers bowed before the queen, it showed how much they _____ her leadership. *(respected)*

Word Magician Strategy

Students can effectively decode many unknown words in text by actively engaging in the study of word parts and considering possible contextual clues, including short phrases, sentences, and text organizers. Word Magician is a strategy that focuses on what good readers do to help themselves when they are challenged by vocabulary in text. Powerful word solvers search an unfamiliar word for known meaningful roots or look around that word for context clues that support meaning (Herman and Weaver 1988; Au, Carroll, and Scheu 1997). Word magicians use these problem-solving strategies to figure out the meaning of words.

To introduce this word-meaning strategy, the teacher carefully selects one to three words from the text, keeping in mind that the words *must be contextually supported*. When choosing the words, the teacher looks for context clues such as embedded definitions, descriptions, examples, explanations, synonyms, or even antonyms. Sometimes the clues will specifically point to the meaning of the word; other times, the clues will require readers to infer the meaning from a broader context. The selected words may also provide the reader with morphological support by containing known roots that will enrich the students' understanding of the word.

When students encounter one of the words the teacher has selected for word-meaning practice, the students apply the two strategies of "looking in" and "looking around" the unknown word in order to figure out its meaning. First, prompt the students to look in the word for the biggest chunk or part they are familiar with. In this case, students are asked to identify known meaningful word roots (prefixes, suffixes, base words) and consider how those parts add to their hypothesis of the meaning of the word. When students identify a word part they know, be sure to ask, "What does it mean?" If students do not know the meaning of a particular prefix, suffix, or base, take advantage of this opportunity to teach students the root. To be successful in this first phase of the Word Magician strategy, students must be able to identify a root and its meaning. This recognition gives them the information they need at this time to solve the targeted word. However, not all words will contain chunks that students know. When that happens, they simply need to move on to the next step that good word magicians take to figure out the tricky word.

> Avoid asking students to look for a "little word" in the big word. This prompts students to randomly search for little words in longer words rather than looking left to right through a word for the biggest part or root they know the meaning of. For example, in the word *scared*, students could find several little words: *a, car, red, care, are,* and *scar*. However, none of these little words will help readers determine the meaning.

The second strategy builds on the initial looking in exploration. In this strategy, the word magicians look around a word for any context clues that confirm or add to the ideas about the word's meaning that they derived from "looking in the word." Many students sit with confused looks when teachers ask them to find context clues to support word meaning. Asking students to look around a word for clues, or "proof," to a word's meaning is a clear, simple direction for exactly what good readers do to solve those tricky words in a text. Students locate and underline or highlight, mark with sticky notes, or verbally identify any contextual links or clues that support the word's meaning while considering any prior information they gained from looking in. Students share any proof from the text they think supports the word's meaning and justify their thinking by providing a meaning for the word that would fit the context. The proof identified can be words, short phrases, or even support from text organizers. Once again, a key point for this portion of the Word Magician strategy—and one that is difficult for many students—is finding specific proof. Teach students that context goes beyond the sentence that the word is in, especially in higher text levels. Students must be able to locate clues in larger chunks of text that support a more complete understanding of a particular vocabulary word. Engage students in rich instructional discussions about how to think about word usage and textual clues. Actively probe and prompt for thinking that develops strong word magicians.

If readers are still unable to determine the meaning of a word after completing the first two steps of Word Magician, allow students to use a dictionary or other reference sources to confirm the meaning or deepen their understanding of the targeted word. In many situations (such as during a state reading assessment or while reading in a doctor's office), looking up a word to determine its meaning is not an option, so it is essential that readers become proficient at using the look in and look around steps of the Word Magician strategy. Knowing how to use this strategy enables students to solve word meanings whenever possible.

STAR Model Lessons

The lessons in this section use the Word Magician strategy to model and build proficiency in looking in and looking around a word to determine its meaning. I have provided "teacher talk" to illustrate the language teachers should use to scaffold the strategy for students. Three nonfiction selections are used to illustrate application of the Word Magician strategy:

- *Cell Phone Agreement*: This text is a synopsis of a cell phone contractual agreement with Ring-A-Ding Wireless Service. It includes a number of text organizers, characteristic of this type of nonfiction text, that highlight the company's information and special plan features. This sixth-grade instructional text poses several vocabulary challenges. The word *contract* is an example of a term that contains both meaningful word parts and context clues to support readers as they figure out its meaning. This word is used in the Word Magician STAR Model Lesson to illustrate how the strategy is taught during the reading when students first encounter the word in the text.

- *A Visit to a Publisher:* This text's level is 2.0 (beginning of second grade). *A Visit to a Publisher* has a table of contents so students can read the text in smaller meaningful chunks. The text font is still large to support the reader at this level, but now many pages have more than one paragraph of text. Along with other supportive text organizers, some of the new content vocabulary is bolded, alerting the reader to the importance of the term and indicating that the word is also included in a glossary at the back of the text.

- *Volcanoes: Volcanoes* is a high-interest nonfiction text (text level 2.2). This text also has a table of contents, glossary, and various other text features to support students' construction of meaning as they read. Multiple text clues and photographs help the reader determine the meaning of *eruption* in this chapter. In addition, the teacher can teach the base *rupt* to help students apply the meaning of this word part to their concept of the word *eruption*.

Figure 5.2 STAR Model Lesson

STAR is a lesson structure based on the gradual release of responsibility model (see Chapter 1). A STAR lesson is comprised of four levels, each of which provides students with varying levels of support leading them toward independence in using the selected strategy.

- Level 1: Modeled Strategy Use: I Do
- Level 2: Shared Strategy Use: We Do
- Level 3: Guided Strategy Use: You Try
- Level 4: Independent Strategy Use: You Do

The lesson description includes the comprehension strategy, a list of critical attributes (specific understandings for the teacher as to what is essential to understand about teaching the comprehension strategy as well as specific language to use when teaching the strategy), a list of materials, and the text.

STAR Model Lesson 1: Word Magician—Cell Phone Agreement

Comprehension Strategy

- understanding word meaning in text

Critical Attributes

- Student identifies the unknown Word Magician word in the text.
- Student looks in the identified word for known chunks or parts.
- Student looks around the identified word for specific context clues.
- Student develops a hypothesis of what the word means in the text.
- Student may look up a word in a reference book, such as a dictionary, to verify or add to its meaning (not included in this STAR Model Lesson).

Materials
- nonfiction text at students' instructional reading level (Note: Provide students with a copy of the text to write on or have small sticky notes, highlighter tape, or an overhead transparency sheet and pen available for marking each organizer)
- markers (a different color for recording in each column of the chart)
- teacher-made chart to record students' thinking (see Figure 5.3 below)
- a Word Magician's hat and wand (optional, but fun!)

Figure 5.3 Word Magician Strategy Chart

The mystery word	What I see when I "look in" the word	What I see when I "look around" the word	What I think the word means

Figure 5.4 Sample Cell Phone Agreement

1

Cell Phone Agreement

Welcome to **Ring-A-Ding Wireless Service**.
Included in your package is a Teletech Ultra-Slim 55x phone with:

- 1.5 megapixel camera
- TXT messaging
- Picture messaging
- Voice dialing
- Speakerphone
- Broadband Internet **capability**
- Instant messaging

This is a one-year service agreement for our Ring AllOver™ national calling plan. It has unlimited long distance in the United States (no roaming charges). You have 450 monthly minutes in your plan. You will be charged $0.45 for each extra minute. Nights and weekends are free.

Night Hours: Monday–Friday 9 P.M.–6 A.M.
Weekend Hours: Friday 9 P.M.– Monday 6 A.M.

Other charges may apply, including tolls, taxes, surcharges, and other fees.

You can cancel your contract before the end of the **initial** 12-month period. There will be an Early **Termination** Fee of $150.

Description of Features

3-Way Calling
Allows you to talk with two people at the same time. (Not available in some areas.)

Voice Mail
Callers can leave you a voice message when you can't answer the phone.

Call Forwarding
Lets you forward calls to another number. When activated, your wireless phone will not ring.

Call Waiting
Lets you know when someone is trying to reach you while you are on another call.

Caller ID
Allows you to see the caller's phone number before you take the call. If the caller is in your phone book, the phone will also **display** the caller's name.

THT Messaging
TXT Messaging is a two-way text-messaging service. Send and receive text messages of up to 160 characters. Messages are shown right on your two-way messaging-capable phone. There is a charge of $0.10 for each message received and $0.10 for each message sent.

For more information
Please see the Customer Agreement. You may also want to speak with a sales representative. Service is subject to the Customer Agreement. Read the agreement before starting service.

Ring AllOver™ National Calling Plan
Allows you to talk with any Ring-A-Ding customer anytime (in the United States and Puerto Rico).

Total due upon signing:
$34.95 Teletech Ultra-Slim 55x
$39.99 first monthly charge
$74.94 TOTAL

Source: Teacher Created Materials 2008

Level 1: Modeled Strategy Use—I Do

Good readers sometimes come to a word in a text and do not know its meaning. Just skipping words and reading on without solving the meaning of those unknown words can quickly get a reader confused about the big ideas of the text. Today, I am going to teach you a strategy called Word Magician that can help you figure out the meaning of an unknown, tricky word.

The first thing that a good word magician does is look in a word. Look at the word that I am writing in the first column on our chart—*contract*. Let's look in this word to find a chunk or part we know—a root. The first chunk or root I recognize is *con-*. We have talked about the meaning of this prefix before. It means "with, together." I think that knowing this chunk will help me understand the meaning of *contract*.

There is another root of this word that I have heard before—*tract*. I need to think. What does *tract* mean? If I am not really sure what a word chunk means, it will not help me. However, I think I do know this Latin root. It means "pull" or "drag." Now, if I put these two parts together, the word *contract* may mean something that you pull together. I will write down my thinking in the second column (see Figure 5.5 below).

Figure 5.5 Word Magician Chart—Look in the Word

The mystery word	What I see when I "look in" the word	What I see when I "look around" the word	What I think the word means
contract	*con* = with, together *tract* = pull, drag		

The next thing that a good word magician does is look around the word in the text for any clues or proof that will help me add to my thinking about what *contract* means. I will reread any text chunks that talk about this contract. I am looking for words or short phrases that point to the meaning of the word *contract*. I am going to underline those clues when I find them. The title is *Cell Phone Agreement*. The whole text is about this agreement. An agreement is when two people or groups decide to do something together. That's like pulling together to do something. I am going to underline *Agreement* in the title.

In paragraph two, when I read the first sentence, I see the phrase *one-year service agreement*. Now I know that this particular agreement is between the person who wants a cell phone and the cell phone service company. This agreement is for one year. I will underline this phrase as another clue to the meaning of *contract*.

In the fifth paragraph, I can reread the sentence that the word *contract* is actually in, and I learn that you can cancel a contract. This contract is for a 12-month period, or a year. I will underline *cancel* and *initial 12-month period*. Let's write all our clues on the chart (Figure 5.6 below).

Figure 5.6 Word Magician Chart—Look Around the Word

The mystery word	What I see when I "look in" the word	What I see when I "look around" the word	What I think the word means
contract	*con* = with, together *tract* = pull, drag	*agreement, one-year service agreement, cancel, initial 12-month period*	

Now I need to write what I think *contract* means in the last column. If I think about what I learned from looking in and looking around this word, then I think I am ready to say what *contract* means. I think a contract is an agreement that pulls two people or groups together for a certain period of time. In this article, the cell phone plan purchaser makes a contract or agreement with the cell phone company to buy cell phone service. Now I can write what I think *contract* means in the last column (Figure 5.7 below).

Figure 5.7 Word Magician Chart—Predicted Word Meaning

The mystery word	What I see when I "look in" the word	What I see when I "look around" the word	What I think the word means
contract	*con* = with, together *tract* = pull, drag	*agreement, one-year service agreement, cancel, initial 12-month period*	*a one-year agreement with Ring-A-Ding Wireless Service to buy a cell phone calling plan*

Level 2: Shared Strategy Use—We Do

Let's find another word that we can use our Word Magician strategy to determine its meaning. In the fifth paragraph, where we came across the word *contract*, there is another tricky word—*termination*.

- What is the first thing that good word magicians do? *(Look in the word for chunks or parts they know.)*
- What do you know? (Possible responses: *The suffix is* -tion, *that means "state of," so the state of or act of terminating. I have seen a movie about a Terminator; he stops all the bad stuff that happens. I have heard the part* term, *but I do not know what it means.*)

Well, the only part that we seem to know for sure is that *-tion* is a suffix that can mean "state of, characterized by." Let's write that in our chart. Maybe we will find out if a *Terminator* who stops or ends bad things is somehow related to the word *termination*. What is the next thing that good word magicians do? *(Look around the word for clues to what the word means.)*

112

- Does anyone see any clues or proof for what *termination* might mean? (Prompt students if they need support. Possible responses: *You have to pay money, or a fee, if you do it early. I think it has something to do with canceling or stopping the cell phone service contract. You have to pay a fee if you cancel the agreement before the end of the 12-month period.*)

- So what clues should I write in the chart? (*cancel your contract, before the end, early, fee*)

- Let's look at the last column of our chart. What do you think I should write here to explain what the word means? When we looked in the word, we determined that *termination* has to do with the state of or act of terminating. In the article, the word *termination* is being used to describe a fee that the cell phone company charges if the cell phone user cancels or ends the contract early. Do we think *termination* is when someone or something stops, ends, or cancels something? Let's write the meaning of *termination* in our own words in the last column.

Level 3: Guided Strategy Use—You Try

Let's try to figure out the meaning of one more word using our Word Magician strategy. The word *national* is in two places in our text—the second paragraph and in the heading "Ring AllOver™ National Calling Plan." With your partner, use the Word Magician strategy to look in and look around the word and determine what you think the word means.

- Look at the word *national*. With your partner, discuss the first thing that a word magician does to figure out the meaning of a word. What do you see when you look in this word?

    Students often identify the chunk, nation, *in this word, but verify that they actually know what it means by asking, "What does nation mean?" Responses heard before include, "A nation ... is ... well, it's like ... a nation," and "A nation ... it's in our social studies book." These answers do not reflect a clear understanding of the concept behind the word and therefore do not help the reader.*

- What else does a good reader do to figure out the meaning of a word?

- With your partner, see what proof you can find for the meaning of the word *national*. (*Possible responses: second paragraph—"in the United States;" under the heading, "Ring AllOver™ National Calling Plan"—"in the United States and Puerto Rico"*)

- Now work with your partner to decide on a meaning for the word *national* in this text. Be ready to share your thinking with the group.

Concluding the STAR Lesson

To close the STAR lesson, ask students to identify the critical steps and attributes of the Word Magician strategy. Write the steps for using this strategy on a STAR Points chart as shown in Figure 5.8 below. Discuss these questions with students: When might a reader use this strategy? Would a reader ever use this strategy in math, science, or social studies? Why? How would that look?

Figure 5.8 STAR Points Chart for the Word Magician Strategy

STAR Points

Word Magician:

A During-Reading Strategy

1. Identify a tricky word you do not understand.

2. Look in the word for chunks or parts you know.

3. Look around the word for clues that point to what the word means.

4. Think about the word now. What do you know? What is the best meaning for the word in this text?

5. If necessary, use a word resource to look up the word or to learn more about the word.

✦ *Pause and Ponder* ✦

Using a nonfiction text of your choosing, plan a series of vocabulary lessons based on this STAR model. What did you learn about your teaching style and language as you presented the lessons to students? How did students respond to the activities?

How is vocabulary instruction presented in the reading program you are currently using with students? In what ways do the attributes of those lessons compare to the critical attributes of the first STAR Model Lesson in this chapter?

What factors do you take into consideration when you select vocabulary for explicit instruction? In what ways do you encourage students to become "conscious" of words? ✦

STAR Model Lesson 2: Word Magician—A Visit to a Publisher

The chart on page 116 (Figure 5.9) illustrates the use of the Word Magician strategy with a lower-level text. The chart was developed through the same process described for the previous selection, *Cell Phone Agreement.*

A Visit to a Publisher is a 2.0-level text. The word *editor* is featured for Word Magician strategy instruction or practice because it has meaningful word parts and there are several context clues on this page of text. After students act as magicians with this word, they can verify their responses by looking up the word in the glossary at the end of the book.

Figure 5.9 Word Magician Chart for "Editor"

The mystery word	What I see when I "look in" the word	What I see when I "look around" the word	What I think the word means
editor	*edit* = fix up writing to make it "reader friendly" *(students may know this root from process writing)* *-or* = one who	*works for magazine publisher, makes choices about what goes in, makes sure writing is best*	

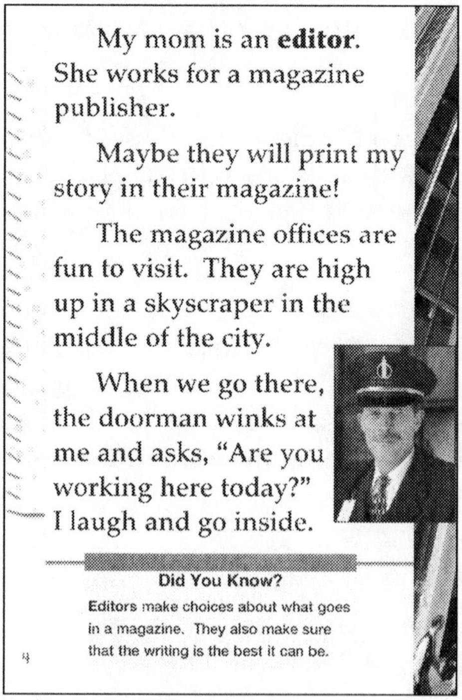

My mom is an **editor**. She works for a magazine publisher.

Maybe they will print my story in their magazine!

The magazine offices are fun to visit. They are high up in a skyscraper in the middle of the city.

When we go there, the doorman winks at me and asks, "Are you working here today?" I laugh and go inside.

Did You Know?

Editors make choices about what goes in a magazine. They also make sure that the writing is the best it can be.

Source: Rice 2004

STAR Model Lesson 3: Word Magician—Volcanoes

Another example of the Word Magician strategy, used with a lower-level text, is shown in Figure 5.11 on the next page. *Volcanoes* (see Figure 5.10) is a 2.2-level instructional text. The meaning of the word *eruption* is supported by text clues and the photographs. The teacher can teach the meaning of the base *rupt* to provide students with additonal information for determining word meaning. This base can be found in other words such as *interrupt, corrupt,* and *rupture.*

Figure 5.10 Excerpt from *Volcanoes: Time For Kids Nonfiction Readers*

Eruption!

An eruption happens when magma, ash, rock, and gases are released from a volcano. Sometimes an eruption comes in a blast. Sometimes it comes in a slow ooze.

If a volcano might erupt, it is called **active**. If we think it will not erupt now or in the future, it is called **dormant** (DOR-mənt). Dormant is another word for asleep.

12

Think what happens when you shake a can of soda. When you open it, the soda might blast out or just overflow down the sides. It depends on how much pressure has built up.

13

Source: Armour 2004

Figure 5.11 Word Magician Chart for "Eruption"

The mystery word	What I see when I "look in" the word	What I see when I "look around" the word	What I think the word means
eruption	*rupt* = break	*magma, ash, rock, and gases are released from a volcano; blast, slow ooze*	

Level 4: Independent Strategy Use—You Do

At this level, the teacher provides a variety of settings for students to autonomously try on the role of word magician. Through literacy centers/stations and other independent engagements with text, students learn to flexibly and fluently apply this strategy as they become effective word magicians. During the You Do phase of the gradual release of responsibility model, the teacher can observe and assess students' proficiency in using the Word Magician strategy and adjust the level of support or provide further instruction on building word meaning from text.

1. Give students (individually or with partners) an independent-level text with two to three words identified for Word Magician practice. On a laminated Word Magician chart (see example in Figure 5.3, on page 108), have students use an overhead pen to record their thinking in the chart as they use the Word Magician strategy to identify the meaning of each of the identified words.

2. Provide each student in a small reading-discussion group with three sticky notes. Students assume the role of word magician as they independently read the text and use a sticky note to identify one to three tricky words in the text where they might need to use the Word Magician strategy to figure out a word's meaning. Later on, students meet as a group to discuss their selected words and try out the strategy with those words together.

3. Students play various word games that focus on word roots, word context, or word meaning, including published word games, word wheels, making words with cards, word sorts, word riddles, word puzzles, and so on.

Differentiation Notes

After the STAR Model Lesson is presented to students, differentiate the strategy by considering the text level and students' familiarity with the vocabulary of the text topic. Identify only one or two words for students to use to practice the Word Magician strategy. Some students will need shared, interactive support several more times as they try out the strategy, while more proficient students may practice the strategy one or two times in a guided context and then be ready to apply it to their independent reading. Below-level students or English language learners may benefit from not only highlighting text clues when looking around a word but also visualizing the information by sketching their mind pictures of the clues.

Summary

Teachers need to continue to engage students in powerful vocabulary-building experiences as they encounter new text topics and concepts, especially in the content areas. Many words must be explicitly taught and experienced in a variety of contexts before students can demonstrate a deep understanding of them. The Word Magician strategy does not help students comprehend every word they encounter as they read. Still, this strategy offers students positive, concrete steps to take when meaning breaks down as they read, especially when the problematic words have a meaningful, known root or the text provides sufficient context clues. Students must be given many opportunities to apply the strategy of Word Magician in a guided context with the teacher before they will automatically apply this strategy and use it independently in literacy centers, self-selected reading, or a testing situation. Students who have strategic options for exploring word meaning as they read—other than just skipping the word and moving on—will be better equipped to understand vocabulary, a critical building block of comprehensible, enjoyable reading.

✦ *Pause and Ponder* ✦

"Words are things, and a small drop of ink,
Falling, like dew, upon a thought, produces
That which makes thousands, perhaps millions, think."
(Lord Byron, *Don Juan*, cto. 3, st. 88).

What images came to mind as you read the quote from Byron? If appropriate, share the quote with your students and invite them to share the images they envisioned as they heard the words.

Words matter—in talking, reading, writing, listening, thinking, and learning. Think about the many ways words are used in your classroom—how you use words and how your students use words. Talk with your students about the wonderful words they encounter and the different ways those words are used. ✍

Using Text Features to Determine Importance, Develop Main Ideas, and Create Text Summaries

"Readers need to know enough about text structure and content to make use of whatever cues are in the surface text, yet not too much lest they think they know everything in the text and therefore do not need to pay attention to the material at all" (Goldman and Rakestraw Jr. 2000, 325).

Considerations from Research

- Text features provide cues to the relative importance of ideas in the text.
- Examining text features helps readers understand the author's purpose.
- Targeted use of text organizers helps readers make self-to-text connections.
- Pausing to think about the ideas after reading a text or a portion of it enables readers to better comprehend the ideas in the selection.
- Being aware of the explicit organization of a text aids readers in determining main ideas—recognizing main ideas that are stated and those that have to be inferred.

- Text features provide signals that help readers summarize text—clues about ideas to keep, ideas to delete, or ideas that could be substituted in a summary.

Hand students a nonfiction text and say, "Get ready to read." Note what students do to prepare themselves to read. Do they sit up straighter, fold their hands, and look at you? Great—they are attentive, and that behavior is certainly preferable to slouching and sighing. But that is not what you are looking for in these readers. They may look around at others in the group to see what they are doing in response to the request. Maybe students look at an illustration or two. Or perhaps they just jump into the text and start reading. At least they are engaged. Many students consistently seem to pick up a nonfiction text and start reading it without doing any purposeful action to set up meaning beforehand.

What a teacher would love to see in response to "Get ready to read" are students who begin to preview the text organizers to determine some of the big ideas of the text before reading. This strategy of surveying text organizers becomes critical in maximizing meaning before reading, especially when students are asked to read without teacher support or a text introduction (for example, in a testing situation). Without instruction and practice, students simply may not know how to preview a text to set up meaning before they read. They are also unlikely to recognize the effectiveness of this strategy in supporting their reading.

Authors use text organizers to draw readers into nonfiction text, point out important information, and even highlight the main ideas. Text organizers take many forms in nonfiction text—headings, subheadings, graphics, and various design elements. These textual and visual clues set students up for determining the relative importance of ideas, locating information, targeting vocabulary, identifying key concepts, establishing the author's purpose, and developing tentative main ideas about the text. Authors use text organizers literally to say to readers: "Look at this! This is important information. Why do you think I put this here? How does this help you make sense of the text before and as you read?"

One of the features of nonfiction text is that it is dense; that is, it is full of facts, details, and concepts. Some students become bogged down in this type of text and have difficulty determining which information is the most important. They often tend to see all the details as equal and cannot isolate the big ideas or significant points from the lesser ones. The inability to determine importance in nonfiction text goes on to affect other comprehension strategies, such as articulating a main idea, identifying significant supporting details, summarizing a text, finding text proof to respond to inferential questions, drawing conclusions, and determining word meaning from context. Taking the time to preview a text, noting the text organizers—terms in titles, captions and headings, text layout, graphics/visuals—and what they might be telling the reader, helps students begin to pull out some of the important ideas of a text before reading (Hoyt 2002).

> **Missing the Main Point**
> A teacher stops by a student who just finished reading a story about a boy who made some wings after studying a book about flight and tried them out by jumping off his garage roof. The boy broke his leg. The teacher comments to the student, "What a problem!" The student carefully studies the picture accompanying the text, looks up at the teacher, and says, "Yes, that boy has on red socks."

Before modeling a text-previewing strategy for students, decide on a consistent language for describing the strategy and *always* call the strategy by that name. Text Preview, Text Survey, and Text Walk are labels frequently used to describe the previewing strategy. For the purposes of this book, the strategy will be called a Text Walk. Whatever the strategy is called, it involves examining all the text organizers provided by the author in order to set up meaning and determine main ideas before reading.

To help students become familiar with the various ways that authors organize text, teachers use a wide range of materials—read aloud text, enlarged text, magazines, newspapers, advertisements, catalogs, menus, trade books, and other types of functional, nonfiction text. Students need to recognize every text organizer that signifies meaning as they take their text walk. Figure 6.1 on the following page presents an overview of nonfiction text features. In Chapter 9, I provide more detailed descriptions of text features and expository text structures and how to use these to build students' reading comprehension.

Figure 6.1 Nonfiction Text Features

Category of Features	Types of Features
Content Features	Titles, Headlines, Headings, Subheadings, Labels, Captions, Questions and Answers, Vocabulary Lists, Glossary, Table of Contents
Graphic Features	Graphic Organizers (e.g., Venn Diagram), Photographs, Illustrations, Sketches, Diagrams, Charts, Graphs, Maps, Tables, Figures, Timelines, Cross-sections, Insets
Format Features	Varied Fonts (e.g., Times, Arial, Courier), **Bold**, *Italics*, <u>Underline</u>, Text Color, Bulleted Lists, Numbered Lists, Columns, Sidebars, Marginal Notes

Familiarizing Students with the Text Walk Strategy

As students work with a variety of instructional or read aloud texts, draw their attention to new and familiar text organizers. These examples can be made visible in a couple of ways. A wall chart titled "Text Organizers We Found" (see Figure 6.2 on the following page) can be developed with examples of text features posted and labeled. New examples can be added regularly as students discover them in texts they are reading.

Figure 6.2 Text Organizers We Found Wall Chart

Text Organizer	Name	Purpose
Here Comes China! Chapter 2 • Adaptation in Living Things	Title (Newspaper: Headline)	Catch reader's attention with a big idea/main idea
Welcome to life in the greenhouse **The Country Has Become a Very Important Nation**	Subtitle	Give more information about title and big/main idea
HUMAN-MADE CLIMATE? **THE HEAT IS ON!**	Heading	Tells the big/main idea of a text section/ chunk
	Photograph/ caption	Helps reader visualize important information and provides details to support big text ideas
Not long ago China was thought of as a poor country. Today, China has become a **manufacturing** giant. Its factories make billions of dollars worth **of goods**. These goods are sold around the world. For example, many of the clothes, toys, and shoes sold in the U.S. and other countries are made in China. — Words to Know: adaptation, camouflage, mimicry	Bold word	Points to important concept vocabulary in text
	Map, globe	Shows important places or locations in text
A Look at China Size: 3,705,406 square miles. China is the world's fourth-largest country, after Russia, Canada, and the United States. **Population:** More than 1 billion **Capital:** Beijing **Language:** Mandarin Chinese is the official language.	Inset box	Gives the reader additional details about the topic

Students can also make a big book with examples of various text organizers or generate their own examples for each text feature they recognize (see Figure 6.3 below). These examples may encourage many students to experiment with using text organizers in their own writing after seeing examples in published authors' work.

Figure 6.3 Sample Pages from a Big Book of Text Organizers

Modeling a text walk is an effective way to focus students' attention on the various features in nonfiction text. Select a reasonable chunk of text to use to model the text walk. A single-page or two-page spread in a text for older students is a sufficient amount of text to preview at one time. Because texts for younger students are much shorter, teachers may choose to preview the entire text at one time. Teach students to go from the top of the page down to the bottom so they will not miss any text features that might inform the reader. Initially, have students circle or place a small sticky note by each text feature that they preview. Note features of different kinds of text and show students how to text walk selected features. For example, columns are often used in newspaper and magazine articles. Use an article to show students how to text walk each column from top to bottom.

> **The Crime of "Assumicide"**
> Do not commit "assumicide" when students encounter a new example of nonfiction text. Assumicide happens when the teacher assumes students know something or thinks that surely the students learned this something last year! Some nonfiction selections are overflowing with text organizers, and students need a purposeful, consistent plan for conducting their text walks.

By surveying the text organizers, students can develop a sense of context for their reading as well as begin to determine importance in the text. However, be aware that a text walk can quickly become a mechanical task if students only circle or note all of the text features without thinking about the information they convey. After examining each text organizer, students must ask themselves, "What do I now know about the text/topic?" and be able to provide a response that reveals the insights they have gained. With each additional preview of a new organizer, students add information to their ideas about the text. Text walking is not a predicting activity; it is based on what students know from their preview of the text organizers. This strategy supports readers in attending to what is important in the text even before they begin to read the body of the text.

After walking the text and its organizers, students can form a tentative main idea, or hypothesis: Is the text going to be about a "who" or a "what"? What information does a survey of text features reveal about the who or what? Write students' tentative main idea in a chart. Then ask students what questions they have or what information they still do not know after their text walk. Add their questions to the chart with their tentative main idea. This text walk gives students a purpose for reading the text—to find answers to their questions and verify or revise their tentative main idea.

✦ *Pause and Ponder* ✦

Give a small group of students a nonfiction text to read. Before reading, ask students to get themselves ready to read. Jot down the student behaviors you observe as students respond to your directions.

What did you find out about these students? What text features, if any, did they note? How did they use this information to help them identify the big ideas of the text? How would an effective text walk enrich their understanding of the text before they read? ✦

STAR Model Lessons

The STAR Model Lesson was introduced in Chapter 5. In this section, I present four STAR lessons designed to teach selected comprehension strategies. The lessons and their corresponding strategies are outlined in Figure 6.4 below.

Figure 6.4 STAR Model Lessons

STAR Lesson Title	Comprehension Strategy
Lesson 1: Taking a Text Walk to Preview a Text for the Main Idea	Determine importance of using text organizers
A Before-Reading Strategy	Develop a tentative main idea statement

Figure 6.4 STAR Model Lessons *(cont.)*

STAR Lesson Title	Comprehension Strategy
Lesson 2: Using a Text Walk Puzzle to Preview Text Organizers and Develop a Main Idea Statement	Determine importance of using text organizers
A Before-Reading Strategy	Develop a tentative main idea statement
Lesson 3: Read a Little, Think a Little	Determine importance in order to summarize and verify the main ideas of a text
A During-Reading Strategy	Monitor meaning during reading
Lesson 4: Pluses, Lines, and Stars	Determine importance and verify main ideas of a text
A During- and After-Reading Strategy	Monitor comprehension

Two nonfiction selections are used to illustrate the Text Walk strategy:

• "A Killer Quake in Asia"

This text is one of two choices for a newspaper article titled "A Killer Quake in Asia." One text is written on a fourth-grade level, and the other text, which is visually similar with the same text organizers and photographs, is at about a third-grade level. These leveled texts allow the teacher to differentiate the content and make it accessible to students at different reading levels. "A Killer Quake in Asia" contains a variety of text organizers for the students to preview and use to determine the main ideas of the text before reading.

- *A Trip to the Hospital*

A Trip to the Hospital is a first-grade-level text from which I have selected a short chapter called "The Ambulance" to illustrate the Text Walk strategy. This text contains a number of text organizers, including titles, bolded vocabulary, an inset box, and a photograph that the students can preview to determine the big ideas of the text before they read.

STAR Model Lesson 1: Taking a Text Walk to Preview a Text for Main Ideas

Comprehension Strategies

- determine importance using text organizers
- develop a tentative main idea statement

Critical Attributes

- The student "walks the text" and identifies each individual text organizer, moving from top to bottom in the text.
- The student stops after each text organizer and asks, "Now what do I know (about the main ideas of the text)?"
- The student articulates a tentative main idea statement after conducting the entire text walk.
- The student asks questions about the text and identifies what he or she does not yet know about the topic (purpose for reading).

Materials

- nonfiction text on students' instructional reading level (provide students with a copy of the text to write on or have small sticky notes, highlighter tape, or an overhead transparency overlay sheet and pen available to mark each organizer)
- markers (a different color for recording in each column of the chart)
- teacher-made chart to record students' thinking (see Figure 6.5 below)

Figure 6.5 Chart to Summarize Student Thinking from a Text Walk

Text Organizer	Now What Do I Know?	Questions

Figure 6.6 Sample Nonfiction Text for Text Walk Strategy

World News

October 9, 2005   Section A

A Killer Quake in Asia

Deadly Shocks Tear Through Pakistan, India, and Afghanistan
By Dawn Frost

Survivors search the wreckage of a destroyed building in Islamabad, Pakistan's capital.

KASHMIR, October 9—A strong earthquake struck here. It happened yesterday. At 8:50 A.M. **tremors** ran through three countries. People felt them in Pakistan and India. They felt them in Afghanistan, too. In just minutes, thousands died. Towns were ruined. Leaders fear that 40,000 people may be dead.

Northern Pakistan had the worst damage. The epicenter of the quake was near Muzaffarabad. It is in Kashmir. (The epicenter is a spot on the surface. It is right over the center of the quake.) Two nations say that they own this area. They are India and Pakistan.

A **shift** caused the quake. This happened along a fault line. A fault line is a place where **massive** pieces of Earth's crust meet. These plates move. They move about 1.6 inches (4.06 cm) a year. A sudden slip between the plates caused the quake. Strong aftershocks rocked the area. They felt like small quakes. This happened on and off for days.

"It was so strong that I saw buildings swaying. It was terrifying," said one man. He works near New Delhi. It is the capital of India. Some big buildings fell down there.

Bad weather has slowed rescue efforts. Landslides have blocked roads. Too much rain has made it hard for planes to land. Rescue workers cannot get to some mountain villages. In cities, millions are stranded. Some have no shelter or electrical power. Others have no food or water.

The quake wrecked hospitals. It left people with no clean water to drink. Health workers fear that **unsanitary** conditions will spread sickness.

One concern was whether problems between India and Pakistan would hurt relief efforts. India and Pakistan have fought for years. They both want to control Kashmir. Yet India offered to help Pakistan. It was hit harder. And Pakistan accepted India's aid. The two nations will work together. This will help those living in the damaged areas.

Summarize and Synthesize / Determine Importance

Science

8

Source: Teacher Created Materials 2008

Level 1: Modeled Strategy Use—I Do

Good readers set themselves up to read a new text with the most meaning possible. I am going to show you how I get myself ready to read and think about the big ideas of a text. The author gives me signals that say, "Look at this. This is important information." These signals are called *text organizers*. We have been looking for examples of text organizers and putting them on our "Text Organizers We Found" chart.

What are some of the text organizers we find in the texts we read? (*Students give some examples.*) After I look at and think about all the text organizers in a text, I will have a good idea of the main ideas of the text. That way I can read with meaning from the beginning.

I am going to look at this text and see if I can find any text organizers that this author used to show me what some of the main ideas are in this text. I will start at the very top of the text and go down to the bottom so I do not miss any text organizers.

If I start at the top of the text, the first text organizer I see is the name of this section, *World News*, which is also called Section A, and a date, October 9, 2005. Circle these text organizers on your text (or mark it with a small sticky note). (*Record this text organizer in the first column of the group chart. If possible, cut out the text organizer from a copy of the text and tape it on the chart.*)

Now what do I know? I think this is a newspaper article about something that happened in the world. News in a newspaper is often not happy or pleasant, so this article might be about something not very positive. Also, since it is the front story of the first section of the newspaper, Section A, it is probably a really important story in *World News* for October 9, 2005. (*Write what the reader knows so far based on this text organizer in the second column of the group chart—see example.*)

What are my questions so far? Let me think. I wonder what was so important that it made the front page of the newspaper. (*Write this thought in a question in the third column on the chart.*)

Level 2: Shared Strategy Use—We Do

Let's continue to move down the text. I see a new text organizer. What is it? (*The headline—in a newspaper, the title of the article is called the headline—*"A Killer Quake in Asia.")

Circle the headline. Let's put that text organizer in the chart. Now what do I know? Help me think about this question. Do I know where in the world this news came from? (*Asia*) What happened in Asia? What does the author mean by a "quake"? (*Establish that this article is about an earthquake that occurred in Asia.*) What do we know about this earthquake from the headline? What do you think it means when it describes the quake as a "killer quake"? (*People were killed, so it must have been a really bad earthquake.*)

This must be a problem-solution text structure, but there might not be a solution to this terrible problem. What questions do we have now? (*Generate several questions with the students, modeling how to ask questions based on what the reader knows up to this point: How many people were killed? Where in Asia did the earthquake happen? What else happened because of this earthquake?*)

Now let's look at the rest of the text. I can see it is written in two columns. When I read a text like this, first I will text walk the first column top/down, and then I will go back up to the top and text walk the second column from top to bottom.

That means the next text organizer that I see and circle is the subtitle of the article—"Deadly Shocks Tear Through Pakistan, India, and Afghanistan." (*Record this text organizer in the group chart.*)

Now what do I know? Do I know what countries in Asia were affected by the earthquake? (*Pakistan, India, Afghanistan*) What do I think the author means by deadly shocks? (*The shocks tell about the earthquake and what it did;* deadly *tells the reader again that people were killed.*) What about the word *tear*? I can tear paper. What does the author mean by the subtitle "Deadly Shocks Tear Through Pakistan, India, and Afghanistan?" (*Solicit students' responses to the question "Now what do I know?" on the group chart.*) What are our questions now? (Possible responses: *Was there more than one earthquake? Just how deadly was the earthquake? Write students' questions in the group chart.*)

We can circle the author's name and the place where the article was written and the date on our group chart. Now we know for sure that this is a newspaper article about an earthquake that happened on October 9 in Kashmir.

There are three bold words in this column to circle—*tremors, shift*, and *massive*. Ask students to note these words and discuss their meaning if they do not know them. Discuss what these bold words tell the reader about the topic, recording students' comments in the second column of the chart.

Level 3: Guided Strategy Use—You Try

Ask students to move to the top of the second column of the text and continue the text walk on their own for the next two organizers (photograph and caption). Students think about what they now know based on information from the text structures. Have younger students share their thinking orally with a partner, teacher, or the group. Older students can write down their ideas on a whiteboard and then share their responses with the group.

Students should finish up their text walk with the final bold word, *unsanitary*, and share any comments to add to the group chart. Figure 6.7 on pages 135–136 is an example of a completed chart based on the first three steps in this lesson.

Figure 6.7 Text Walk Chart for "A Killer Quake in Asia"

Text Organizer	Now What Do I Know?	Questions
Title of newspaper section—*World News*, October 9, 2005, Section A	This is a nonfiction newspaper article about something that happened in the world on October 9, 2005 that was important enough to report in the first section of the newspaper.	What part of the world will be featured in this article? News articles are often about bad things that have happened. Will the article be about something bad?
Headline—"A Killer Quake in Asia"	This is bad news. An earthquake happened in Asia, and it killed people. This text has a problem-solution structure, but we don't know yet if there is a solution.	Where in Asia did the earthquake happen? How many people did it kill?
Subtitle—"Deadly Shocks Tear Through Pakistan, India, and Afghanistan"	The three countries in Asia that were affected by the earthquake were Pakistan, India, and Afghanistan. The shocks were deadly and tore through these countries.	Were the people surprised by the earthquake? Was there more than one earthquake? Just how deadly was this earthquake?
Byline—By Dawn Frost, Kashmir, October 9, 2005	This is the author of the article and the country where the story was reported and written on October 9, 2005.	What did Dawn Frost see in Kashmir that she reports in her article?

Figure 6.7 Text Walk Chart for "A Killer Quake in Asia" *(cont.)*

Text Organizer	Now What Do I Know?	Questions
Bold Words— *tremors, shift, massive*	These words tell more about the earthquake. *Tremors* happen when the earth *shifts* during earthquakes. *Massive* means "really large or huge."	Was this a massive earthquake?
Photograph	There are people looking all over this big pile of rocks and what looks like a wrecked building. Some of the people are dressed differently. Some people look like they are wearing uniforms. They look like they are searching for people in this destruction.	Who are all of these people? Are they looking for people who might still be alive under all that rock?
Caption— "Survivors search the wreckage of a destroyed building in Islamabad, Pakistan's capital."	The people who did not die are called survivors. Rescue workers are looking for other survivors under the destroyed building. The damage must have been bad in Islamabad. Since this is Pakistan's capital, the uniformed men might be in the military or policemen.	Did the rescue workers find any survivors?
Bold Word— *unsanitary*	**The prefix** *un-* means "not." So after the earthquake, maybe the cities were not sanitary or clean.	What are some of the things that made the city unsanitary?

Ask students to reread the "Now What Do I Know?" column of the group Text Walk chart in order to generate a tentative main idea statement for the article—a hypothesis for the main idea based on the "data" they have collected. What is this text mostly about? To help students get started on framing the main idea, give them a word or phrase to begin their main idea statement, such as "A killer quake in …" or "People in Pakistan, India, and Afghanistan …" At the bottom of the group chart, record several possible ways to express the main idea of "A Killer Quake in Asia." (*Examples of possible main idea statements: A killer quake in Asia causes death and destruction; People in Pakistan, India, and Afghanistan are killed by an earthquake while rescuers search the wreckage for survivors; An earthquake in Pakistan, India, and Afghanistan kills people and causes damage to buildings.*)

Next, have students reread the questions they asked when they previewed the text organizers. These questions become the students' purpose for reading the text. As they begin to read the text, the students look for text information that will answer the questions they posed before reading. Students are now set up to read the text with meaning and a better understanding of the big ideas of the article. As they read, students often refer back to the text organizers to support their comprehension and help them locate text information.

Concluding the STAR Lesson

To close the STAR lesson, ask students to identify the critical steps or attributes of this strategy (how to walk a text and determine a tentative main idea). Write the steps for using this preview strategy on a STAR Points chart (see Figure 6.8 on the following page). Discuss these questions with students: When might a reader use this strategy? Would a reader ever use this strategy in math, science, or social studies? Why? How would that look?

Figure 6.8 STAR Points Chart—Taking a Text Walk to Preview a Text for Main Ideas: A Before-Reading Strategy

STAR Points

Taking a Text Walk to Preview a Text for Main Ideas:
A Before-Reading Strategy

1. "Walk" the text from top to bottom.

2. Look at each text organizer.

3. Ask myself, "Now what do I know?"

4. Ask myself, "What questions do I have?"

5. Ask myself, "What is this text mostly about?"

6. Create my hypothesis for the main idea of the text.

Differentiation Notes

After the STAR Model Lesson is presented to students, differentiate the strategy by attending to the level of scaffolding necessary for students to feel comfortable completing a text walk and developing a tentative main idea independently. Some students will need shared, interactive support several more times as they try out the strategy, while more proficient students may practice the strategy in a guided context and then be ready to try text walks independently with a new text.

The text walk may be made easier or more difficult by changing the text level or the number or simplicity of text organizers provided by the author. Below-level students or English language learners may benefit from a more familiar text topic as they learn how to conduct a text walk.

STAR Model Lesson 2: Using a Text Walk Puzzle to Preview Text Organizers and Develop a Main Idea Statement

Comprehension Strategies

- determine importance using text organizers
- develop a tentative main idea statement

Critical Attributes

- The student walks (previews) the text-organizer puzzle pieces one at a time in sequential order.
- The student stops after each text-organizer puzzle piece and asks, "Now what do I know (about the main ideas of the text)?"
- The student articulates a tentative main idea statement after conducting the entire text walk puzzle.
- The student asks questions about the text and identifies what he or she does not yet know about the topic (purpose for reading).

Materials

- consumable nonfiction text on students' instructional/ independent reading level with the text organizers numbered in the order they are presented or previewed in a text walk
- puzzle pieces made from text organizers that are cut out from the text, put in sequential order, paper clipped together, and placed in an envelope (Figure 6.9 on the following page illustrates the text puzzle for *A Trip to the Hospital*)
- teacher- or student-made chart to record students' thinking— optional (see Figure 6.7, pp. 135–136)

Text

  A Trip to the Hospital, the text used in this lesson, is provided with Lesson 3 later in this chapter (p. 150). In this STAR Model Lesson, the students only see the prepared text puzzle pieces one at a time and not the complete text. Six puzzle pieces are used in this lesson:

- the book's title—*A Trip to the Hospital*
- a chapter title—"The Ambulance"
- boldfaced words—uniforms, hospital
- a text inset—Think About It
- a picture
- boldfaced words—stretcher, broken

Figure 6.9 Text Puzzle for *A Trip to the Hospital*

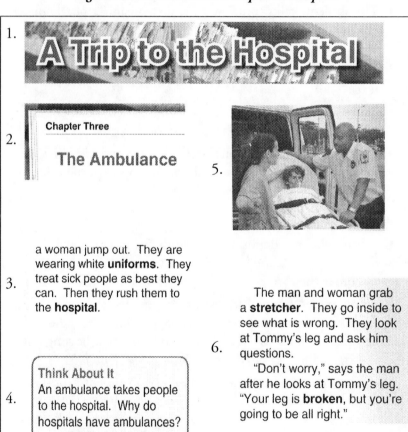

Source: Teacher Created Materials 2008

Level 1: Modeled Strategy Use—I Do

We have been using text organizers to take a text walk before reading in order to identify the information that the author gives us about the main ideas. Let's read and review our STAR Points chart (Figure 6.8, p. 138) to recall how good readers can come up with a hypothesis, or good guess, for the main idea of a text by taking a text walk before reading.

Today, instead of looking at the entire text, we will use a Text Walk Puzzle to preview the text and decide on the possible main idea. Once again, if we think about the clues the author gives us in the text organizer, we can read text with better understanding of the topic and big ideas.

Here is the first text-organizer puzzle piece. (*Put the first puzzle piece in front of the students so they can see it clearly.*) Let's read it: "A Trip to the Hospital." Now what do I know about this article? Let's see—this article must be about someone who makes a trip to the hospital. Maybe this text will be about a problem, like a person getting sick or getting hurt. Going to the hospital could be the solution to this problem. I wonder who is going to the hospital and why he or she is going there. (*Students share their responses, personal connections they have about going to the hospital, and questions they have about the text so far. Remember that at this point, the students will only have seen the first piece of the text puzzle.*)

Level 2: Shared Strategy Use—We Do

Let's look at the next puzzle piece. It says, "Chapter Three: The Ambulance." As good readers, what should we do first? (*Think about what we know now.*) I think I know several things.

What do you know? (*This is a chapter from a book about a trip to a hospital. This chapter is about the ambulance. The ambulance must be a part of taking a trip to the hospital.*)

Does anyone know what an ambulance is? We do not have a picture to look at yet or any words that explain what the word *ambulance* means. If we don't know what an ambulance is, we can keep looking at the puzzle pieces to see if another piece might help us. Before we do that, we need to think about any questions we have. (*Students share any questions they have: Who is hurt or sick? Why did someone call an ambulance? Why do hospitals use an ambulance?*)

Level 3: Guided Strategy Use—You Try

Here is the next puzzle piece. It has two boldfaced words—*uniforms* and *hospital*. With your partner, talk about what you now know about the text from these boldfaced words, and then think about any questions you have.

The fourth puzzle piece shows the reader an inset box labeled "Think About It." We can read the words in the box. What does this box tell readers about ambulances? Think about the question in the box. Do you have any answers for this question, or do you think the text will help us answer this question?

With your partner, look at the fifth puzzle piece. It is a picture. Talk about what you see in the photograph and what you think about it. Does this picture give us any more information about ambulances? Do you have any questions after seeing this puzzle piece? (*Students talk in pairs and then share their thoughts with the group.*)

Here is the last puzzle piece. It has two boldfaced words from the text. These words are *stretcher* and *broken*. Think aloud with your partner about what these two words tell you about this chapter called "The Ambulance." (*Help students understand the meaning of* stretcher, *and point out the stretcher in the photograph.*) Do you have any questions left to ask?

Now we need to think about all the text puzzle pieces together and what we have learned about the big ideas from looking at all these text organizers. We need to predict—create our hypothesis for—the main idea of this chapter after thinking about the text puzzle pieces. Who would like to start us off with a main idea sentence for this text? (*Work with the students to develop a main idea statement for the text: "An ambulance takes people to the hospital when they need help." "One part of a trip to the hospital can be taking an ambulance when you are hurt."*)

142

Differentiation Notes

After the STAR Model Lesson is presented to students, differentiate the strategy by attending to the level of scaffolding necessary for students to feel comfortable completing a text puzzle and developing a tentative main idea independently. Some students will need shared, interactive support several more times as they try out the strategy, while more proficient students may practice the strategy in a guided context and then be ready to try text puzzles independently before reading a new text. The text puzzle may be made easier or more difficult by changing the text level or the number or simplicity of text organizer puzzle pieces that the students have to preview. Below-level students or English language learners may benefit from a more familiar text topic as they learn how to use a text puzzle to develop a tentative main idea.

Level 4: Independent Strategy Use—You Do for Text Walks or Text Puzzles

1. Students work individually or with a partner to preview a new independent-level nonfiction text/text chunk using a text walk or a teacher-prepared text puzzle and then develop a main idea statement. Then students read the text and verify or adjust their main idea hypothesis after reading.

2. Students work individually or with a partner to preview a new instructional-level nonfiction text/text chunk before a guided-reading or small-group reading lesson on that text by using a text walk or text puzzle. The students come to the reading lesson ready to share their questions (purpose for reading) and hypotheses for the main ideas of the text.

3. Laminate a large chart on poster board for a text walk or text puzzle (see Figure 6.5, p. 130). Provide students with a nonfiction text or text puzzle on their instructional or independent reading level to preview and think about the text organizers. Students work with partners to think aloud and record their thinking in the chart with an overhead pen.

4. Students fill out a chart (see Figure 6.10 below) to explain their before-reading plan for a nonfiction text. Students can present their plans in their small reading groups and discuss their strategies and the main ideas of the text.

Figure 6.10 A Before-Reading Plan for Students

My Before-Reading Plan

Text Title: _____

Think about your strategy for getting ready to read this text. Write your ideas about what you will do before reading below:

1. _____

2. _____

3. _____

4. _____

5. _____

Try out your strategy. How did your before-reading strategies help you better understand the big ideas of the text as you read?

_____

_____

_____

_____

_____

Students must be given many opportunities to preview a text for main ideas in a guided context with the teacher before they will automatically apply this strategy and use it independently in literacy centers/engagements, self-selected reading, or a testing situation. Students who text walk a passage on a test before reading, using whatever information the author provides (even though sometimes the only organizer may be a title), have a better understanding of the length, organization, context, and possible big ideas of the reading selection. Students who recognize that previewing the text includes asking why the author included each text organizer are set up to determine some of the important ideas of the text even before they begin reading.

Read a Little, Think a Little Strategy

At the stage of independent strategy use, students are set up to actually read with meaning as they actively verify the main ideas, determine/summarize the important details, and use text clues to answer any questions they had before reading. The expression "read a little, think a little" describes the process in which students read a text or a portion of it, pause to think about what they have read, and possibly exchange ideas with their classmates when they rejoin the small reading group.

After students reassemble, teachers often question them about the content of the text only to be met with such responses as "I don't know," "I'm not sure," or "I don't remember." Did these students read the text? In most cases, with the possible exception of the student who tried to fake the reading process with just a surface skimming of the text, students probably read the text, especially if the text was on their instructional or independent level.

So what happened? Why do these students struggle with responding to the teacher's questions?

Perhaps the reason lies in the fact that the students *read* the text, but they did not *think* about what they read. Many students do not actively engage with the text, especially a nonfiction text, as they read. They do not have an authentic, internal conversation about the text as they read, stopping to ask questions such as:

- What did I just read?
- What did I think was important?
- Did anything confuse me—a word? Ideas?
- Do I have any questions?
- What do I think might happen next? What might I find out now?

Consequently, these same students are unable to engage in a meaningful conversation with the teacher and their peers about their thinking after reading the featured text. Teachers can encourage and support students' comprehension by thinking aloud after students read a chunk of text and identifying main ideas, summarizing important details, clarifying concepts or word meaning (rereading if necessary), asking questions about the text, making predictions about what might happen next, and using the author's words to visualize what he or she is saying or explaining to the reader (Stauffer 1980; Palincsar and Brown 1985).

If students are not processing and interacting with text as they read, teachers need to model the thinking that good readers do when they encounter a new text. A powerful reading strategy that helps students to develop and sustain comprehension across a nonfiction text is to divide the text into smaller chunks, stopping after reading each chunk to think about and assimilate what was just read. Natural text breaks, such as paragraphs or groups of related paragraphs under a subheading, can provide students with "markers," or reminders to process that text in small, meaningful chunks.

Modeling the Read a Little, Think a Little Strategy

To model the Read a Little, Think a Little strategy, after students read an identified text chunk, the teacher explains how a good reader stops and summarizes what was just read, focusing on what was important in that chunk (determining importance). Then the teacher demonstrates how good readers ask themselves, "What was the big idea here? What important information did the author just give me? What information was interesting but not necessarily the most important?" If students are unable to summarize the chunk of text and identify the important ideas, they should reread the section to gain more information. The teacher shows students how to think about concepts or vocabulary that may be unfamiliar or confusing (tricky parts) by searching for context clues or text organizers that help the reader discern meaning. The teacher can use the comprehension strategy of visualization to demonstrate how a good reader forms mental pictures of what the author is trying to convey with words (see Chapter 7).

Next, show students how good readers ask a question of themselves or the author and continue reading to find out more information. The students make a reasonable prediction as to what might happen next in the text or discuss what they might find out next based on what they have already read. After the teacher and students have read and processed the entire text together, they return to the tentative main idea (hypothesis) that the group generated after their text walk. They then revise that main idea based on any new important information gained from reading the actual text.

The teacher models the Read a Little, Think a Little strategy and provides interactive practice many times in a small group setting before the students show evidence of owning this strategy. By engaging students in a short, clarifying conversation about each chunk of text before continuing reading, students learn to process meaning as they go along rather than only thinking about a text after they are done reading. Using Read a Little, Think a Little as a comprehension strategy actively supports students in being "risk takers" in their thinking as they monitor their own meaning-making by asking questions when something they read does not make sense.

STAR Model Lesson 3: Read a Little, Think a Little

Comprehension Strategies

- determine importance to summarize and verify the main ideas of a text
- monitor meaning during reading

Critical Attributes

- After doing a text walk and developing a tentative main idea statement, the student determines how to divide the text into short, meaningful chunks for Read a Little, Think a Little.
- The student reads a text chunk and stops to summarize the important details of the content. The student rereads the text chunk if necessary and makes a mind picture—visualizes the content.
- The student articulates the big ideas of that text chunk.
- If possible, the student clarifies any confusing concepts or vocabulary.
- The student asks questions about the text chunk to focus his or her reading.
- The student makes predictions about the next text chunk.

Materials

- nonfiction text on students' instructional/independent reading level (**Note:** students have already previewed the text organizers and developed a tentative main idea and a purpose for reading)
- Read a Little, Think a Little cards produced on colored cardstock for each reader (see Figure 6.11 on the next page)
- sticky notes to identify the end of each text chunk or pencils to bracket each text chunk if using consumable text

Figure 6.11 Read a Little, Think a Little Cards

Read a Little, Think a Little Cards	1. Can I summarize what I just read? 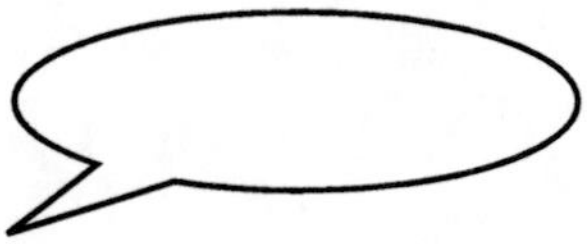
2. What is the most important thing I just read—the main idea? 	3. Are there any confusing ideas or words to think about?  word
4. Can I ask a question? 	5. Can I make a prediction? 

**Figure 6.12 Sample Nonfiction Text for
Read a Little, Think a Little Strategy**

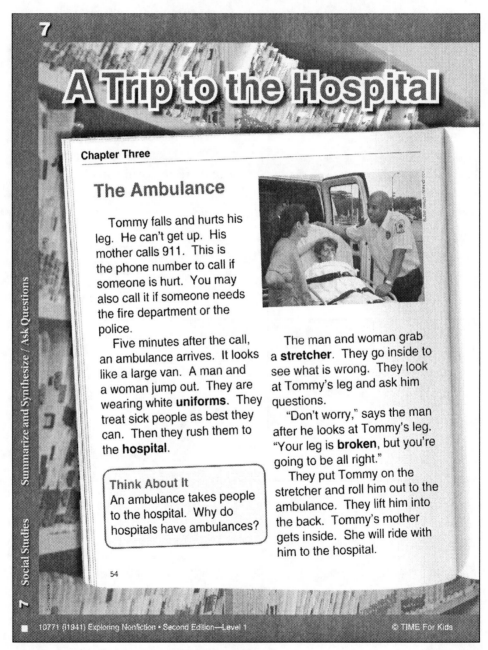

A Trip to the Hospital

Chapter Three

The Ambulance

Tommy falls and hurts his leg. He can't get up. His mother calls 911. This is the phone number to call if someone is hurt. You may also call it if someone needs the fire department or the police.

Five minutes after the call, an ambulance arrives. It looks like a large van. A man and a woman jump out. They are wearing white **uniforms**. They treat sick people as best they can. Then they rush them to the **hospital**.

Think About It
An ambulance takes people to the hospital. Why do hospitals have ambulances?

The man and woman grab a **stretcher**. They go inside to see what is wrong. They look at Tommy's leg and ask him questions.

"Don't worry," says the man after he looks at Tommy's leg. "Your leg is **broken**, but you're going to be all right."

They put Tommy on the stretcher and roll him out to the ambulance. They lift him into the back. Tommy's mother gets inside. She will ride with him to the hospital.

54

7 Social Studies   Summarize and Synthesize / Ask Questions

10771 (i1941) Exploring Nonfiction • Second Edition—Level 1   © TIME For Kids

Source: Teacher Created Materials 2008

Level 1: Modeled Strategy Use—I Do

We are going to try something that good readers do to make sure they understand what they read. We are going to monitor our comprehension—how effectively we are building meaning as we read. Rather than just reading the whole text at one time, we are going to read a little and then stop and think about what we read. When we stop and think after reading a text chunk, we summarize what we just read—retell the important details—and then we think about what is the big or main idea of that part of the text. Next we think about any confusing ideas or tricky words we read to make sure what we read makes sense. We ask questions about what we read, and finally, we make predictions about what will happen next or what we will find out next. We have a lot of great strategies to use to identify the most important ideas of what we read!

I have some cards for us to use to remember the steps of our new strategy, Read a Little, Think a Little. These steps are written on cards for each of you to use. Let's read each card in order, and then we will try out using the cards with our text *A Trip to the Hospital*.

I will show you how to use the Read a Little, Think a Little strategy cards with the first chunk of our text. We have already done our text walk and have created our hypothesis for the main idea. On your text, put a bracket around the first paragraph as a reminder to stop and think about that text chunk when we are done reading. (*Read the first paragraph to the students.*)

Now I will look at the first card. It says, "Can I summarize what I just read?" I think this part explains that Tommy has hurt his leg, so his mom called 911 so someone would come and help Tommy. I can picture what this looks like in my mind: I can see Tommy with his hurt leg and his mom on the telephone trying to get help.

Now I can look at the second card. It says, "What is the most important thing I just read—the main idea?" I think that the main idea is that Tommy is hurt and 911 is the phone number to call for help.

The third card asks me to think about any confusing or tricky ideas or words in this part. Well, I know that I am supposed to call 911 only when I have a big problem. I guess the people who answer the phone must ask questions to determine whether to send the fire department or police to help hurt people. I guess that Tommy's mother did a smart thing by calling 911.

The next card says, "Can I ask a question?" I have a few questions. How badly is Tommy's leg hurt? Did he break it? Who will come help him? How long will it take to get to Tommy's house? I hope that when I read on I will find out the answers to my questions.

Now I am ready for the last card. I am supposed to make a prediction based on what I just read. What do I think I will find out next? I think the next part will tell me about who will come to help Tommy and what they will do about his problem.

Level 2: Shared Strategy Use—We Do

We can do the next text chunk together as we "read a little, think a little." Put a bracket around the second paragraph as a reminder to stop and think after we read this part. Let's read it together.

Read the first card with me. How do you want to summarize or retell the most important details in this part? (*An ambulance comes in five minutes to help Tommy. A man and woman wearing uniforms get out of the ambulance. They are the people who will help Tommy and take him to the hospital.*)

Now let's read and try the second card—what is the main idea of what we just read? (*People in uniforms in an ambulance take sick or hurt people like Tommy to the hospital.*)

What do we do next to make sure we understand this part of the article? Are there any tricky ideas or words in this part to think about? (*What is an ambulance? Are there any words or pictures to help us know what an ambulance looks like or does? What is a uniform? Which person in the photograph arrived in the ambulance? How do you know?*)

Now let's look at the fourth card. What questions do we have about what we just read? (*Why can't the people in the ambulance just fix Tommy? Why does he have to go to the hospital? How do you think Tommy feels?*)

The last card reminds us to make a prediction. What do you think will happen next? What do you think we will find out next about Tommy's trip to the hospital? (*Tommy will get some help at the hospital so his leg will get better. Tommy may be worried about what will happen to him at the hospital.*)

Level 3: Guided Strategy Use—You Try

Put a bracket around the last three paragraphs. Now you will work with a partner to use the Read a Little, Think a Little cards for the last text chunk. We will practice using each card one at a time with our partners. After you think about the question on the card with your partner, we will talk about your thinking. Then we will move onto the next card. When we are done, we will think about what we have learned from the text. (*Students work in pairs through each card. Drop in and listen to the students' conversations, prompting students to think aloud about their processing when they need support. After each step, have students stop and share before moving on to the next card.*)

Concluding the STAR Lesson

To close this STAR lesson, students review the steps of the Read a Little, Think a Little strategy, describing in their own words how readers can think about the questions on the cards to help them better understand what they read. Write the steps for using the Read a Little, Think a Little strategy on a STAR Points chart (see Figure 6.13 on the following page). Discuss these questions with the students: When might a reader use this strategy? How could this strategy help readers better understand what they read?

**Figure 6.13 Star Points Chart—Read a Little, Think a Little:
A During-Reading Strategy**

STAR Points

Read a Little, Think a Little

A During-Reading Strategy

1. Summarize in my own words the important details of the text chunk I just read. Reread and make a picture in my mind if the text did not make sense.

2. Ask myself, "What is the most important thing I just read?"

3. Ask myself, "Are there any tricky words or confusing ideas I need to think about?"

4. Ask myself, "Can I ask any questions about what I just read?"

5. Ask myself, "Can I make a prediction about what will happen next or what I will find out next?"

Differentiation Notes

After the STAR Model Lesson is presented to all students, model it in small reading groups with instructional text that matches the students' reading levels. If necessary, move down to an independent-level text so students are freed up to focus their full attention on comprehension.

Create a risk-free environment where students feel that their approximations—attempts at responding to the questions—are valued as steps to becoming authentic comprehenders of text.

Continue to think aloud for struggling students, especially for summarizing the important details of each text chunk, identifying confusing words and ideas, and finding text proof to support their understanding. Only focus on one or two steps of this comprehension strategy at a time rather than using all five steps.

For advanced readers, differentiate the text level or put the strategy cards into a literacy center for students to use independently with self-selected texts. After these students practice with the Read a Little, Think a Little cards, discontinue the use of the cards and let the students guide their own discussion about each text chunk.

✦ *Pause and Ponder* ✦

How do teachers create a risk-free environment where students feel free to express their thoughts even if they think they might be wrong? What can teachers do to support students in framing and extending their thinking through conversation about text? Consider such factors as wait time, specifically affirming responses, extending thinking by providing prompts, and demonstrating or modeling.

What features of your classroom make it conducive to communication and experimentation? ✧

Level 4: Independent Strategy Use—You Do

1. Students work with a partner on an independent-level text and complete a text walk of the text organizers before reading. Students identify a chunk of text to read silently. After the students read the text chunk, they discuss the questions on the Read a Little, Think a Little cards. After reading and processing the text, the students write the main idea on a piece of paper along with a few important details. Students then use the main idea and supporting details to create a part-to-whole graphic organizer to show the relationship between the details and the main idea (see Figure 6.14 on the following page).

Figure 6.14 Part-to-Whole Graphic Organizer

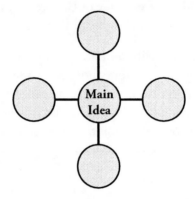

2. Students select a text on their independent reading level. After completing a text walk and developing a main idea hypothesis, the students break the text into chunks and then read it one chunk at a time. Students stop after each part to use the Read a Little, Think a Little cards and think about the text while having an internal conversation about the big ideas of that text. After completing the text, students meet together in small groups to discuss the effectiveness of this strategy in supporting comprehension as they read.

Using Annotation to Support Read a Little, Think a Little

As teachers employ the Read a Little, Think a Little strategy in their instruction, they need to scaffold increasing responsibility to the students for having a conversation about the meaning of each text chunk. Eventually, this "comprehension conversation" will happen in the students' heads as they read—becoming automatized as a reading skill—and they will employ good reading tools during independent reading or in a testing situation.

Along with the Read a Little, Think a Little strategy, teachers can show students the power of annotating small chunks of text with their thoughts during reading (Harvey and Goudvis 2000). This written record of their thinking can support students' understanding when they return to the text to determine main ideas, locate and review supporting details to summarize text, and find proof for their responses to questions without having to reread the entire text.

Students can make notes directly on a consumable copy of a text or they can use small sticky notes for each text chunk. Students' notes should be brief and focus on the big ideas of the text chunk, writing only words or short phrases instead of complete sentences. Students may also choose to jot down connections they make to the text information or sketch mental images they have as they read. Show students how powerful notes can help them scan the text after reading for information and locate details without having to reread the entire text. Annotating text, while processing that text chunk for meaning using the Read a Little, Think a Little strategy, helps students sustain meaning throughout their reading and recall the thinking they did as they read. Consequently, this strategy allows students to participate fully in authentic conversations about the text after reading and respond to questions about text using their notes as a guide.

Once again, learning to annotate text effectively and use that annotation to support comprehension must be modeled many times by the teacher in a small group setting. Students who have trouble determining importance in a chunk of text will also have difficulty writing notes about that chunk of text that effectively capture the big/main ideas. The more experience students have with Read a Little, Think a Little conversations about text, the better they will become at ascertaining what is important in each text chunk. For students who continue to struggle with determining importance, the teacher can introduce Pluses, Lines, and Stars (Lesson 4 on the following pages) as a supportive beginning notation strategy.

✦ *Pause and Ponder* ✦

When reading a text for specific, relevant information, such as searching for ideas to present to your peers in a meeting or critical details that might be assessed on a graduate-level education exam, what strategies do you use to identify critical information and concepts that you will need to remember? Do you annotate text? Highlight text? Use sticky notes? Write on index cards? Have you noticed any of your students annotating text in any way? What are your students currently doing to support comprehension as they read? ❧

STAR Model Lesson 4: Pluses, Lines, and Stars

Comprehension Strategies

- determine importance and verify the main idea(s) of a text
- monitor comprehension

Critical Attributes

- After doing a text walk and writing a tentative main idea statement for the text, the student determines how to divide the text into short, meaningful chunks.

- The student reads a text chunk and stops to identify the most important fact or detail in the text chunk. The student reads the sentence containing that most important fact or detail and places a small plus (+) next to this part of the text chunk.

    Note: Please refrain from saying, "Put a plus (+) by the main idea of the paragraph or text chunk." This direction leads students to assume that every paragraph/text chunk has a stated main idea. As students move up in text levels, the main idea is more often implied or inferred from the context. As teachers, we avoid teaching students shortcuts that will not work in all contexts. Students must learn how to effectively determine the big ideas of text without tricks. Pluses, Lines, and Stars is an initial annotation strategy to support students who cannot yet infer the most important fact or detail of a text and put it into their own words.

- After the student has multiple, successful experiences with marking the most important fact or detail with a plus (+), add the star notation. The student places a star by the fact or detail he or she thinks is the most interesting in that text chunk. The place in the text chunk where each student chooses to place a star is up to the individual student; the fact or detail that each student finds the most interesting is the opinion of that student. The star notation gives the student something to do with that interesting detail that often distracts the struggling reader into thinking it is the most important detail in the text chunk.

- Add the line notation when the student is becoming adept at using the plus to signify the most important fact or detail. The student underlines the fact or detail that best supports, or "holds up," the plus (+) statement—basically, the most important supporting detail. The line notation is the least "exact" notation. Since all the other details in the text chunk are supporting details, there may be some debate over which supporting detail is the most important or most effective in holding up the big idea of the text chunk. The critical factor in deciding where to place the line notation is the student's thoughtful evaluation of the supporting details. As long as the student can defend his or her thinking, there may be more than one acceptable place to put the line notation.

- After reading the text, the student re-evaluates the main idea hypothesis developed after the text walk and revises it.

- The student reads the revised main idea statement for the entire text and then reads each of the plus (+) statements marked in the text. After reading these statements, the student has simply summarized the big ideas of the text.

- For a richer summary, the student reads the revised main idea statement and then reads each plus (+) and line notation in sequence.

Materials

- consumable copies of nonfiction text on students' instructional/independent reading level (**Note:** students have already previewed the text organizers and developed a tentative main idea and a purpose for reading)
- pencils, markers to annotate text
- sticky notes or a blank transparency and overhead markers to annotate the text if it is not consumable (after the initial STAR Model Lesson on Pluses, Lines, and Stars)

Text

"A Killer Quake in Asia" (The text for this lesson is presented on p. 132)

Level 1: Modeled Strategy Use—I Do

Note:

- The following example is the initial lesson for the strategy of Pluses, Lines, and Stars.
- Only the plus (+) annotation will be used in this first model lesson.

We have done our text walk and developed our hypothesis for the main idea of this article, which I have written on our chart: *An earthquake in Pakistan, India, and Afghanistan kills people and causes damage.* We want to find out how big the earthquake was, how many people were killed, and if the survivors found anyone under the wrecked buildings. Now, that we have our purpose for reading, we are ready to read the article to find the answers to our questions and identify the most important facts and details.

We are going to learn a way to mark (annotate, code) text in order to help us locate and think about the most important big ideas in the article. We are going to read and think about the text in smaller, meaningful chunks as we always do as good readers. However, today we are going to add a special written symbol or notation to help us remember the big ideas so we can summarize those ideas after we are finished. A summary of a nonfiction text includes the main idea of the whole text—which we have already considered—and the most important details. As we read each text chunk, we will use the plus (+) symbol to mark the big idea or most important detail of each chunk. As we try out this new strategy of marking our text for the most important facts or details, I will be the "banker" of the pluses (+). For each text chunk we read and think about, I will tell you how many pluses (+) we can "spend" in each section. Usually I will only give you one plus (+) per chunk, but depending on how many big ideas there are in that part of the text, sometimes I may give you two pluses (+).

I will model our new strategy first so you can see how I think about where to put my plus (+) to show what I think is the most important fact or detail of the first text chunk. We put brackets around our first text chunk, so let's bracket the first paragraph. The brackets will remind us to stop and think about the most important fact or detail in this part. I will give us one plus (+) for this first text chunk.

(Read the first paragraph aloud to students. Stop and comment when there is a tricky or unknown word or when one of their questions generated before reading is answered—in this case, the magnitude of the earthquake and how many people were killed.)

My, this was a really enormous earthquake! It is very sad to think about how many people lost their lives. That is a detail that answers one of our questions, but I am not sure that it is the most important detail. I think that it may be more important to mark the detail that tells the problem in article. I think that I will put my plus (+) here: *A huge earthquake struck this region yesterday at 8:50 a.m.* Let's read what I marked with a plus (+) together. Yes, I think that is the most important fact or detail because it tells the problem of the whole text.

Level 2: Shared Strategy Use—We Do

Now let's bracket the next paragraph as our new text chunk. We will read this chunk together. I think we will have only one plus (+) to spend in this part, so as we read, help me think about what is the most important detail. We can stop reading at any tricky parts or words that we need to think about.

(Read the next text chunk together, stopping to talk about any vocabulary that was not discussed before reading. The teacher may also want to engage students in a short visualization of how an earthquake happens.) Let's think together about where we want to put our plus (+). What do we think is the most important detail? (*The worst damage was done in northern Pakistan.*) This important detail tells where the most destruction occurred.

Okay, we will try one more chunk together. This time, we will bracket a bigger text chunk, but I am still only going to give us one plus (+) to use. I know we can do it if we really think about the big idea as we read. After we read, we will hear your ideas about what you think is the most important fact or detail. (*The quake was caused by a shift along an active fault line.*) This detail sets up the cause of the problem.

Level 3: Guided Strategy Use—You Try

Now it is your turn to try putting a plus (+) by the most important fact or detail. Bracket the next two paragraphs. Read this text chunk to yourself, but this time, after you read, you will have two pluses (+) to spend because there are two important details in this chunk. You may work with a partner after you read to decide where you will put your two pluses (+). I may ask you questions or give you suggestions to guide your thinking as you work.

This time, the first plus (+) goes in front of "Bad weather has slowed rescue efforts," and the second plus (+) goes in front of "Health workers fear that unsanitary conditions will spread sickness." (Ask students to share the thinking behind their decisions about their annotations.)

The final chunk of text that we will bracket and think about is the last paragraph. Read the chunk to yourself and decide where you will put the last plus (+) for the article. This time, work by yourself, and I will drop by to ask you about your decision about where you want to put your plus (+). Be ready to explain your thinking to me. (*Students should put their plus (+) by "The two nations [India and Pakistan] will work together."*)

Now we can go back and see if our hypothesis for the main idea of the whole article was correct: *An earthquake in Pakistan, India, and Afghanistan kills people and causes damage.* What do you think? Do you think that this statement is the main idea of the article, or do we need to modify it a bit after reading the article?

(*The tentative main idea can still be used, or students can add a little more important information. For example: An earthquake in Pakistan, India, and Afghanistan kills people and causes damage while aftershocks and weather slow rescue efforts.*)

After reading a nonfiction text, good readers go back and summarize the big ideas of the text to help them remember the most important information. A summary of a nonfiction text includes the main idea of the entire text and the most important details. We have our main idea, and we put pluses (+) by the most important facts and details. So all we have to do to create a summary of our text is read the main idea statement on our chart and then read the plus (+) statements we marked in our text. If we did a good job of selecting our plus (+) details—the big ideas of the article—then we will have a great summary of what we read. Read the main idea and plus (+) statements from the article in sequential order. Did reading our main idea and the plus (+) statements give us a good summary of the big ideas of this text?

With your partner, explain in your own words our new strategy of using a plus (+) to mark the most important fact or detail in each text chunk. Then we will write the steps of this strategy on a group chart (see Figure 6.15 on the following page). How can this strategy help you as a reader? Where and when can you use this strategy again?"

Figure 6.15 STAR Points Chart—Determining Importance and Summarizing Nonfiction Text: A During-and After-Reading Strategy

STAR Points

Determining Importance and Summarizing Nonfiction Text:

A During- and After-Reading Strategy

1. Write your hypothesis for the main idea of the text after doing a text walk.

2. Identify and read a text chunk.

3. Ask yourself, "What is the most important fact or detail?"

4. Put a plus (+) by the most important fact or detail. Sometimes there will be more than one fact or detail to mark with a plus (+).

5. Repeat steps 2–4 for each text chunk.

6. After reading, fix up or revise your main idea of the text if necessary.

7. Read your main idea and each of the plus (+) statements you marked to form a summary of the text.

Figure 6.16 Annotated Version of "A Killer Quake in Asia"

8

World News

October 9, 2005 Section A

A Killer Quake in Asia

Deadly Shocks Tear Through Pakistan, India, and Afghanistan

By Dawn Frost

KASHMIR, October 9—A strong earthquake struck here. It happened yesterday. At 8:50 A.M. **tremors** ran through three countries. People felt them in Pakistan and India. They felt them in Afghanistan, too. In just minutes, thousands died. Towns were ruined. Leaders fear that 40,000 people may be dead.

Northern Pakistan had the worst damage. The epicenter of the quake was near Muzaffarabad. It is in Kashmir. (The epicenter is a spot on the surface. It is right over the center of the quake.) Two nations say that they own this area. They are India and Pakistan.

A **shift** caused the quake. This happened along a fault line. A fault line is a place where **massive** pieces of Earth's crust meet. These plates move. They move about 1.6 inches (4.06 cm) a year. A sudden slip between the plates caused the quake. Strong aftershocks rocked the area. They felt like small quakes. This happened on and off for days.

"It was so strong that I saw buildings swaying. It was terrifying," said one man. He works near New Delhi. It is the capital of India. Some big buildings fell down there.

Bad weather has slowed rescue efforts. Landslides have blocked roads. Too much rain has made it hard for planes to land. Rescue workers cannot get to some mountain villages. In cities, millions are stranded. Some have no shelter or electrical power. Others have no food or water.

Survivors search the wreckage of a destroyed building in Islamabad, Pakistan's capital.

The quake wrecked hospitals. It left people with no clean water to drink. Health workers fear that **unsanitary** conditions will spread sickness.

One concern was whether problems between India and Pakistan would hurt relief efforts. India and Pakistan have fought for years. They both want to control Kashmir. Yet India offered to help Pakistan. It was hit harder. And Pakistan accepted India's aid. The two nations will work together. This will help those living in the damaged areas.

8 Science Summarize and Synthesize / Determine Importance

10774 (i1977) Exploring Nonfiction • Second Edition—Level 4 © TIME For Kids

Source: Teacher Created Materials 2008

This annotated example of "A Killer Quake in Asia" (Figure 6.16, p. 165) shows all the elements of the Pluses, Lines, and Stars strategy. From this example, teachers can see how each symbol has been introduced to the students and practiced on a guided/independent level. The instructional steps include introducing the plus (+) annotation first, followed by the star annotation, and lastly, the line annotation.

Differentiation Notes

The critical attribute of this strategy's effectiveness is whether students are able to determine the most important fact or detail in a text chunk. The Pluses, Lines, and Stars annotation strategy is an initial nonfiction summary strategy for struggling readers because students do not have to paraphrase the significant details in their own words.

In this strategy, students have to weigh the importance of stated facts and details in a text chunk and evaluate their significance to the topic. However, since everything in nonfiction is a fact or detail, the teacher will need to provide many opportunities for struggling readers to talk about which details are more important than others.

This strategy requires higher-level thinking on the part of students and provides the less proficient student, who cannot yet summarize text in his or her own words, a place to begin. Begin by using independent-level text with these students, giving them the opportunity to focus all their attention on determining importance and selecting the big ideas in order to summarize the text.

Level 4: Independent Strategy Use—You Do

1. Students work in pairs to use the Pluses, Lines, and Stars strategy (or whatever portion of the strategy they currently control as learners; they may only have used the pluses (+) annotation up to the point of independent practice). Provide each pair with an individual copy of an independent-level nonfiction text already marked for text chunks and note how many pluses (+) they can use for each text chunk.

2. Students use annotated text that they coded in a group lesson to create a part-to-whole graphic organizer that summarizes the text.

Summary

When students focus on determining importance and identifying the main ideas of a text by using such strategies such as Text Walk, Text Puzzles, Read a Little, Think a Little, and Pluses, Lines, and Stars, they are able to engage in authentic conversations about text. The students actively set themselves up for reading with meaning, and they process text as they read—summarizing the big ideas as they go. With practice, students automatize these good strategies, and they are ready to think even more deeply about what they read as they move into making inferences and drawing conclusions about text.

→ *Pause and Ponder* ←

"We need *thoughtful* learning. We need schools that are full of thought, schools that focus not just on schooling memories but on schooling minds. … We need educational settings with thinking-centered learning, where students learn by thinking through what they are learning about" (Perkins 1995, 7).

Literacy teachers spend a lot of time teaching students about text features and how to use them to support predictions, link prior knowledge to text content, and build understanding. Students' proficiency in using text organizers is essential as they encounter more challenging texts in content areas. In what ways do you help students see the relationship between the strategies they learn in language arts and the application of those strategies when they read texts in math, science, and social studies?

Assemble a collection of nonfiction texts in math, science, and social studies (textbooks as well as other nonfiction resources). With your students, examine the text organizers in these materials, noting features that are common across the texts and those that are distinctive. Have students create charts with examples of text features from some of these materials. ↩

Chapter 7

Visualizing the Text

"Although reading can lead to abstract thought, the thought depends at its base on concrete, highly visualized experiences of the individual readers. All thinking proceeds from the concrete to the abstract, from the visible to the invisible" *(Wilhelm 2004, 14).*

Considerations from Research

- Visualization is a unique constructive aspect of reading. The reader goes beyond the author's words, re-enacting the brain's capacity for cognitive breakthroughs.
- Visualization accommodates a range of learning modalities; images can emerge from any of the senses.
- Visualization is integral to the act of inference. Mental images can help support links between prior knowledge and text content as well as connections within the text.
- Visualization may be influenced by the nature of material being read, heard, or viewed. The impact of visually dense material (e.g., Web-based or other digitally presented content) on the ability (or need) to form mental images is the focus of newer research (Wolf 2007).

Many years ago, I read an article in an education publication that stated that up to two out of five people may not make a picture in their mind—visualize—when they read. While the source of this statistic is long forgotten and is unsubstantiated by any other source found to date, the mere consideration of how many students might not visualize text ideas and concepts when they read has stuck with me. What if 20 percent of students in classrooms do not actively create mental images of what they read? What if this number was more accurately reduced to, say, one in 10 students? That statistic would still be significant in a classroom of 20 students. Consider those students who perform poorly when attempting to comprehend text and the possible impact the reading strategy of visualization could have on their comprehension. Would the inability to create mind pictures during reading partially explain why some students "read" with 100 percent accuracy on grade-level text yet are unable to identify main ideas, summarize important information, or develop inferences? What about those students who prepare for a class discussion or exam by reading the text again and again and again and still appear unprepared to share their thinking about what they have read? Could these students be trying to "study" by memorizing the text rather than creating a big picture in their minds and linking significant text details to their visual schema? If the ability to visualize during reading can improve reading comprehension for students, how can teachers illustrate this apparently "invisible" strategy through reading instruction and monitor students' proficiency in creating pictures in their minds as they read?

Teachers can demonstrate the ability to see mental images during reading by thinking aloud as they read text and stopping periodically to share their personal mind pictures. Many students who do not engage in active visualization as they read are not even aware that this is a strategy that can help them better understand what they read. These students need opportunities to try out visualization in a risk-free environment so that they can recognize the effectiveness of this strategy in supporting them in making meaning during reading. Students

Benefits of Visualization Strategies
Research shows that the ability to create mental images during reading provides mental "pegs" on which to hang memory for text information and allows students to use those pegs to organize and store meaning (Sadowski 1984; Long, Winograd, and Bridges 1989). Strong reading comprehension grows from automatic visualizing that brings together students' various mental images to build an understanding of the whole text. Once students can visulaize text, they can retrieve information, make inferences, and draw conclusions from the mental images they constructed in response to text.

should note that not everyone's mental images in response to text are exactly the same. Teachers can model how readers use sensory clues, rich text details, and their own prior experience and background knowledge to construct mental images while reading. Since readers' mind pictures represent the ideas and words from a text, teachers can show the link between those ideas and words and their own mental images by sketching them and identifying the text clues that sparked those images. Then students have the opportunity to explore their own mind pictures in response to text and share those images with others.

Most teachers can likely readily identify characteristics of students who are not strong visualizers of text content. These students may appear to be unfocused or inattentive while reading in small groups. They may demonstrate weak auditory memory and faulty comprehension, missing main ideas and significant details as well as relationships such as cause and effect. Students who do not create images as they read may struggle with problem solving and responding to questions, especially inferential questions. These students tend to ask questions that have already been answered and often have trouble following written directions. Although students who do not link text with mind pictures may be able to decode text well, they are more likely to read and reread text as they attempt to understand what they read and process the bigger ideas (Bell 1991). Students who do not visualize are not usually interested in self-selected reading in the classroom or at home. Therefore, they do not get needed independent reading practice, exposure to a variety of texts, or the intrinsic pleasure of reading an engaging text.

While none of these characteristics in isolation may indicate a significant problem with students' ability to visualize, a combination of "symptoms" may cue teachers to explore students' proficiency with this vital reading strategy and provide instruction that will help them incorporate visualization into their repertoire of strategies. After assessing how students use visualization as they read, scaffold students into this strategy based on their effectiveness in creating images as they respond to text. Move from pictures to words to sentences to paragraphs to passages as students become more capable in developing mind pictures and sharing and explaining their mental images during and after reading. Students who become active visualizers of text enjoy describing their mental images with others as they use visualization to develop a greater understanding of and stronger connections to text. Sketching—a nonlinguistic representation of students' ideas in response to text—provides another venue for students to share their mind pictures and personalize text content.

✦ *Pause and Ponder* ✦

Think about the students in your classroom. Do you have any students who might not be visualizing as they read? How do you know? Do these students exhibit any of the characteristics previously mentioned? As you consider the STAR Model Lesson for visualization and the variations that follow, select instructional goals that correlate with your students' strengths and instructional needs in effectively integrating visualization as a tool for comprehending text. ✦

STAR Model Lessons

The STAR Model Lesson format was presented in Chapter 5 to teach word-meaning strategies and again in Chapter 6 to teach students how to use text features to increase comprehension. In this chapter, I describe a model lesson with two variations to illustrate ways in which to improve students' ability to use visualization to strengthen comprehension. These lessons focus on two comprehension strategies:

- constructing and adjusting mental images—"mind pictures"—through visualizing written text clues
- clarifying and modifying mental images by asking questions

Three nonfiction selections—one photograph and two texts—are used to demonstrate the visualization activities:

- A photograph from *Fishers Then and Now* (Zamosky 2007), a social studies-themed book about how the life of fishers has changed over time. The illustration selected from this primary-level text (level 1.5) depicts a sailing ship from the past, so students will probably not immediately visualize this type of boat. They will be able to use the text clues to add to and revise their mind pictures of the boat as they read and visualize the details provided in each succeeding sentence of the text.

- "Life in the Abyss Zone" is a chapter excerpted from the book *Life in the Ocean Layers* (Lockyer 2009), which is a text in a series of mathematics readers. This particular text is written at a 4.7 text level. This section has rich, descriptive language to support students as they form mental images of the text content.

- "States of Matter" is a section of text from the science leveled reader *Inside the World of Matter* (Weir 2007), text level 4.5. The specific information provided in the text helps students picture the big ideas and significant supporting details about the different states of matter.

STAR Model Lesson 1: Framing a Mind Picture

Comprehension Strategies

- Construct and adjust mental images—mind pictures—by visualizing written text clues
- Clarify and modify mental images by asking questions

Critical Attributes

- The student listens to a series of written text clues, provided one at a time, about the subject of a simple picture that is hidden from the student's view.
- The student attempts to capture a mental image—mind picture—of the unseen picture from the clues provided.
- The student stops to adjust his or her mental image after each clue and describes his or her current image and the

adjustments made after considering each additional clue.

- The student asks questions to clarify and modify his or her developing mental image.

- After all the clues are revealed, the student describes his or her final mental image and identifies the words and phrases in the clues that contributed to the mind picture.

- The student views the actual picture and notes how the clues in the text helped develop his or her visualization of the picture's subject.

- The student discusses how visualization helps readers develop mental images, or mind pictures, to make sense of a text, clarify the ideas presented, and adjust their thinking as new information is presented.

Materials

- a picture or photograph with a simple, single subject that is placed in a paper or wooden frame (see Figure 7.1 on page 176).

    Note: For students just beginning to try out the strategy of visualizing, select a picture with no color and no extraneous details (for example, a black-and-white picture found in a coloring book).

- Three to eight sentences with text clues that describe the picture or photograph, written on sentence strips or a chart or projected on a screen.

    Note: The clues move from general to more specific clues about the subject of the picture. The number of clues provided depends on the students' proficiency in constructing and maintaining a mental image as multiple details are introduced. Each clue provides only one piece of information. Use sensory language and spatial clues to describe the picture. Reveal only one clue at a time.

- markers
- a camera to use as a prop during I Do (optional)

Level 1: Modeled Strategy Use—I Do

Sometimes as we read, the author provides pictures or photographs to help us picture what the words are telling us. However, as good readers, we also use the words and sentences in the text to snap mind pictures with our "brain cameras" in order to create and "frame" our own pictures of the information and ideas in the text. (*Show the camera prop, if desired, to represent the idea of a brain camera.*)

If I read the sentence "The man loved his dog," my brain camera snaps a picture of a dog. The mind picture that I frame in my brain is a picture of my dog, Maggie. I can see my soft, furry, long-eared Maggie wagging her tail and looking at me with her deep, dark-brown eyes as she stands by the front door begging for a walk.

Then I read in the book, *"His huge, black dog barked loudly as if to say, 'I love you, too!'"* Now I realize that I have to use my brain camera again to change my mind picture based on new text clues provided by the author. The dog in this book is not just like Maggie, my dog. Another mind picture snaps into my mind to fit this new information. Now my framed mental picture looks like Atticus, my son's dog. Atticus is huge and black with shiny dark eyes that look adoringly at his owner, especially when my son is getting ready to throw Atticus a ball.

Visualizing what the author tells me through text clues helps me picture the meaning of the text in my mind so I can remember what I read. Finding new clues as I read keeps those mind pictures changing as I adjust my thinking. I find myself linking those framed pictures together to create kind of a mental "picture album." Snapping pictures with the camera in my brain also helps keep me engaged in the text so I will keep reading.

Today, we will see how we can use text clues to snap our own mind pictures as we read. Here is a simple picture in a frame that is hidden right now. (*Show students the back of the framed picture used for this model lesson.*)

Figure 7.1 Framing a Mind Picture

THE LIBRARY OF CONGRESS

Source: Zamosky 2007

We will examine a series of clues about this picture, but we will only see one sentence at a time. After we read the sentence, we will think about any words or phrases—clues—that can help us make a picture in our minds with our brain cameras. Then we will think about or frame our mind pictures and share some of our thinking. We can ask questions or share our "I wonder …" thoughts to clarify our thinking and help bring our mind pictures into focus. After we have seen all the clues, we will share our final mental images and then look at the real picture to see how focused we were able to make our own mind pictures.

I will read the first clue on this paper strip so you can listen and identify any details that help you begin to build a mind picture for what is in the real picture that I've hidden: *Fishers began to use a boat to go out into the water.* Let me think about any clues that help me use my brain camera to snap a mind picture. I used to go fishing with my dad sometimes, so I guess we were *fishers*. I will underline that clue in the sentence. I will also underline the words *boat* and *water*. The word *began* gives me a clue, too. This word tells me that this is an early type of boat used when fishers first started to go out from shore to fish.

I have a picture in my mind now. Think about the picture that you have in your mind. What does your boat look like? Is it big or little? Who is fishing in your boat? Where is the boat? (*Allow some think time.*) I see my dad and me holding our fishing poles as we sit on the wooden seats in our boat on the lake. I am in a green rowboat that is small and kind of flat. It sits low on the water. It has two oars to row the boat around a lake. I bet early fishers used a boat like the one I am picturing. Tell me about your mind pictures of the boat. The boat that you are visualizing probably does not look just like my boat. That is okay. All we know now from the clues is that there is a boat on the water that fishers began to use to find fish. (*Students share their mental images. Ask questions to get some of the students to elaborate on the details of their mind pictures.*)

Level 2: Shared Strategy Use—We Do

Now we are ready to look at the second clue. Let's read this clue and see how the details might help us focus our mind picture: *Over time, boats got bigger and took fishers farther out to sea.* This new sentence has some clues that require me to change my picture with my brain camera. Which text details give us more information about the boat and fishers we are picturing? (*bigger, farther out to sea*) How will you change your mental image based on these new clues? Will your boat still move in the water the same way? Is your boat bigger? What do the fishers look like? How are they fishing? We have some new information that helps us continue to develop our mind pictures. Let's take turns describing our new mind pictures.

(*Students share their visualization of the boat and fishers. Ask questions to help the students clarify their mind pictures. Share your mind picture as another example of how readers picture text details.*) Now my boat has changed. I don't think a rowboat would be good for going far out into the ocean. I think that my boat will have a motor like a speedboat. I do not know yet if these fishers had a motor in their boat, but that is the kind of boat that I am seeing in my mind. The fishers on my boat—there are two men—are still using fishing poles.

Level 3: Guided Strategy Use—You Try

Look at the third sentence on the chart and read it to yourself: *Early wooden boats were called sailboats because they had sails and were powered by the wind.* As you read, think about the clues that tell you more about the hidden picture. Which words or phrases really help you focus your mind picture? *(early wooden boats, sailboats, sails, powered, wind)* Change your mind picture as you consider this new information. I will give you some time to develop your mind picture before we share.

Drop in on several students, and ask them to identify the text clues that helped them create a more focused mind picture and make adjustments to their mental image. Have students talk about their thinking with a partner. Then highlight the text clues that the students used to visualize and let them share some of their new mind pictures as well as some of their questions or wonderings about what the boat in the hidden picture might look like.

Repeat the above process with the fourth and final clue: *Gusts of wind filled the two enormous square sails in the middle of the boat and two smaller triangular sails at the front of the boat as the fishers pulled in fat fish caught on long fishing lines.* After students identify the text clues that helped them focus their brain camera and share their final mind pictures with their partners or the group, review all the underlined clues in the text. Tell students that their mental images may not be exactly like the hidden picture, but if they considered all of the text clues, the framed mental picture they snapped with their brain cameras should reflect the big details of the actual picture. Show students the hidden picture and lead them in a reflective conversation about the strategy.

Concluding the STAR Lesson

To close the STAR lesson, ask students how using their brain cameras to develop mind pictures helped them better understand the images that the words of the text were creating in their brains as they read. Let students explain in their own words how readers change or adjust their mental images as they continue to read a text. Discuss how using the strategy of visualization—making mind pictures—during reading can be used in other contexts, such as reading in the content areas or writing a descriptive text. To review with students what they did as they used their brain cameras, develop a STAR Points chart (see Figure 7.2 below).

Figure 7.2 STAR Points Chart—Framing a Mind Picture:
A During-Reading Strategy

STAR Points

Framing a Mind Picture:

A During-Reading Strategy

1. Read the identified text chunk carefully.

2. Ask yourself, "What are the clues in the text that help me use my brain camera to snap a mind picture of what I just read?"

3. Frame your mind picture based on those clues.

4. Ask yourself, "Do I have any questions or wonderings that would help me bring my mind picture into focus?"

5. Read the next identified text chunk carefully.

6. Ask yourself, "Did any clues in this new text chunk require me to change or adjust my mind picture? Do I need to snap any new mind pictures based on the new information or clues I just read?"

7. Continue reading the text in chunks, changing or adding to your picture album of framed mind pictures as you read.

8. When you are finished reading, revisit your mind pictures in the picture album you've created in your brain. Review the text information by thinking about the collection of mind pictures you snapped as you read.

Level 4: Independent Strategy Use—You Do

1. Provide a variety of simple photographs or illustrations mounted in paper frames on a nonfiction topic with each photograph/illustration hidden from view in a folder. For each photograph or illustration, paper clip a white envelope to the folder containing a series of numbered paper strips with a sentence or short text chunk on each that describes the photograph or illustration. Students work with a partner to practice the strategy of visualizing using the steps on the STAR Points chart. Students read each strip provided about the hidden photograph or illustration one at a time as in the STAR Model Lesson, underline the clue words and phrases, share their mind pictures, and discuss their questions or wonderings. After processing all the clues, students view the actual framed visual and have a conversation with their partners about their mind pictures. Students should focus their conversations on the process they used to visualize the framed picture or illustration.

2. **Note:** This variation of the STAR Model Lesson needs to be modeled and explained to students before it is put into an independent, You Do context. Provide a variety of simple photographs or illustrations in paper frames on a nonfiction topic and five plastic chips or markers. Working with a partner, one student selects a framed picture to examine and describe verbally to his or her partner. This student gives oral clues to describe the picture's content. Each single clue is represented by one of the five chips or markers, and only one clue is provided at a time. The clue-giver allows his or her partner time to process the information given in each clue and snap a mind picture before providing the next clue. The clue-giver attempts to use rich, specific language to describe the framed picture. When all five clues have been given, the student receiving the clues describes his or her final framed mind picture to the clue-giver, who then reveals the actual picture. The partners discuss which clues provided the most specific information to help the listener snap an accurate mind picture. Students consider what other

pieces of information might have helped the listener visualize the unseen picture more effectively. Then students exchange roles and try the activity again.

3. **Note:** This activity or any variation needs to be modeled for students before it is put into an independent You Do context. Adapt the previous activity by using colored blocks instead of pictures. Select two sets of matching blocks, five to eight blocks per set depending on the level of the students. Check to make sure students know the names of the colors and shapes represented by the blocks and are familiar with such spatial descriptions as *above, below, beside, over, next to, to the right of, to the left of,* etc. Students work in pairs, sitting one behind the other, each with a set of matching blocks. The student sitting at the back uses the blocks to create a design on the floor. The only rule for the activity is that each block must touch at least one other block. The student constructing the block design describes it to the student sitting in front of him or her, providing only one clue at a time, such as: *"Place the blue triangle block right below the yellow hexagon block with the point of the triangle pointing down like an arrow"* or *"Put the blue square block to the right of the purple rectangle block."* The student sitting in the front of the pair moves his or her blocks one at a time, following the directions in order to visualize and replicate the block design described by the partner. When all the clues have been given and the visualizing partner's blocks have been placed, the two students move aside and compare their two designs. The partner who visualized the block design shares which clues were the most effective in helping him or her develop a mind picture of that design. Then the students exchange roles. With practice, students use more specific directions to help their partners better visualize the design to be copied. Increase the difficulty of this task by increasing the number of blocks. Make the visualizing easier for students by using only one shape of block for the activity, such as three to five multicolored square blocks.

STAR Model Lesson 2: Sketching Mind Pictures

After students complete the initial STAR Model Lesson for Framing a Mind Picture and demonstrate that they can identify the critical attributes of the strategy of visualization, their strategy practice can be extended into broader contexts. The following adaptation incorporates sketching of mind pictures. Sketching helps students firm up their mind pictures and attend to the text details they use to develop their images. As additional text clues are revealed, students adjust the sketches of their mind pictures. Their sketches reflect their personal ponderings of the text content and concepts and the meaning they build from the printed page through visualizing. Sketching—the nonlinguistic representation of the big ideas of text as perceived by the students—"recasts" the information into a system other than language. This action of sketching engages students as they interpret the new knowledge through a different format—a process that Short, Harste, and Burke (1996, 528) call "transmediation."

Materials

- a short paragraph with rich imagery and descriptive language written on chart paper or projected on a screen so only one sentence is revealed at a time
- a fiction text example follows the description of the procedure (see pp. 183–185) (**Note:** in order to successfully scaffold students through their initial interactions with this strategy variation, I have selected a fiction text which is likely more familiar to students than a nonfiction text.)
- a whiteboard, dry-erase marker and eraser for each student

Procedure

- Give each student in the group a whiteboard, marker, and eraser. Tell the students that they will practice using their brain cameras to snap mind pictures in response to a chunk of text. As they read, students change or add to their mind pictures until they have finished reading the entire text chunk and "developed" their final snapshots or mental images.
- Reveal the first sentence of the text. Ask students to identify

specific words or short phrases that help them focus their mind pictures. Circle those words and phrases in the sentence.

- Students sketch their mind pictures on their whiteboards. Remind students that a sketch is not a full-blown illustration, so stick figures and simple details are acceptable to record their ideas.

- Give students a chance to share with a partner the sketched mental image they snapped with their brain cameras and discuss how readers visualize some of the details of a text in different ways. However, students need to check their mind pictures to make sure they included the critical clues they circled in the text.

- Read the next sentence and repeat the above process. Rather than erasing their entire sketch, encourage students to modify their sketches based on the new text clues or add new details to their original mind pictures. Students share their revised mental images with one another. Have a conversation with the students about how good readers adjust or change their mental images as they read.

- Read the rest of the text one chunk at a time following the steps outlined above until students have formed a final mind picture based on the entire text's clues.

- Discuss how good readers use text information to visualize as they read. Students share their thinking about this strategy and how good readers create powerful mental images to focus their reading and effectively comprehend text.

Fiction Text

Note: The initial model text is a short fiction paragraph. Select a text based on students' independent or instructional reading level. After teachers take students through this lesson example, they can use nonfiction text to demonstrate the strategy.

Figure 7.3 Fiction Text and Examples of Possible Student Mind Pictures

The house stood in the middle of a tiny island.

Students identify and circle these clues that help them visualize— house, middle, tiny island—*and then sketch their mind pictures.*

The island was surrounded by a river that went all around the house.

Students identify and circle these clues that help them visualize— surrounded, river, all around—*and adjust their sketches based on the new clues.*

The house had a gigantic wooden door that creaked.

Students identify and circle these clues that help them visualize— gigantic, wooden, door, creaked—*and adjust their sketches based on the new clues.*

Ivy crawled up the sides of the house as if reaching for the sky above.

*Students identify and circle these clues that help them visualize—*ivy, crawled, sides, reaching for the sky—*and adjust their sketches based on the new clues.*

A large tower rose from each corner of the house, and on top of each tower were turrets that looked like rows of teeth with every other tooth missing.

*Students identify and circle these clues that help them visualize—*large tower, each corner, on top, turrets, rows of teeth with every other tooth missing—*and adjust their sketches based on the new clues.* **Note:** If students do not know the vocabulary in the text, their ability to visualize is challenged. In this sentence, if students do not know the meaning of the word *turrets*, they still have the text clues that describe what turrets look like.

Figure 7.3 Fiction Text and Examples of Possible Student Mind Pictures *(cont.)*

Thin, red, triangular flags, raised on a pole above every tower, fluttered in the breeze.

Students identify and circle these clues that help them visualize—thin, red, triangular flags, pole above every tower, fluttered—and adjust their sketches based on the new clues.

Suddenly, the great wooden door began to lower over the river as the king appeared on his horse to enter his home, the castle.

Students identify and circle these clues that help them visualize—great wooden door, lower over the river, king, horse, castle—and adjust their sketches based on the new clues. **Note:** With the final text details, the students' original mental images of a house on an island have evolved into a king's castle.

✦ *Pause and Ponder* ✦

Use the selection, "Life in the Abyss Zone", in a lesson that you plan based on the strategy variation for Framing a Mind Picture described in STAR Model Lesson 1 (p. 173 of this chapter). ✦

Life in the Abyss Zone

The abyss zone [layer of the ocean] is pitch black and almost freezing. At the bottom of this zone, the ocean floor is like a huge muddy plain. Millions of plankton skeletons have helped form this thick layer of mud. But there is life here in the abyss. Worms, starfish, giant sea spiders, and crabs live on the ocean floor. Some fish also live here. They eat food that sinks down from the ocean layers above. Vents of hot, gushing water are also found on the ocean floor. The water is around 662 degrees F (350 degrees C). It is amazing to think that animals can live near these vents. Giant clams and tubeworms feed on the bacteria that live in these hot waters.

Read the text "Life in the Abyss Zone." Write the text on chart paper or project the text onto a screen. Cover the paragraph so only one sentence is revealed at a time (sometimes two sentences may be grouped).

Here are some questions to guide your observations during the lesson:

- Which critical text details or clues in each sentence help a reader focus his or her mind picture?
- How does a reader's mind picture develop or change after reading each sentence?
- What impact does understanding the vocabulary of nonfiction text have on visualization?
- How can using this strategy with nonfiction text help students understand how text information strengthens reading comprehension?

STAR Model Lesson 3: Read It, See It

Framing a Mind Picture becomes an anchor strategy that students consistently employ as they read nonfiction text, using all the available specific text details to build mental images that support meaning. The Framing a Mind Picture STAR Model Lesson 1 in this chapter (p. 173) with its variations and the STAR Points chart (Figure 7.2, p. 179) target the critical attributes of visualization and provide students with valuable contexts for practicing and enriching this reading strategy. Students then gain more independence in creating mental images as they read, process, and draw conclusions throughout an entire text chunk or passage as modeled in the STAR Model Lesson variation Read It, See It.

Materials

- premade eight-page stapled paper booklet for each student
- pencils
- nonfiction text on students' instructional reading level divided into seven short text chunks

Text

"States of Matter" text presented in Figures 7.4 and 7.6–7.7

Level 1: Modeled Strategy Use—I Do

On the front page or cover of the booklet, have students write the title of the text section at the very top of the page. **Note:** "States of Matter" is the title of the section from which the example is taken.

Read the first text chunk to students. Stop at the end of the text chunk and think aloud about the most important text clues that help readers frame a mind picture about the big ideas presented.

On the second page of the booklet, sketch any mind pictures of the significant details discussed. Then label the sketches and write a one-sentence caption that "frames" the mind pictures and captures the big ideas of that text chunk. Give students the opportunity to sketch their mental images for the same text chunk in their own booklets, writing labels and a caption on the page under their sketches.

Figure 7.4 "States of Matter" Text Chunk 1

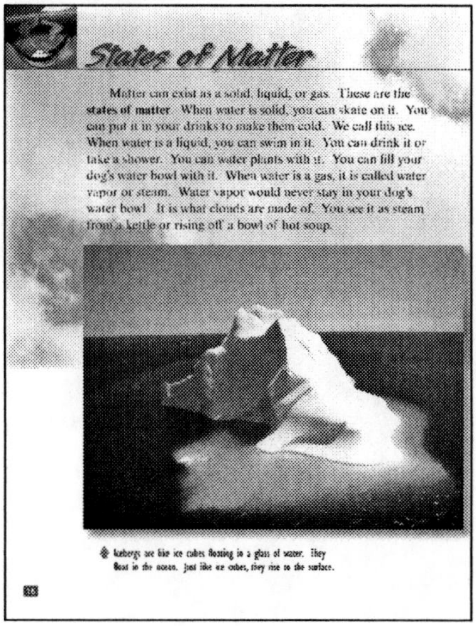

States of Matter

Matter can exist as a solid, liquid, or gas. These are the **states of matter**. When water is solid, you can skate on it. You can put it in your drinks to make them cold. We call this ice. When water is a liquid, you can swim in it. You can drink it or take a shower. You can water plants with it. You can fill your dog's water bowl with it. When water is a gas, it is called water vapor or steam. Water vapor would never stay in your dog's water bowl. It is what clouds are made of. You see it as steam from a kettle or rising off a bowl of hot soup.

Icebergs are like ice cubes floating in a glass of water. They float in the ocean. Just like ice cubes, they rise to the surface.

Source: Weir 2007

This first chunk of text helps me think about the three states of matter. I can picture skating on ice when I was a little girl; I was not very good! I also see water as a solid in my glass. I like a lot of ice cubes to make my drink really cold. I will quickly sketch those two mind pictures and write the label *solid—ice*. I read about water being a liquid, and I snap a mind picture of swimming in a pool. I also see my dog's water bowl. It's almost empty, so I better fill it! I will sketch those mind pictures and write, *liquid—water*. This last part talks about water when it is a gas, and I first picture the clouds in the sky. Then I make a mental picture of the steam coming off my cup of hot chocolate. I sketch these mind pictures and add the label *gas—clouds, steam*. Now I need to think about a caption for all my sketches and try to frame the big idea that holds my mind pictures together. I think I will write, *Solid, liquid, and gas are the three states of matter.*

Figure 7.5 Teacher Sketches for "States of Matter" Text Chunk 1

Level 2: Shared Strategy Use—We Do

Read the second text chunk with students. Engage students in a discussion of the important details of this text chunk, and let them explain any mental images they have after reading those details. On the third page of the booklet, students make quick sketches of their mind pictures. Help students create a caption for the main ideas of the images they sketched.

Figure 7.6 "States of Matter" Text Chunk 2

Why Does Water Appear Outside My Glass?

On a hot humid day, the air contains many water molecules. These molecules have a lot of energy and move around a great deal. If they hit the sides of a cold glass of water, then they lose some of their energy and slow down. Some of the molecules slow down so much that they don't have enough energy to be in a gas any more. They turn into liquid on the outside of the glass.

Source: Weir 2007

The students sketch their mind pictures of gas molecules hitting the icy glass, slowing down, and turning into liquid molecules. A possible caption might read, *When fast-moving gas molecules hit a cold surface, they slow down and turn into a liquid.*

Figure 7.7 "States of Matter" Text Chunks 3–7

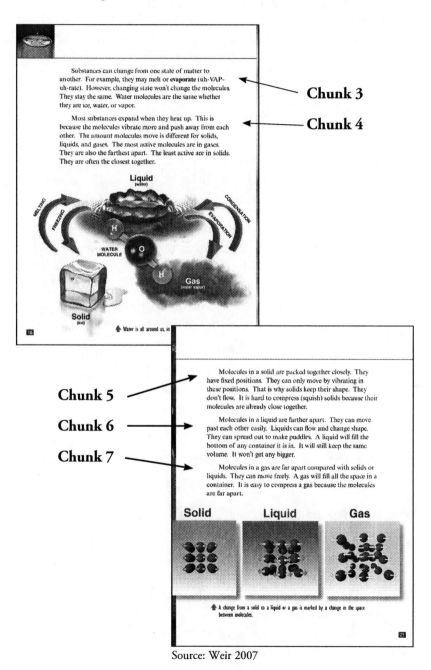

Substances can change from one state of matter to another. For example, they may melt or **evaporate** (uh-VAP-uh-rate). However, changing state won't change the molecules. They stay the same. Water molecules are the same whether they are ice, water, or vapor.

Chunk 3

Most substances expand when they heat up. This is because the molecules vibrate more and push away from each other. The amount molecules move is different for solids, liquids, and gases. The most active molecules are in gases. They are also the farthest apart. The least active are in solids. They are often the closest together.

Chunk 4

Liquid
(water)

MELTING

FREEZING

CONDENSATION

EVAPORATION

WATER MOLECULE

H   O   H

Gas
(water vapor)

Solid
(Ice)

Water is all around us, in

Chunk 5

Molecules in a solid are packed together closely. They have fixed positions. They can only move by vibrating in these positions. That is why solids keep their shape. They don't flow. It is hard to compress (squish) solids because their molecules are already close together.

Chunk 6

Molecules in a liquid are farther apart. They can move past each other easily. Liquids can flow and change shape. They can spread out to make puddles. A liquid will fill the bottom of any container it is in. It will still keep the same volume. It won't get any bigger.

Chunk 7

Molecules in a gas are far apart compared with solids or liquids. They can move freely. A gas will fill all the space in a container. It is easy to compress a gas because the molecules are far apart.

Solid   **Liquid**   **Gas**

A change from a solid to a liquid or a gas is marked by a change in the space between molecules.

Source: Weir 2007

Level 3: Guided Strategy Use—You Try

Students read the third text chunk silently and then work with a partner to talk about their mind pictures. Students sketch their mental images on the fourth page of their booklets, adding labels and a caption after they sketch. Students share their completed page with their partners. The teacher drops in on the students as they work, asking questions and talking to students about the text details that help them visualize the text for their Read It, See It booklets.

Students complete the reading of the text, stopping after each chunk to sketch their mind pictures and write labels and captions about the big ideas depicted in their images.

When students have completed all the pages of their "Read It, See It" booklets, redirect them to the cover or first page of the booklets. Under the title of the text, help students develop a main idea sentence for the entire text. Example main idea statement for "States of Matter": *The three states of matter—solid, liquid, and gas—are determined by the movement of the molecules and the space between them.*

Write the main idea on the booklet's cover or first page. The students then read their entire Read It, See It booklets—mind pictures, labels, and captions—noting how they used visualization to capture the main idea and significant details of the text. In doing so, students will develop a summary of the text.

For another approach to this activity, divide a shorter text into only three or four chunks.

Level 4: Independent Strategy Use—You Do

The Read It, See It strategy can be used in a variety of reading contexts to support students' meaning making. In science, as students read the steps of a science experiment, they visualize each step, sketch their mind pictures, and label their sketches or write the steps in their own words before conducting the actual experiment. The Read It, See It booklet provides students with a record of their thinking in social studies as they read a text section about the events leading up to a historic event. They can use the pages of the booklet to make a visual timeline that describes the most important events. In math, students create a Read It, See It booklet to illustrate and summarize the steps of a process they use to solve a particular type of math problem.

Differentiation Notes

After presenting the initial STAR Model Lesson on visualization, differentiate the strategy by adjusting the level of scaffolding necessary as students demonstrate proficiency in creating mental images to remember details, make inferences, and draw conclusions from text. When students need extra support for understanding how readers snap mind pictures, start with simple pictures and then let students try to visualize words. Move from words to short phrases to a sentence or two and then to a paragraph or short text chunk as students become more efficient at framing their mind pictures and sharing their thinking.

When reading aloud, be on the lookout for rich sensory text details and think aloud how these details help readers make mental images. Ask students to use their brain cameras to snap text passages that inspire strong images. Adapt the Act It Out activity from Chapter 4 (p. 78–81) to a during-reading strategy by engaging students in acting out a portion of text, turning visualized mind pictures into physical images through movement.

For English language learners and below-level students, remember that comprehending the vocabulary of nonfiction text affects visualization, and frontloading to build background before reading is critical if students are going to successfully interpret vocabulary and create mind pictures. (See Chapter 4 for strategies to set students up to read with meaning.)

More-proficient students move quickly from strategy practice to an independent awareness of the importance of visualization in their reading comprehension. These students enjoy using sticky notes as they read to sketch some of their critical mind pictures or to mark text chunks that have powerful sensory language that supports visualization. Provide these readers with a selection of interesting objects or artifacts. The students choose an object and write a descriptive paragraph with specific sensory details without naming the object. Students read their paragraphs, anticipating that the other students can use the details provided in the paragraph to visualize and guess the mystery object.

Summary

The wonderful message for teachers is that the reading strategy of visualization can be brought to light for students who are unaware of its power to create a more vibrant reading experience. Through modeling the significant connection between text clues and making mental images that "recast" that text information, teachers illustrate how visualizing helps readers monitor meaning and incorporate new learning into their knowledge base. Comments such as "Here's what I am seeing with my brain camera" and "Let me sketch my mind picture for you" permeate a classroom where students celebrate visualization as an active strategy in their repertoire of comprehension strategies.

✤ *Pause and Ponder* ✦

Students today are surrounded by visual images. Observe the visual aspects of several texts you use with students or ones they use in other areas of the curriculum. In what ways do you think visually dense materials affect students as they read these texts? How closely do you think students attend to these visuals and the relationships between visuals and text? How do you think highly visual resources affect students' ability to form their own mental pictures? ᴓ

Chapter 8

Asking Questions and Making Inferences

"Interpretive understandings are generated by the reader, who makes inferences and connections from information presented in the text. The process calls on the reader to use personal knowledge and experiences to make meanings beyond the stated facts" (Stead 2006, 75).

Considerations from Research

- Rich questions probe beneath the surface of understanding and require students to make an inference, offer a reflection, give and justify an opinion, or ask their own questions.

- Self-questioning or questioning the text enables readers to make sure they are understanding what they read.

- Making inferences is often a challenge for struggling readers. Poor inferencing may be attributed to a lack of background knowledge, difficulty with integrating personal information with text information, difficulty with recognizing relationships among ideas within the text, and not realizing that inferences are "necessary and permissible" (Allington and McGill-Franzen 2009, 563).

- Asking questions and making inferences provide evidence of the reader's active engagement with text. These actions demonstrate that the reader recognizes that sometimes text needs to be "reprocessed in order to make sense of it" (Pressley 2005, 197).

While driving down the road, you hit a busy intersection that is considerably backed up and moving at a snail's pace. You are running late, so you survey the situation, craning your neck over and around the cars stopped in front of you to ascertain the cause of the delay. Is it a car accident, an emergency vehicle in the way, a broken traffic light, or just a heavier-than-usual flow of cars? Depending on the source of the delay, you mull over your choices and picture their impact on your attempt to get to work: wait it out, turn around and find another possible route, *(Is there another route?)*, turn off on a side street *(Where does that street go?)*, or just go home and forget it. Finally, you make your decision and act on it.

Consider the many thought processes that quickly engage your brain as you work through this familiar experience. First you use your prior knowledge of traffic patterns and possible causes of delay. You entertain questions and the responses of the people in the cars in front of you, perhaps even visualizing each possibility, and you examine the "evidence" as you predict the results of each choice you can make. Finally, based on your observations, you infer the best possible course of action, and acting on your prior knowledge and the available evidence, you draw a conclusion and respond.

The example above illustrates the critical relationship that exists between predicting, visualizing, questioning, and inferring when evaluating information to draw conclusions. Similarly, successful readers draw upon these resources as they work through text to make meaning. In reading, students must evaluate the information and how it is presented in a text in order to develop inferences. To infer, students make connections; predict, visualize, and determine the main ideas and important details; ask, interpret, and answer questions; ascertain the author's point of view or bias; and form tentative theories, conclusions, or judgments about the impact of the information (Macceca 2007; Keene and Zimmermann 1997). No wonder making inferences is one of the most difficult comprehension strategies to take on as a reader!

When students begin reading text, especially nonfiction text, making connections to the "known" provides them with a framework of prior knowledge from which to make reasonable assumptions about the content in the text. Predictions about a text—one type of inference—are not just random guesses about the content; they are reasonable hypotheses based on links readers make between their background knowledge and any text clues they examine. As students move through the text, they confirm, revise, modify, or abandon prior predictions to formulate new predictions. The ability to make reasonable predictions before and during reading enables readers to create expectations about the content, set individual purposes for reading, increase curiosity about the text, and sustain motivation to continue reading (Ryder and Graves 2003). These behaviors serve to increase comprehension.

Examining Questions

Questions that students and teachers pose before reading provide a context for wondering about a text and making predictions. Provocative questions draw students into a nonfiction text and help them link what they already know about a topic to the new content (Ryder and Graves 2003). Questions also promote students' curiosity about the text and keep them motivated to read on and seek answers through an internal dialogue with the author, the text page, and themselves (Hoyt 1999; Zimmerman and Hutchins 2003). Students formulate questions as part of the Text Walk strategy described in Chapter 6. These student-generated questions, whether literal or inferential, serve as a framework for establishing a purpose for reading. They also set students up to acquire information that will answer their questions as they read.

Ways to Share Student Questions

Many teachers encourage students to share their questions or wonderings before, during, and after reading by recording them on a chart. A Wonder Wall chart features an open-ended column with the heading "I wonder… ."

If desired, other columns may be added to the charts. For example, you can add one for the students' predictions and one for answers to the questions or wonderings discovered as students read. The questions from the charts guide students as they read. While reading, they can stop periodically to refer back to the questions, taking time to discuss and record any answers addressed by or inferred from the text, as well as record new questions that arise.

Figure 8.1 below shows an example of a first-grade Wonder Wall. The students are framing their wonderings as questions. The chart presents the students' questions about pandas. Question marks on the chart were circled by different students. The teacher focused on the question words with students and underlined the question word in each sentence. Then students read *Pandas* (*Level 1.4, Nonfiction Readers, Emergent Level*) in teacher-guided small groups. The teacher read aloud the text *Giant Pandas* (Stone 2002) to the class. Then the students returned to the Wonder Wall to see if any of their questions or wonderings were answered by the texts.

Figure 8.1 Our Wonder Wall About Pandas

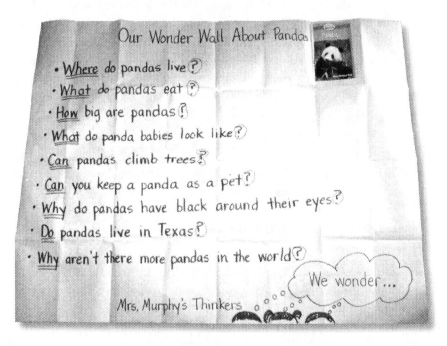

Questions and Queries is another type of chart that the teacher or students can use to record questions—before, during, and after reading. Figure 8.2 shows student questions related to the selection "A Killer Quake in Asia" (for this text, see Chapter 6, p. 132). The students developed questions before, during, and after reading the selection.

Figure 8.2 Our Group's Questions and Queries for "A Killer Quake in Asia"

Before reading:	During reading:	After reading:
How many people were killed? What causes an earthquake? What were other effects of the earthquake? Why didn't more people survive the earthquake? Were the survivors able to save anyone?	Why were so many people killed by the earthquake? Why couldn't the rescue workers save more people? Did other countries offer to help the survivors of the earthquake? Why did the two countries—India and Pakistan—not get along? What were their differences?	Did India and Pakistan working together actually help the survivors and clear the destruction? Have there been any other big earthquakes in this area since then? Where else in the world have there been really bad earthquakes like this one?

Often, students expect to find answers to their questions stated explicitly in the text. Students soon learn that this is not always the case. Answers to literal questions can be found in the text, either in text organizers or within the body of the text. But many questions require students to read between the lines, or infer an answer from the text clues and what they think about those clues based on their background knowledge. As students develop proficiency in reading, they learn that answers to questions can be determined in various ways:

- finding the answer specifically in the text
- inferring an answer by using text details in combination with background knowledge and personal interpretation
- recognizing that a question can only be answered with further reading and research in resources beyond the text

Teachers increase students' inferential understanding by familiarizing them with the types of questions that require them to think beyond the literal level and connect textual information to their knowledge base. By posing inferential questions, teachers focus students on critical thinking and enable them to better recall and understand text concepts and content (Duke and Pearson 2002).

"Good questions work on us, we don't work on them. They are not a project to be completed but a doorway opening onto greater depth of understanding, actions that will take us into being more fully alive" (Block 2001, 39).

Therefore, from the earliest school years, teachers use both literal and inferential questions, making sure to emphasize higher-level questions to help students comprehend text deeply. Although teachers may ask a series of literal, on-the-lines questions to see if students actually read and understood a text, teachers gain greater insight into students' comprehension by asking inferential questions. These questions require students to use literal text details to draw conclusions and make generalizations about the information presented. These same teachers recognize the powerful link between comprehension and student-generated questions. Engaged readers stay focused as they ask questions to analyze the text information, determine the author's intent, clarify meaning, and make predictions, critically evaluating what they read and drawing conclusions about the content and its significance to their own lives (Keene and Zimmermann 1997).

Students need to know how to think about a text and the answers it provides to questions on both the literal and inferential levels. In order to effectively process the depth of a question and share their thoughts, students need instruction to delineate between the two types of thinking—*literal* (right there, on-the-lines thinking) and *inferential* (think about it, between-the-lines thinking). Engagement with different levels of thinking and questions, initiated by both teachers and students, encourages independent, active readers who employ questioning and inferential thinking throughout their reading experience to better understand and talk about text.

✦ *Pause and Ponder* ✦

Making inferences requires readers to understand the difference between something stated explicitly and something stated implicitly. Consider how you teach students to develop inferences as they read.

- How do you support students as they think through a text?
- What kinds of questions do you ask students during your reading instruction?
- What kinds of questions do students ask?
- How effective are students in framing and responding to literal-level or inferential questions?

Choose one or two texts that your students read in other areas of the curriculum. Select texts that include questions as text features to guide readers. With your students, examine some of the questions and discuss whether the answers are likely to be stated explicitly or whether the students will have to infer the answers. ✑

STAR Model Lessons

Using the STAR Model Lesson format, I now describe a model lesson with three variations to illustrate ways in which to teach students these comprehension strategies:

- using inference as a strategy to think about and process the meaning of nonfiction text visuals
- establishing the difference between on-the-lines literal thinking and between-the-lines inferential thinking

Three nonfiction selections—photographs as well as text—are used in the model lessons:

- Photographs from *Workers* (Rice 2003), a short text (emergent reading level 1.2) about various familiar workers in the community. The photographs clearly depict some of the aspects of different professions, enabling the students to use the photograph to make inferences about each worker.
- Photograph from *Natural Disasters* (Noonan 2009) a mathematics concept book at text level 4.6. The text has rich photographs that depict some of the natural disasters and their effects. The photographs have ample details to support the students as they make inferences about the content.
- Excerpt from *Causes of the Revolution* (Mulhall 2005), a 5.4 level text that describes multiple events leading up to the American Revolution. Each two-page spread discusses different distinct causes for the revolution. In addition, the book contains a wide variety of text features to further support the students in understanding the main ideas and making inferences about the book's concepts.

STAR Model Lesson 1: On-the-Lines/Between-the-Lines Reading Detectives

Comprehension Strategies

- use inference to think about and process the meaning of nonfiction text visuals
- establish the difference between on-the-lines literal thinking and between-the-lines inferential thinking

Critical Attributes

- The student examines the text visual (photograph or illustration) on the page.
- The student stops after each page with a text visual to ask, "What is right there on-the-lines in this photograph? What do I see?"
- The student identifies the literal, on-the-lines information provided by the text visual.
- After thinking about the literal information, the student asks, "What might be between-the-lines in this photograph? What do I think about what I see?"
- The student provides any inferences, linking between-the-lines thinking to the literal information provided in the photograph (text visual) and explaining any interpretations or conclusions.

Materials

- nonfiction book with supportive photographs for the content

Note: For the initial STAR Model Lesson, use a wordless nonfiction book or a book with limited text, covering any text with sticky notes. Provide each student with a copy of the book or project the pages of the book on a screen one page at a time using a document camera.

- props to reinforce the two types of thinking (optional)
- a pair of fun plastic reading glasses to represent right there, on-the-lines literal thinking

- a magnifying glass to represent the think-about-it, between-the-lines inferential thinking done by "reading detectives"

- a hat made with a stapled paper strip with a picture of a pair of reading glasses and a picture of a magnifying glass, one picture attached to each side of the hat, to represent the two kinds of thinking

Note: Younger students like the "reading detective hat," turning the hat to the appropriate symbol as they engage in that type of thinking. A picture of a pair of reading glasses can symbolize on-the-lines thinking for a reading detective—representing clues that are right there in the photograph—and a picture of a magnifying glass can symbolize between-the-lines thinking since the reading detective must look closely and think beyond the specific text details.

- a reading detective response signal made from a plastic drinking straw with a picture to represent each of the two kinds of thinking

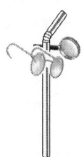

Note: Staple a picture of reading glasses and a picture of a magnifying glass back-to-back on each side of a straw. Students hold and turn the straw to the appropriate symbol as they engage in that type of thinking.

Figure 8.3 Nonfiction Content Support Photographs

Figure 8.3 Nonfiction Content Support Photographs *(cont.)*

Figure 8.3 Nonfiction Content Support Photographs *(cont.)*

Source: Rice 2003

Level 1: Modeled Strategy Use—I Do

Literal-Level Reading

As we read, we think about all the clues the author gives us to help us make the most meaning we can. We are like reading detectives as we look at those clues to see what is there to give us information about the text. One kind of thinking that good reading detectives do is right there, on-the-lines thinking. This kind of thinking is also called literal-level thinking.

Note: Put on the reading detective glasses or hat. For the rest of this STAR lesson, the reading glasses and magnifying glass will be used as examples for incorporating teaching props.

Today we are only going to look at the visual clues that authors give readers through photographs in a text. I am going to look at the photograph and the title on the cover of the book. The title will be the only word we see today. Now, using my reading detective on-the-lines reading glasses, I will tell you what I see in this photograph. I will need to be careful to stay on-the-lines and tell just what I see, not what I think.

Let me look at the photograph. I see a man dressed in a yellow jacket and pants with some bright yellow stripes on it. The jacket looks like it is made of some shiny, slick material. He is wearing a hard, black hat with two yellow patches on it and a flashlight attached to the side of it. The man has a smile on his face. He has his arm around a spotted, black and white dog that is wearing a red bandana. The man and dog are sitting on the front part of a red truck that says *FIRE* on it. I see that the title of the book is *Workers*.

What do you think? Did I do a good job of staying on-the-lines and only telling what I see in the photograph? Did I leave anything out?

Inferential-Level Reading

Now I am ready to try out my reading detective magnifying glass. The magnifying glass reminds me that readers do another kind of thinking: reading between the lines. When I read between the lines, I think about what I see—the clues provided by the author—and what I know. I put my thoughts together and tell what I think the meaning of the text might be in my own words. When I do this kind of between-the-lines thinking, I make an inference about the text. Let's use our magnifying glass to look at the clues from the photograph and read between the lines to make an inference. I will think about each thing that we noted as we read on the lines.

When I see a truck that is red with the word *FIRE* on the front, I know that this must be a fire truck. I have seen many fire trucks just like this. The man sitting on the truck is wearing clothes just like firefighters wear. The yellow clothes are his uniform. These clothes look shiny and thick. I think that man is a firefighter, and he needs these special clothes to protect him from the fire and probably the water that firefighters must use to put out fires. He also has that hard hat. I bet that hat protects his head from anything that falls in the fire. He has a light on his hat so he can see in the fire. Fire makes light, though, so maybe he needs the flashlight on his hat when he looks through the smoke that fire makes. The yellow stripes on the firefighter's uniform remind me of the stripes on our crossing guards' jackets. The stripes probably help people see the firefighter in the dark. The firefighter has a smile on his face. He must really like his work. I think he is also smiling because he likes his dog. I know that dogs cannot fight fires, so I have to think about why there is a dog sitting on the fire truck. Maybe the dog is around to be a friend to the firefighter when he is not working, or maybe the dog is a kind of symbol for the firefighters. The name of this book is *Workers*, so I think that the book will be about people who have different kinds of jobs. I wonder if one of the jobs in the book will be a teacher. That is what I do for my work.

How did I use the clues that are right there on the lines to help me think and read between the lines and draw conclusions about the photograph?

I use what I see and what I know from my own experience and make inferences about the photograph and the title.

Level 2: Shared Strategy Use—We Do

Let's look at the photograph on page two. We can put on our reading detective on-the-lines glasses to describe what we see right there in the photograph. Be careful to stay right on the lines and tell just what you see. I will start us off: I see a lady wearing glasses standing behind an open white truck or van. What clues do you see?

Students discuss what they see in the photograph. Possible responses: *The lady is wearing a blue cap and blue shirt. She has an eagle on her hat and sleeve. She is holding envelopes with a rubber band around them and a magazine. She has boxes in back of her truck.*

If a student switches to reading between the lines with a comment such as "The lady is bringing the mail," say, "Oh, now you are reading between the lines. We will need our reading detective magnifying glass for the kind of thinking you are doing." Discuss the student's inference from the photograph clue with the group, and then return to using the reading glasses to look for literal, on-the-lines clues.

You did a nice job looking for clues that were right there on-the-lines in the photograph. Now let's switch to our reading detective magnifying glass to read between the lines and think about the text clues and what we know from our own experience. Here is an inference I can make by reading between the lines with my magnifying glass: *I think the envelopes the lady is holding and the boxes she has in her truck are the mail that needs to be delivered to people.*

Now what are some of the things you are thinking as you use your clues to read between-the-lines? Possible responses: *The lady is wearing a uniform. The lady is a mail carrier who brings mail to your house. The eagle in the uniform's patches represents the United States, so the mail carrier must work for the U.S. Post Office. The lady is wearing glasses so she can see the addresses on the envelopes. The mail carrier is smiling, so she must enjoy delivering the mail.*

Repeat this model with students using page three of the text—a photograph of a trash collector.

Level 3: Guided Strategy Use—You Try

Ask students to turn to the photograph on page four—a photo of an electrical power or telephone lineperson. The students continue using their reading detective strategies on their own before sharing their thinking with the group. Students note what they see in the photograph and then use the information and clues to draw conclusions about the worker and his or her occupation. Drop in on students to monitor their understanding of the process and ask questions to clarify or extend their between-the-lines thinking. After the students have completed their on-the-lines and between-the-lines thinking with the photograph on page four, engage the students in a discussion about their observations and inferences.

Now have students work with a partner to read on the lines and between the lines with each photograph remaining in the book. Ask students to first use their reading glasses to explore what they see on the lines in the photograph. Then have students use their reading detective between-the-lines magnifying glasses to discuss their thoughts about the photograph. Continue to drop in on student pairs and clarify the students' thinking processes as they consider the literal and inferential aspects of the text information.

Concluding the STAR Lesson

To close the STAR lesson, have a conversation about the inferences students made and have them share the on-the-lines clues that supported their thinking. Ask the students to identify the critical steps and attributes of this strategy. Write the steps for using on-the-lines and between-the-lines thinking on a STAR Points chart as shown in Figure 8.4.

Discuss these questions with the students: When might a reader use this strategy? Why? Can readers use the strategy of reading on the lines and between the lines with short text chunks to note what important information is right there in the sentences and then make inferences about what was read? How would that look? (See the Think It Through Chart strategy variation later in this chapter on page 216.)

Figure 8.4 STAR Points Chart—On-the-Lines and Between-the-Lines Reading Detectives: A Before- and During-Reading Strategy

STAR Points **On-the-Lines and Between-the-Lines Reading Detectives:** **A Before- and During-Reading Strategy**	
	1. Look at the text visual or read the text chunk. Identify the important information that you see right there, on-the-lines.
	2. Think between the lines about what you see and read in the text, and think about what is right there and what you know.
	3. Ask yourself, "What are my ideas or inferences?"
	4. Share or write your between-the-lines thinking or inferences. Support your inferences with clues from the text and your own background knowledge.

Note: If desired, add visual cues, as in the example above, to the STAR Points chart, such as a picture of the reading glasses by step 1, a picture of the reading detective magnifying glass by step 2, a picture of a lightbulb by step 3, and a picture of a pencil by step 4.

Step 4: Independent Strategy Use—You Do

Note: These activities provide opportunities for the teacher to observe students applying the On-the-Lines/Between-the-Lines strategy.

1. Provide a variety of photographs or illustrations on a nonfiction topic. Students work with a partner and select a photograph or illustration to practice being On-the-Lines/Between-the-Lines Reading Detectives, following the steps on the STAR Points chart.

2. Offer students a selection of wordless picture books, such as *Tuesday* by David Wiesner or *Good Dog Carl* by Alexandra Day. Students choose a picture book and work with a partner to use the On-the-Lines/Between-the-Lines Reading Detective strategy to read the pages of the text both at the literal and inferential level.

3. Extend the strategy practice by moving students into interpreting different types of nonfiction visuals, including diagrams, cut-away illustrations, or maps with symbols or picture keys. Students use the On-the-Lines/Between-the-Lines Reading Detective strategy to analyze the various visuals and draw conclusions about the content.

STAR Model Lesson 2: Tell Me What You See/Tell Me What You Think

Several variations of the Reading Detectives STAR Model Lesson can be used to reinforce the strategy with text visuals and to move the strategy into text reading. These additional activities support students as they work with actual text, developing strategies for both literal, on-the-lines thinking and inferential, between-the-lines thinking. After students have developed a basic understanding and "hook" for remembering the different kinds of thinking, they can begin to extend the strategy into drawing conclusions about text visuals with Tell Me What You See/Tell Me What You Think and text reading with Think

It Through charts. These variations of the Reading Detective STAR Model Lesson are described in this lesson and the one that follows.

Materials

- photograph or primary-source document such as a map, diagram, illustration, political cartoon, etc.
- What I See and What I Think individual charts (see Figure 8.5) or a group chart
- pens, pencils, or markers

Figure 8.5 What I See and What I Think Chart

What I See	What I Think

Procedure

- Distribute the What I See and What I Think charts for students to use to record their thinking.
- Display the photograph (or other selected primary source) for students to study.
- Under the column titled What I See, ask students to use their on-the-lines thinking to peruse the photograph and write a bulleted list of at least five things they see. If preferred, the teacher can write the students' responses on a group chart.
- Provide students with the opportunity to share their literal-level observations about the photograph.
- Now ask students to put stars next to the three things in the What I See column that they think are the most important or interesting in the photograph.
- In the column titled What I Think, have students write their thoughts—their between-the-lines inferences—for the three things they starred in the first column.

- Discuss the items that students starred and the inferences they drew about those things in the photograph. Ask students to support their thinking with any details from the photograph and any prior knowledge they used to think between-the-lines.

✈ *Pause and Ponder* ✦

Figure 8.6 Tell Me What You See/Tell Me What You Think Photograph

Source: Noonan 2009

Examine the photograph presented in Figure 8.6. Use the Tell Me What You See/Tell Me What You Think strategy as you work with students to create their chart for this photograph. Make sure you stay on-the-lines in your first column, and try not to make any inferences before you move to the second column to consider and write your inferences.

How can using this chart help students understand the difference between literal and inferential thinking? What details in the photograph influenced your inferences? How does your background knowledge on a nonfiction topic or concept affect your inferences? ✖

Tell Me What You See/Tell Me What You Think becomes a strategy that students employ consistently as they read nonfiction text and encounter all the rich visuals these texts provide readers to support meaning. Tell Me What You See/Tell Me What You Think is a targeted strategy for students to utilize as they preview text organizers. Studying text visuals and considering what can be seen and inferred from those visuals contributes to establishing the big ideas of the text prior to reading.

STAR Model Lesson 3: Think It Through Chart

The Think It Through chart (Figure 8.7, on the following page) moves the strategy of On-the-Lines/Between-the-Lines Reading Detectives from responding to text visuals to analyzing meaning at the text level. When using the Think It Through chart, teachers ask students to apply literal text clues and background information connections to nonfiction text concepts in order to answer questions and generate new ideas and inferences. The Think It Through chart, which can be used both during and after reading, reminds students to stop and think about text chunks to ponder questions, consider text information and new ideas, and draw conclusions. This chart provides a way for students to establish some distinct steps for developing an inference:

1. Focus on the stop-and-think, inferential question in the first column.

2. Search for the text clues in the second column.

3. Apply the thinking process and connect the text clues with what you know in the third column.

4. Record any inferences or conclusions you draw from the text in response to the question.

Initially, the teacher provides the inferential questions about the selected text chunks for the Think It Through chart. As students become more proficient in asking "heavyweight" questions that require them to infer answers, those questions are also included on the chart. Students need many opportunities to experience a supported walk-through of the steps represented by the What I See (Looking) and What I Think (Thinking/Connecting) columns before they can utilize the chart independently and evaluate text information to make effective inferences as they read.

Materials

- copies of a nonfiction text on students' instructional reading level or small sticky notes, highlighter tape, or an overhead transparency and overhead pen for students to mark text proof
- markers
- teacher-made chart to record students' thinking (see Figure 8.7)

Figure 8.7 Think It Through Chart

Asking	Looking	Thinking/ Connecting	Ideas/ Inferences
		Hmmm…	
		Hmmm…	

Text

Excerpt from *Causes of the Revolution* (see Figure 8.8, p. 218)

Procedure

- Select a short nonfiction text chunk. The students preview any possible text organizers (see Chapter 6) and then read the text chunk to determine the big ideas and most significant supporting details.
- Write the first question in the first column on the Think It Through chart. Students read the question to determine what kind of thinking they will need to do in order to answer it. Be sure that only inferential questions are recorded in the chart.

- Move to the second column of the chart to remind students that they now need to return to the text to look for clues or text proof that will help them answer the questions. Students mark any clues they find by underlining, highlighting, or marking the text with sticky notes. Write the identified text clues in the second column of the chart, noting the page and paragraph number. The text clues are paraphrased or placed in a bulleted list. The teacher can start the text sentence or phrase and use an ellipsis to indicate that some of the text in the text clue has been omitted.

- Direct students' attention to the third column. Tell them that they will not write anything in this column. The column heading and the "Hmmm…" comment in the box remind students that part of thinking through a between-the-lines question is thinking about the text clues and connecting the facts and details of the text with their background knowledge. When connecting what they are thinking with what they read in the text, students are making inferences.

- In the last column, write the students' ideas and inferences in response to the question in the first column. At this time, students explain their thinking from the third column and how it supports their answers to the question.

- Once students have had several group experiences with the Think It Through chart, try letting them work in partners or independently to write their own comments in the columns either during or after reading.

Figure 8.8 Excerpt from *Causes of the Revolution*

Stamping Out the Stamp Act

The French and Indian War was very expensive for Britain. The **government** decided it needed to raise some money. So **Parliament** (PAR-luh-muhnt) passed a special tax just for the American colonists. It was called the Stamp Act.

The act required people in America to buy a special stamp to put on all printed paper. This included things like newspapers, marriage licenses, and even decks of playing cards.

Ouch!

Some of the colonists' behavior was very cruel. A few tax collectors were even tarred and feathered. They had sticky, hot tar put all over their bodies. Then they were coated with feathers. This was very painful.

This made the colonists very angry. "We are citizens, too!" they thought. They did not want to pay a tax that the people in England did not have to pay.

So the colonists did an unexpected thing. They refused to pay the tax. Many of them gathered in large mobs and scared off the men who were sent to sell the stamps. By the time the act was officially supposed to start, there was no one left to collect the money.

Taxation without Representation

The people in the colonies had no **representatives** (rep-ri-ZEN-tuh-tivz) in Parliament. This meant they never got to vote on any of Britain's laws. They decided they did not want to pay taxes unless they had a say.

▼ Protest of the Stamp Act

No *Stamped Paper* to be had.

Source: Mulhall 2005

Figure 8.9 Think It Through Chart for *Causes of the Revolution*

Asking 	Looking 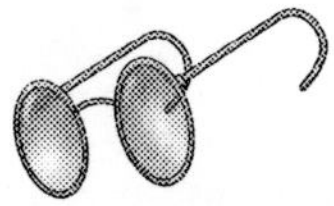	Thinking/Connecting 	Ideas/Inferences 
How could the protest of the Stamp Act affect Britain's relationship with the colonists?	*The government (Britain) decided it needed to raise some money* (p. 8, #1). *They (colonists) refused to pay the tax* (p. 9, #2). *Scared off men who were sent to sell stamps* (p. 9, # 2).	Hmmm...	Since the colonists refused to pay the Stamp Act taxes and drove off the tax collectors, Britain had no way to raise money to pay for the French and Indian War. Britain was probably very frustrated with the colonists and wanted them to behave and pay the taxes. Now Britain might feel like it has to use force to convince the colonists to follow British laws and pay taxes.

Figure 8.9 Think It Through Chart for *Causes of the Revolution (cont.)*

Asking	Looking	Thinking/ Connecting	Ideas/Inferences
Why did Britain enact the Stamp Act to raise money?	*A special tax just for the American colonists (p. 8, #1). Required people in America to buy a special stamp to put on all printed paper … even decks of playing cards (p. 8, #2.).*	Hmmm…	Since Britain needed a lot of money, they selected a tax for all of the American colonists to pay. Everyone had to pay a tax on every piece of printed paper. There were many printed things in America that everyone would need, like marriage licenses and newspapers. Britain thought it could raise a lot of money fast because so many people in the colonies used printed paper, and many people would have to pay the tax.

Differentiation Notes

After the STAR Model Lesson is presented to students, differentiate the strategy by adjusting the level of scaffolding necessary to ensure students are able to frame reasonable inferences and draw conclusions.

Use everyday experiences, such as the example provided at the beginning of this chapter, to illustrate for students how they are constantly using inference in their lives to make predictions, answer questions, formulate ideas, and draw conclusions.

English language learners and below-level students need multiple opportunities through shared, interactive contexts to try out the above strategies with text visuals and shortened text chunks that are only two to three sentences long.

More-proficient students may move quickly from strategy practice in a guided context to partner or independent practice of Tell Me What You See/Tell Me What You Think or the Think It Through chart. This strategy application may be made easier or more difficult by changing the text level or the familiarity of the text topic of the nonfiction selection.

STAR Model Lesson 4: Ask Me

One final strategy variation for students to practice asking higher-level questions and responding to those questions using their between-the-lines thinking is called Ask Me. In Ask Me, the students generate their own questions about the text, trying to ask their partner heavyweight questions that are not explicitly answered in the text. Hearing other students' questions in response to the text inspires new questions in readers and helps

Sometimes students encounter a state reading assessment or a testing situation where the answers to the questions are based entirely on the text used in the assessment. Every correct response to a test item, whether it requires literal or inferential thinking to answer, is based on textual proof, not the students' background knowledge. In fact, an incorrect response can be a plausible choice based on students' prior experiences. Being able to support an inference with text evidence is an essential comprehension element assessed on many reading tests. Students learn how to "prove" their answer choices by returning to the text clues, as well as "disprove" incorrect choices. Students understand that those incorrect responses can trick readers if they are not careful thinkers who use text support for reading between the lines.

221

them understand that asking questions is a powerful tool to monitor comprehension during reading. As students hear and evaluate their peers' responses to the questions, they become aware of new types of thinking required to understand the content and the author's message more deeply. These types of thinking involve the ability to reason, which includes identifying similarities and differences, summarizing, synthesizing, and generating and testing hypotheses (Marzano, Pickering, and Pollock 2001).

Materials

- nonfiction text on students' instructional reading level divided into three short text chunks
- recording sheet and pencil or pen
- group chart for recording and coding questions and answers
- markers

Procedure

- Students work with a partner to read the text. One reader assumes the role of the *questioner*, and one reader becomes the *responder*.
- Both readers identify the text chunk they will read, and then they each read the text chunk silently. (See the Read a Little, Think a Little strategy on p. 145 of Chapter 6.)
- Working with their partners, the questioners ask the responders one or two questions about the text chunk. The questioners try to ask inferential questions—questions that require the responders to read between the lines.
- Both partners reread the text chunk before the responders answer the questions. The responders search for text proof to support their responses to the questions asked by the questioners.
- The responders share their answers with their partners and explain any inferences they made using the text clues and what they knew about the text concepts. The partners discuss the answers and thinking processes of the responders.

- The questioners use their recording sheets to jot down confusions the partners had about the text content or any "tricky" words.

- The partners share with the group their questions and answers and the thinking they did to come up with their responses. The teacher writes down the students' questions on the group chart and, with the students, codes the questions as on-the-lines questions or between-the-lines questions. If the questions cannot be answered by the text, star them for further reading or research.

- The partners exchange roles before reading the next text chunk, and they continue to read, ask questions, and develop responses.

- At the end of the third text chunk, students review the kinds of questions that were asked and answered during reading and discuss how asking questions can help readers monitor their own understanding and improve their reading comprehension.

Summary

Readers use various cognitive levels as they make meaning from texts. Higher levels of reading strategies include asking and answering questions, making inferences, and drawing conclusions—critical tools for students to own as they process and comprehend text. Explicit, consistent language that describes how to integrate these strategies into reading, as well as sufficient time for students to try on these strategies across many contexts, is essential for students as they encounter more challenging nonfiction texts. Reading between the lines enriches readers' experiences with text as they move beyond the words on the page to consider the possibilities behind those words.

→ *Pause and Ponder* ←

How would you describe yourself as a reader? Do you read widely and often? Do you find it easy to abandon a book? Do you read some books more than once? Think about some of your favorite books, when you last read them, and the context in which you read them. What if you were to return to those books today? How do you think your reading would be different? Would you ask the same questions you did the first time you read the book? Would you make the same inferences?

The characters remain the same and the words do not change, but you, the reader, change. How do these observations help you think about what you do with your students as you help them become self-sufficient readers? What part does rereading play in your life and your students' lives? ✒

Chapter 9

Recognizing Nonfiction Text Structures and Author's Purpose

"Understanding how information is arranged and organized within the text can enhance students' ability to organize information to be put into memory" (Spencer 2003, 755).

Considerations from Research

- Effective readers use both text-driven and knowledge-driven processes.
- Text-driven processing involves the use of the text content and organization as the basis for making meaning.
- Students who are more knowledgeable about text structure are able to recall more textual information than those who are less knowledgeable.
- Explicit instruction in text structures improves both comprehension and recall of text details.
- Visual representations of text structures foster comprehension and memory of text information.

When I was teaching, I went to the library every two weeks and brought back to the classroom between 30 and 40 nonfiction books on different topics, encompassing a wide range of reading levels. The students could not wait for those days when they saw my large red book wagon filled with the new nonfiction books. Everyone sat down on the floor and dove into the books, eagerly perusing the titles, photographs, and other text organizers to discover the new content areas for classroom study and excitedly share what they already knew about those topics. It was a true "book frenzy"—under control, of course—filled with the potential joy of learning something new and sharing it with others. Finally, each student settled down with a chosen book and divulged one intriguing feature of that text, such as "This one has a great diagram of the inside of a castle" or "Wait until you see these great photographs of sharks. There is even a whole chapter on great white sharks!" These students found as much pleasure in selecting a nonfiction text as picking a picture book or novel to read.

With nonfiction text, the students' purposes for reading can determine both why and how they read that text. Sometimes students will read an entire nonfiction text from cover to cover, but frequently, they select to read only those portions of a text that interest them, answer their questions, or provide information they want to share with others. Many students are excited about reading nonfiction and choose interesting text that motivates them as they read for pleasure. One student reads every dinosaur book he can get his hands on, while another student devours books about bridges. A teacher who celebrates nonfiction texts in the classroom and frequently reads this kind of text aloud expands the students' repertoire of reading possibilities to include the wide array of nonfiction texts.

Content-area reading is a powerful tool for acquiring intriguing information that is important to readers, allowing them to extend their prior knowledge and answer questions about that content. Sometimes students read nonfiction text that is designed to walk readers through instructions, outline steps in a process, or enumerate a series of rules so readers will know how to accomplish a task or create a product. In addition, in today's world, a plethora of persuasive nonfiction text bombards readers. Students learn to read this text with a critical stance, identifying the author's point of view, word choice, appeals, and examples. The students read reflectively and challenge the author's stance on the topic to infer the author's intended impact on readers. Students question the power of and societal messages behind the persuasive text and read between the lines to infer and evaluate the author's position. With the multiple information-gathering resources available to readers today, a focus on critical literacy develops responsible readers who learn to determine trusted sources of information and evaluate the underlying messages of text (Beck 2005; Cervetti, Pardales, and Damico 2001).

Knowing About Text Structures

Regardless of students' purpose for reading, when teachers call students' attention to the structure of a nonfiction text, those students are more effective in locating information, recalling the major points of their reading, and comprehending the text overall (Duke and Pearson 2002). The structure of a text serves as a type of "road map" to show students how they can best navigate the nonfiction text with meaning. This road map gives students a sense of direction for their reading, allowing them to take certain expectations into the text. The road map for a particular text structure can be visually represented by a graphic organizer that provides the students with a concrete frame to gather, sort, and organize critical information. Since the brain is a pattern-seeking tool (Kovalik and Olsen 2001), a graphic organizer is a brain-compatible device that allows students to process large chunks of text by representing the text patterns on paper and mapping out the relationships among significant text details. This visual image of the text's structure connects the students' prior knowledge to the new information, integrating a new pattern of critical relationships into the students' prior knowledge and thereby allowing them to access it for new learning.

Before reading, previewing the text helps students consider the best route to travel through the text so they can anticipate the text information and organize it with a textual frame in mind. Such text features as the title, subtitles, headings, photographs and illustrations, captions, maps, graphics, and insets provide students with clues to develop a possible main idea hypothesis for the text (see Chapter 6, Figure 6.1, p. 124) and determine a probable text structure. When students have a tentative text structure in mind as they read, they are freed up to think more deeply about the text connections rather than trying to ascertain the construction of the text. The frame or roadmap established during the text preview can be represented by a graphic organizer drawn on chart paper to reflect the text's organization. Students are now ready to read the text with certain expectations for how the information will be organized and interrelated. As students read, they may note that they need to adjust their text-structure graphic organizer. In addition, students may discover that another text structure coexists with the original structure, such as a problem-solution text with cause-effect relationships or a chronological structure with underlying compare-contrast connections. In cases like this, teachers can continue to develop the primary text-organizer relationship with students or add a second graphic organizer to represent the additional relationship presented in the text.

Before reading, students "pack up" their essentials for their "trip" through the selected nonfiction text. Along with their "map" (graphic organizer), they take sticky notes and pencils to record ideas or visualizations as they read. As students "travel" through the text, they pause at "rest stops"—the end of short chunks of text—and reflect on the information presented thus far. Students share any key points they absorbed in their reading and sketch any mental pictures they captured with their brain cameras (see Chapter 7, p. 179) or write down the big ideas on sticky notes. Students then incorporate their images or notes into the graphic organizer, considering how to lay them out in the organizer to best show the relationships and connections among the text details.

An author's purpose in a nonfiction text is revealed in the structure or organizational pattern of the text information. When students are well-versed on the different types of text structures, they are better equipped to read with meaning, summarize their learning, determine the author's purpose, make inferences, and draw conclusions. Figure 9.1 on the following page lists and defines structures commonly used in nonfiction text as well as words that signal those structures.

Figure 9.1 Nonfiction Text Structures and Signal Words

Structure	Definition	Signal Words
Descriptive/ Enumerative	The main idea is stated or listed and supported by examples.	*also, another, besides, characteristics of, for example, for instance, furthermore, in addition, in particular, moreover, particularly, specifically, such as, to begin with, above, behind, below, between, down, inside, outside, over*
Chronological/ Sequenced	A series of details, ideas, or events are presented in temporal order or in order of importance.	*additionally, after, also, another, beginning, finally, first, following, initially, in the first place, in conclusion, last, next, preceding, second, then, third, when*
Cause and Effect	A cause is stated along with its possible results or outcomes, or an effect is given with its possible causes.	*as a result, because, begins with, caused by, consequently, effects of, finally, for this reason, hence, however, if/then, in order to, leads to, nevertheless, next, since, subsequently, therefore, thus, when/then*
Problem and Solution	A problem is presented along with one or more solutions.	*as a result, because, begins with, caused by, consequently, effects of, finally, for this reason, if/then, in conclusion, last, leads to, next, since, subsequently, therefore, unfortunately, when/then*
Proposition and Support	An idea or position is set forth along with advantages in an attempt to persuade the reader to adopt a particular point of view.	*finally, first, foremost, in conclusion, in summary, in support, last, leads to, most importantly, next, subsequently, therefore, unfortunately, when/then*
Compare and Contrast	The similarities and differences between two or more subjects are described.	*although, but, by contrast, compared with, different from, either/or, even though, however, in comparison, in common, like, neither/nor, on the other hand, similar to, unlike, whereas, yet*

Descriptive Text Structure

One text structure used frequently in nonfiction is descriptive text. This text type provides information on a topic through descriptive facts and details or characteristics and traits. Descriptive text lists or enumerates important features, elaborating on each for the purpose of informing the reader. Sometimes descriptive text includes a progression of ideas that may also be embedded in a chronological sequence. Graphic organizers that serve as maps for descriptive text structures include part-to-whole graphic organizers such as webs, lists, and even a Frayer Model (Frayer, Frederick, and Klausmeier 1969) for text that presents a complex concept.

Figures 9.2 and 9.3, below and on the following page, are examples of graphic representations of descriptive text structures. An adaptation of the Frayer Model is presented in Figure 9.3. This example adds boxes to the bottom of the graphic organizer for students to use to sketch their visualizations of the concept.

Figure 9.2 Graphic Organizers for Descriptive Text Structures

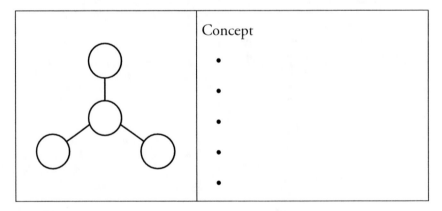

Figure 9.3 Graphic Organizer Adapted from the Frayer Model

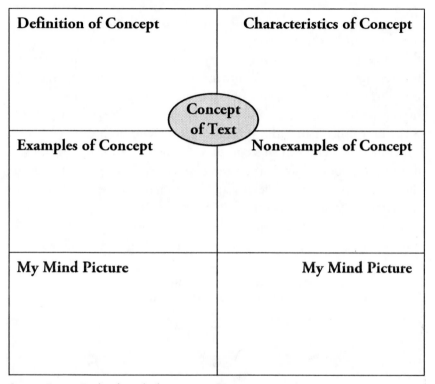

Source: Frayer, Frederick, and Klausmeier 1969

As students read nonfiction text, they notice words that can signal a possible descriptive text structure, such as *also, another, besides, characteristics of, for example, for instance, furthermore, in addition, in particular, moreover, particularly, specifically, such as, to begin with,* and any positional terms, such as *above, behind, below, between, down, inside, outside, over.* While students do not need to memorize these signal words, being familiar with these word clues and noting the presentation format of text organizers help readers confirm the roadmap they've selected to guide their way through the information presented in the text.

Chronological or Sequenced Text Structure

Many students are familiar with a chronological or sequenced text structure because this structure reflects the organization of most fiction text. In nonfiction text, key details, facts, or events can also be presented in chronological order. Concepts and ideas are set forth in a linear or cyclic fashion. Details are arranged in a time-ordered sequence, but they may also be arranged in order of importance. Steps in a process including directions represent a chronological text structure. Students who recognize a chronological or sequenced text organization locate information more quickly in the text and interpret the interrelationships of details and ideas across time or in order of importance. Graphic organizers that reflect a chronological/sequenced text structure include timelines, flowcharts, story maps or boards (for biographies), and cycle charts (see examples in Figure 9.4 below).

**Figure 9.4 Graphic Representations of Chronological
or Sequenced Text Structures**

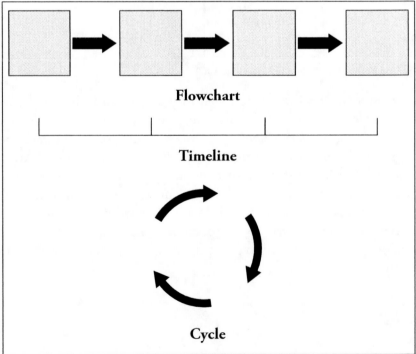

Flowchart

Timeline

Cycle

As in descriptive structures, signal words indicate to a reader that a text is organized chronologically or sequentially. Some of these words include *additionally, after, also, another, beginning, finally, first, following, initially, in the first place, in conclusion, last, next, preceding, second, then, third,* and *when.* When students recognize a chronological or sequenced text, they can quickly locate information in a text based on its order and draw conclusions from the significant details presented.

Cause-and-Effect Text Structure

A powerful text structure found frequently in nonfiction text is cause and effect. Although many nonfiction texts have a cause-and-effect text structure, this structure is also found embedded in other text structures such as chronological/sequenced or problem-solution structures. Cause-and-effect text explores the interrelationships of certain elements and the effects of the impact of those elements on one another. Events are presented along with the consequences of those events. This type of text structure often presents a series or chain of cause-and-effect relationships. While there may be only one cause for one effect in the text, readers more frequently encounter variations of this structure, such as multiple causes for one effect, one cause with multiple effects, or multiple causes and multiple effects. Based on the cause-and-effect relationships presented in the text, the graphic organizer selected shows the pattern of causes and effects. Cause-and-effect charts, chains, and flip books all show the interplay of text details in cause-and-effect relationships. Figure 9.5 on the following page presents examples of graphics for cause-and-effect text structures.

Figure 9.5 Graphic Representations of Cause-and-Effect Text Structures

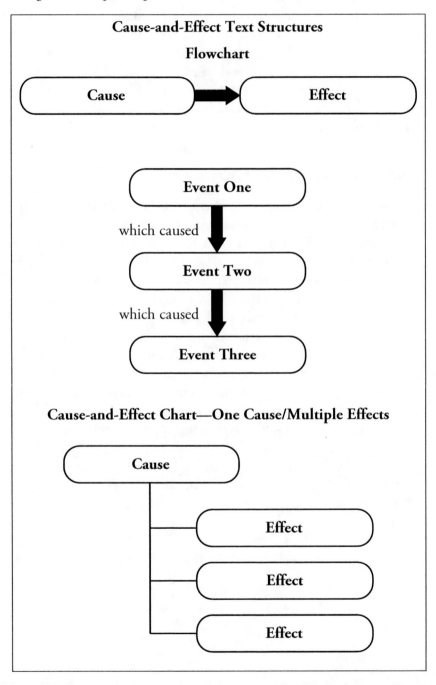

As with other text structures, signal words alert readers to cause-and-effect relationships: *as a result, because, begins with, caused by, consequently, effects of, finally, for this reason, hence, however, if/then, in order to, leads to, nevertheless, next, since, subsequently, therefore, thus*, and *when/then*. When students determine cause-and-effect relationships between text details and record those patterns on a graphic organizer, they map out the connections among the isolated details to create visual patterns that integrate those details into meaningful chunks.

Problem-and-Solution Text Structure

Closely related to cause-and-effect relationships in nonfiction text, the problem-and-solution text structure depicts a problem along with a possible solution. Once again, as in cause-and-effect text, multiple problems and solutions can be set forth by the author. Often the author's point of view or bias enters into problem-and-solution text. The author may want to explore the pros and cons of various solutions, thereby integrating elements of a proposition-and-support text structure into a problem-and-solution text. Readers who experience several problem-and-solution texts quickly learn to recognize the portions of the text that present the problem and then locate any text chunks that contain possible solutions. Signal words for a problem-and-solution text structure include *as a result, because, begins with, caused by, consequently, effects of, finally, for this reason, if/then, in conclusion, last, leads to, next, since, subsequently, therefore, unfortunately*, and *when/then*. The same graphic organizers used to represent the patterns of cause-and-effect text can be used for problem-and-solution text. Figure 9.6 on the following page presents another type of graphic organizer that is useful in examining problem-and-solution structures.

Figure 9.6 Graphic Representation of Problem-and-Solution Text Structures

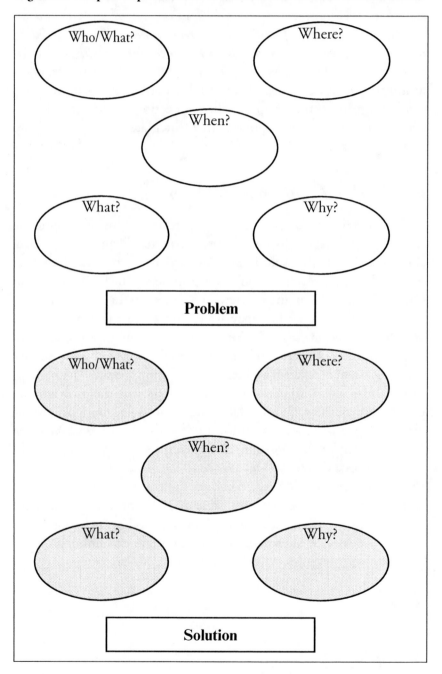

Proposition-and-Support Text Structure

Proposition-and-support text structures challenge readers' thinking because not only are the author's ideas presented, but also those ideas are supported or challenged by the author. The author's point of view or bias greatly influences this text structure; consequently, students must read reflectively between the lines in order to ascertain and evaluate the author's message and intended influence on the reader. In proposition-and-support text, the author usually proposes an idea and provides support for that idea. The author may also present ideas from the opposite point of view and argue against those points in favor of the stated proposition. In an attempt to persuade the reader, authors using this type of text often emphasize the advantages of their solution and highlight the disadvantages of other solutions. Readers need to recognize that proposition-and-support text structures can be used as propaganda to attract the reader to the author's particular point of view. Readers who approach a text with critical literacy eyes in order to infer the author's purpose can then evaluate their own personal stance on the ideas and positions presented. Words that alert readers to a possible persuasive text structure include *finally, first, foremost, in conclusion, in summary, in support, last, leads to, most importantly, next, subsequently, therefore, unfortunately,* and *when/then.* Proposition-and-support text structures can be represented graphically as illustrated in Figure 9.7 on the following page.

**Figure 9.7 Graphic Representations of
Proposition-and-Support Text Structures**

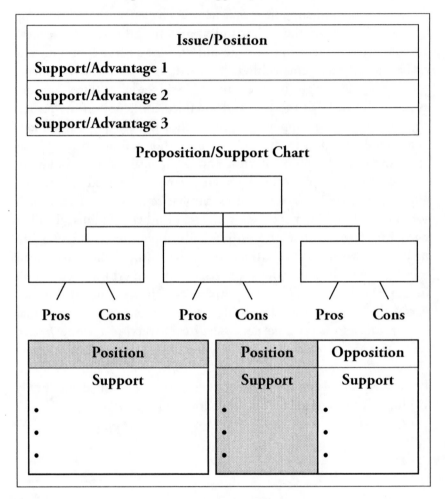

Issue/Position
Support/Advantage 1
Support/Advantage 2
Support/Advantage 3

Proposition/Support Chart

Compare-and-Contrast Text Structure

A final example of nonfiction text structure is the compare-and-contrast relationship. In this structure, the author explores facts and details, topics, events, people's lives and achievements, and concepts for similarities and differences. The author prompts readers to compare and contrast the relationships among text details in order to assimilate those new relational patterns into their current knowledge base for a topic or concept. Since categorization frames an understanding for comparing and contrasting ideas, younger readers can begin with sorting concrete objects as they explore similarities and differences. Early on, students can describe these associations using a Venn diagram graphic organizer. As students move into text, a Venn diagram provides a familiar tool for students to record the compare-and-contrast relationships in text. Later on, students represent compare-and-contrast text structures with other types of graphic organizers (see Figure 9.8 below). Words to target as students determine compare-and-contrast text structures include *although, but, by contrast, compared with, different from, either/or, even though, however, in comparison, in common, like, neither/nor, on the other hand, similar to, unlike, whereas,* and *yet.*

**Figure 9.8 Graphic Representations of
Compare-and-Contrast Text Structures**

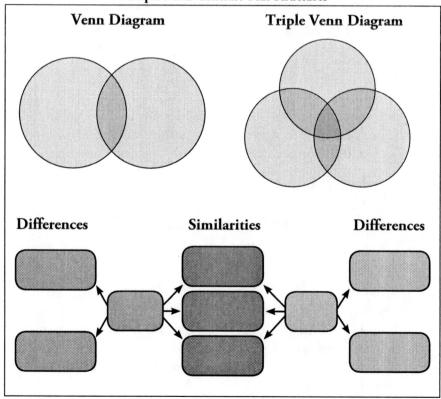

✦ Pause and Ponder ✦

Select a short nonfiction text or text chunk. Preview the text for the clues that point to a possible text structure. Read the text and focus on the clues the author provides the reader to indicate the structure of the text.

What is the structure of the text, and how does that structure support the author's purpose? What clues did the author provide through text organizers, signal words, and actual text to indicate that structure? How does knowing the structure of the text help you create more meaning from the text? What graphic organizer would you select to create a model of the text patterns? Is there another text structure that underpins the predominant text structure? ✦

STAR Model Lesson

The versatility of the STAR Model Lesson format is again demonstrated when teaching students how to determine a text structure. In this model lesson, the Text Walk strategy (see Chapter 6, p. 131) is a prerequisite for the activities involved in determining a text structure and recognizing relationships among ideas in the selection. This lesson focuses on using text organizers and details to:

- determine text structure
- ascertain relationships among important ideas
- differentiate important ideas from less important details
- construct a graphic organizer that reflects the organization and big ideas of a text

This lesson is based on the excerpt "How Is Chocolate Made?" from the nonfiction text *All About Chocolate* (Spielman 2004). This high-interest book (text level 2.4) is divided into six short chapters. The chapter "How Is Chocolate Made?" outlines the steps for making chocolate, which are clearly articulated in the text as well as supported by the photographs on each page.

STAR Model Lesson: Determining a Text Structure

Comprehension Strategies

Determine text structure using text organizers (features) and details to:

- Ascertain the relationships among important ideas
- Differentiate those ideas from less important details
- Construct a graphic organizer to reflect the organization and big/main ideas of a text

Critical Attributes

- The student walks the text, moving from top to bottom identifying each individual text organizer.
- The student stops after each text organizer and asks, "Now what do I know (about the big/main ideas of the text)?"
- The student articulates a tentative main idea statement after conducting the entire text walk.
- The student reviews the possible structures (descriptive, cause and effect, problem and solution, etc.) for organizing nonfiction text and considers how the author uses the text organizers to reflect the text's primary structure.
- The student reads the first paragraph or text chunk and considers any signal words or text details that verify the structure of the text and the author's purpose for writing the text.
- During reading, the student identifies the significant information from the text as indicated by the text structure.
- During and after reading, the student uses the text-structure pattern to locate significant information and incorporate that information into a graphic organizer reflecting the text's structure.

Materials

- copies of a nonfiction text on students' instructional reading level, small sticky notes, highlighter tape, or an overhead transparency and overhead pen for marking text features and annotating text

- markers—different colors for recording on a group graphic organizer
- graphic organizer based on the text's structure drawn on chart paper and hidden from students' view at beginning of lesson (example shown in Figure 9.9 below)

Figure 9.9 Model Graphic Organizer

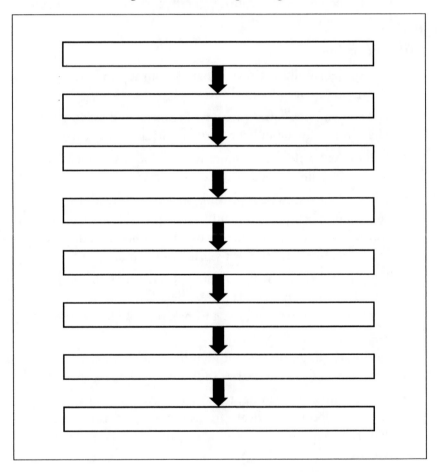

Figure 9.10 Text for "How Is Chocolate Made?"

How Is Chocolate Made?

It takes time and work to make good chocolate.

Ferment means to change slowly. Yeast and bacteria can cause this chemical change.

First, the cacao pods must be picked. Then they are **fermented** for six days.

When they are ready, the pods are split open. The seeds are removed and dried.

They are dried in the sun for about seven days. Sometimes they are dried in special machines instead.

Next, the dried beans are sent to chocolate factories.

243

Figure 9.10 Text for "How Is Chocolate Made?" *(cont.)*

Source: Spielman 2004

Prerequisite STAR Lesson

Taking a Text Walk to Preview a Text for Main Ideas (Chapter 6, p. 130)

Level 1: Modeled Strategy Use—I Do

Let's review how we get ourselves ready to read and think about the big ideas of a text. Remember that the author gives us text organizer signals that say, "Look at this. This is important information." After we look at and think about all the text organizers in a text, we have a good understanding of its main idea so we can read with meaning from the beginning.

Another way text organizers support readers as they make sense of a text before reading is by helping them determine the possible structure of the text. The structure of a text reflects how authors organize the ideas of a text as they present them to readers. The structure of the text is like a pattern or model that authors use to arrange details, creating a text that flows together and builds connections among those details for readers.

There are several types of text structures or writing models authors use when they write nonfiction text. Today we are going to look at a part of the text, *All About Chocolate,* and see if we can use the text organizers and text clues to identify the structural pattern of the text chunk. The text structure helps readers locate information more effectively, and it helps readers highlight the main ideas of the text. We can use the text structure during or after reading our section to create a graphic organizer to record the patterns of the text and help us remember the most important information.

Begin with a Text Walk

We start at the top of this text chunk on page 14 in the book and look at the first text organizer we come across during our text walk—the title of the section, "How Is Chocolate Made?" Let's put a sticky note right here by the title. Now, what do we know about this text? We know that this section will answer the question "How is chocolate made?" I think the author's purpose in this text chunk is to show me the steps for making chocolate. I would like to know how to make chocolate since I love to eat it!

One text structure that authors use to present information is a sequenced text structure. That means the information is presented in order, step by step, or from one event to the next event. The steps for making chocolate will need to be sequenced—presented in order—or the chocolate will not turn out properly. We can continue to review the text organizers to see if they support our prediction that this text chunk will have a sequenced (chronological) text structure.

Let's look at the next text organizer—the photograph on page 14 of the text. Put a sticky note here. Now, what do we know? The photograph shows workers finishing up some chocolate candy, so this picture must show us how the chocolate ends up in a factory just before it comes to the store. On page 15 of the text, what do we see? What do we know? (*The photograph shows someone picking cacao pods from the ground and putting them into a bag. From a previous section of the text [not shown], the students know that chocolate is made from the seeds or beans inside the cacao pods. The inset box provides students with the definition of the word* ferment.) I think this photograph illustrates the first step for making chocolate—picking the cacao pods. Another part of the step must have something to do with fermenting and cacao pods. Do you have any questions? (*Students may ask why the pods are fermented or wonder what will happen next in the process.*)

Level 2: Shared Strategy Use—We Do

Turn to the photograph on the next two pages—pages 16 and 17. Put your sticky note on this text organizer. Now, what do you know? We can take turns thinking aloud about what we see. (*Students may say that they see two boys counting cacao beans or spreading the beans out under a tent. Make sure the students notice that this photograph shows another step in making chocolate*). What do you wonder about this photograph? (*Possible student questions: What are the boys really doing? Why are the boys spreading out the beans?*)

Turn to page 18. Where do you want to put your sticky note? (*Students should put their sticky notes by the illustration.*) Tell me what you see. (*Students note the lady putting the beans into a hole over a fire. Then a brown liquid goes through three layers of a machine and comes out the bottom.*) Tell me what you think. (*Students comment on the beans that are cooked by the fire and then turned into a liquid chocolate that goes through a machine. Students mention that this illustration shows two more steps of making chocolate.*)

I think we are getting close to finishing up the steps of making chocolate!

Level 3: Guided Strategy Use—You Try

Now you can look at the last page of this section—page 19. Put sticky notes on the two text organizers, and think about what you see and what you know now about making chocolate. Next, turn to a partner and share what you are thinking.

Drop in on readers and discuss their reflections on the illustration and the inset. Students' responses should indicate an understanding that these text organizers show another step in making chocolate.

From our text walk, I think that, as a group, we made a good prediction that the structure of this section would have a sequenced structure to show the steps in making chocolate. I have a graphic organizer that provides a model for a sequencing text structure (*show the prepared graphic organizer on the chart paper*). As we read the text, we can write the steps in making chocolate, one step per box, in order from top to bottom on this graphic organizer (*point to the "steps" boxes*). If we do a good job of describing the steps of making chocolate as we read, then when we are finished with the text, the graphic organizer will show the pattern of big ideas in making chocolate. We can read the graphic organizer to help us remember what we read in the text.

As we read, we will look for the steps in making chocolate. We can also listen for signal or clue words the author uses to tell the reader that a step is coming up. These clues might be words like *first*, *next*, and *then*.

Read pages 14 and 15 to yourself and see if you can find a step for making chocolate. Put your finger on at least one step that you find in the text. (*Students read the text. Check to see if the students note the signal words* first *and* then *and locate the first two steps of making chocolate.*) Who can read me the first step of making chocolate? How did you know that it was the first step? Who can find the next step? What word helped you know it was the next step?

I will write the first two steps of making chocolate in the graphic organizer just as you shared with me. You can use two sticky notes to sketch a mind picture of the first two steps of making chocolate. We can put your sketches in order just like a graphic organizer to illustrate the steps (see Figure 9.11 on the following page).

(The students continue to silently read the text, stopping after each page to discuss the signal words that helped them identify the next step of the chocolate-making process. Write each step in the graphic organizer and have students sketch mind pictures on sticky notes to represent each step. The students' sticky notes can be placed next to the appropriate steps on the group graphic organizer, or the students can each build their own visual graphic organizer with their sticky notes to show the sequence of steps.)

Figure 9.11 Graphic Organizer for "How Is Chocolate Made?"

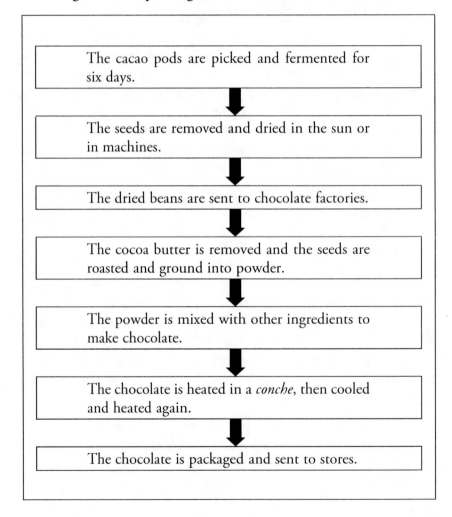

The cacao pods are picked and fermented for six days.

The seeds are removed and dried in the sun or in machines.

The dried beans are sent to chocolate factories.

The cocoa butter is removed and the seeds are roasted and ground into powder.

The powder is mixed with other ingredients to make chocolate.

The chocolate is heated in a *conche*, then cooled and heated again.

The chocolate is packaged and sent to stores.

Concluding the STAR Lesson

After completing the text and the graphic organizer, close the STAR lesson by having students reread the chart and discuss how thinking about the text structure before reading helps readers better understand the author's presentation of the information. Discuss with the students how readers can more easily identify the big ideas when they read nonfiction text with the pattern of the text in mind.

Ask the students how a graphic organizer supports readers' comprehension of the text. Have students identify the critical steps or attributes of this strategy:

- taking a text walk to predict a possible text structure before reading
- reading a text with a text structure in mind to help readers locate important information
- using text information to complete a graphic organizer that highlights the big ideas and patterns of the text

Write the steps for using this strategy on a STAR Points chart (Figure 9.12 on the following page).

- When might a reader use this strategy?
- How could readers use this strategy in math, science, or social studies?
- How would that look?

**Figure 9.12 STAR Points Chart—Determining a Text Structure:
A Before-, During-, and After-Reading Strategy**

> ## STAR Points
> ### Determining a Text Structure:
> ### A Before-, During-, and After-Reading Strategy
>
> 1. Walk the text from top to bottom.
> 2. Look at each text organizer.
> 3. Ask myself, "Now what do I know?"
> 4. Ask myself, "What is this text mostly about?"
> 5. Ask myself, "How is this text organized?" Make a prediction based on my text walk.
> 6. Read each text chunk and look for signal words and text clues that help me understand how the text is organized.
> 7. Use the text organization to locate and identify the most important ideas in the text.
> 8. Record those big ideas in a graphic organizer that matches the structure pattern of the text.

Level 4: Independent Strategy Use—You Do

1. Students work individually or with a partner to conduct a text walk of a new independent-level nonfiction text or text chunk to develop a main idea statement and a prediction of the text structure used by the author. Then students read the text and verify or adjust their predictions using the signal words and text details provided.

2. Students work individually or with a partner to text walk a new instructional-level nonfiction text or text chunk before a guided-reading or small-group lesson on that text. Students make predictions about the text's structure based on the text organizers. Students come to the lesson ready to share their predictions for the text's structure and graphic organizers for that structure to record the big/main ideas of the text as they read.

3. Laminate an enlarged graphic organizer chart for a familiar text structure. Provide a nonfiction text on the students' independent reading level that represents that known text structure. After reading the text, students work in pairs to return to the text to locate information that can complete the graphic organizer. Students record the big/main ideas of the text on the organizer with an overhead pen.

4. Give students a partially completed graphic organizer for a text they read independently or in a small instructional group. Students work individually or in pairs to complete the missing portions of the graphic organizer by returning to the text for proof. An example of this independent extension is the sequential flowchart developed for the text, "How Is Chocolate Made?," with two of the eight events missing. Students return to the text to find the missing steps after locating the provided step that comes right before or right after the missing step. Students present their completed graphic organizers to the group and discuss the strategies they used to locate the missing information.

5. Students use a familiar graphic organizer for a known text structure to create an individual writing plan for a composition. A chronological/sequenced graphic organizer can be used to develop a plan for a personal, nonfiction narrative. A descriptive-structure graphic organizer can help students organize their research on a science or social studies topic and provide a guide for composing a descriptive piece on the nonfiction topic.

A Problem-and-Solution Graphic Organizer

Earlier in this chapter, I described the problem-and-solution text structure (see p. 235). A graphic organizer helps students visualize and understand the relationship between the problem and its solution. The graphic organizer shown in Figure 9.14 on page 253 is based on the text, "A Killer Quake in Asia" (Figure 9.13 on the following page).

Figure 9.13 Text for "A Killer Quake in Asia"

World News

October 9, 2005 — Section A

A Killer Quake in Asia

Deadly Shocks Tear Through Pakistan, India, and Afghanistan
By Dawn Frost

KASHMIR, October 9—A strong earthquake struck here. It happened yesterday. At 8:50 A.M. **tremors** ran through three countries. People felt them in Pakistan and India. They felt them in Afghanistan, too. In just minutes, thousands died. Towns were ruined. Leaders fear that 40,000 people may be dead.

Northern Pakistan had the worst damage. The epicenter of the quake was near Muzaffarabad. It is in Kashmir. (The epicenter is a spot on the surface. It is right over the center of the quake.) Two nations say that they own this area. They are India and Pakistan.

A **shift** caused the quake. This happened along a fault line. A fault line is a place where **massive** pieces of Earth's crust meet. These plates move. They move about 1.6 inches (4.06 cm) a year. A sudden slip between the plates caused the quake. Strong aftershocks rocked the area. They felt like small quakes. This happened on and off for days.

"It was so strong that I saw buildings swaying. It was terrifying," said one man. He works near New Delhi. It is the capital of India. Some big buildings fell down there.

Bad weather has slowed rescue efforts. Landslides have blocked roads. Too much rain has made it hard for planes to land. Rescue workers cannot get to some mountain villages. In cities, millions are stranded. Some have no shelter or electrical power. Others have no food or water.

Survivors search the wreckage of a destroyed building in Islamabad, Pakistan's capital.

The quake wrecked hospitals. It left people with no clean water to drink. Health workers fear that **unsanitary** conditions will spread sickness.

One concern was whether problems between India and Pakistan would hurt relief efforts. India and Pakistan have fought for years. They both want to control Kashmir. Yet India offered to help Pakistan. It was hit harder. And Pakistan accepted India's aid. The two nations will work together. This will help those living in the damaged areas.

Science — Summarize and Synthesize / Determine Importance

Source: Teacher Created Materials 2008

Figure 9.14 Problem-Solution Graphic Organizer for "A Killer Quake in Asia"

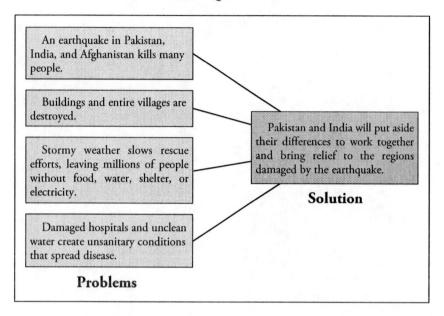

An earthquake in Pakistan, India, and Afghanistan kills many people.

Buildings and entire villages are destroyed.

Stormy weather slows rescue efforts, leaving millions of people without food, water, shelter, or electricity.

Damaged hospitals and unclean water create unsanitary conditions that spread disease.

Problems

Pakistan and India will put aside their differences to work together and bring relief to the regions damaged by the earthquake.

Solution

A Cause-and-Effect Graphic Organizer

Cause and effect is a structure (see p. 233 of this chapter) that appears in many nonfiction texts that students read in school. Here again, graphic organizers enable students to recognize and understand relationships among causes and effects in a text. The graphic organizer in Figure 9.16 on page 255 is based on the selection, *Causes of the Revolution* (Figure 9.15, p. 254). As you read the passage, notice that in addition to the cause-and-effect structure, the selection also has a chronological/sequenced structure.

Figure 9.15 Excerpt from *Causes of the Revolution*

A New Way to Fight Back

The people in England were surprised at the colonists' reaction to the Stamp Act. They could tell that the tax was not going to work. So Parliament **repealed** the act.

Great Britain still needed money, so they passed a new set of taxes called the Townshend (TOWNS-end) Acts. These laws taxed glass, paint, paper, lead, and tea.

▼ English cartoon showing a funeral for the Stamp Act

Made in the U.S.A.

The colonists would not buy British goods. But they still needed many products. So they learned to make them in America. The boycott actually helped the colonists develop some of their first industries.

Sons of Liberty

Around this time, some colonists started a secret new group. The Sons of Liberty met at night. They talked about their unhappiness with the British. They also helped organize some of the boycotts.

▶ Flyer urging citizens to participate in a boycott

Once again, the people in America became angry. Nobody in England had to pay special taxes on these items. The colonists did not see why they should have to do so. Many people gave speeches and wrote articles. They convinced the colonists to try a new way to fight back. The colonists agreed to **boycott** British goods. This meant they would not buy anything made in Great Britain.

The boycott worked. Soon the merchants in England grew angry at losing their business in the colonies. They made the government repeal the taxes.

Source: Mulhall 2005

Figure 9.16 Cause-and-Effect Graphic Organizer for *Causes of the Revolution*

Cause	Effect
The colonists' reaction to the Stamp Act was not positive.	The English Parliament repealed the Stamp Act.
Britain needed money.	Britain passed a new set of taxes called the Townshend Acts that taxed things like glass and tea.
The colonists were angry about the new taxes since no one in England had to pay them.	Colonists protested the new taxes by boycotting British goods.
Since the colonists did not buy British goods, they did not have some of the things they needed.	The colonists developed industries to make the goods they had once bought from England.
The English merchants were angry about losing business in the colonies.	The British government had to repeal the new taxes on the colonists.

Differentiation Notes

After the STAR Model Lesson is presented to students, differentiate the strategy by demonstrating the featured text structure with another text or introducing a new text structure with a different text. Attend to the instructional level of the text and the scaffolding necessary for the students to feel comfortable identifying a known text structure, locating the big ideas using the text structure, and completing a graphic organizer to reflect the significant details of the text. As students gain more experience working with text structures in nonfiction, point out that sometimes a text contains more than one text structure, allowing readers to frame main ideas and important details with more than one graphic organizer.

Many students will need shared, interactive support as they

explore new text structures and analyze various texts through a text-structure framework. More proficient students may practice the strategy in a guided context and then be ready to look for examples of different kinds of text structures in their independent reading. Determining a text structure may be made easier or more difficult by changing the text level, the selected text structure example, or the simplicity or variety of graphic organizers to represent a text structure. Below-level students and English language learners may benefit from a more familiar text topic as they learn about a text structure and construct a graphic organizer.

Summary

Teachers must provide many contexts and opportunities for students to determine the structure of a variety of nonfiction texts before they can expect students to automatically apply this strategy and use it independently in literacy centers/engagements, content-area reading, self-selected reading, or a testing situation. Students who can determine the structure of a text before and during reading are able to more effectively process the relationships among the details of that text as they read. The features of nonfiction text structures, represented through graphic organizers, serve as concrete physical models that demonstrate how authors chose to relate the critical facts and details of a text. Students use their images of the patterns in text to locate and arrange information in a logical manner, develop main ideas, and make inferences from the authors' purpose and presentation of the text. Students who recognize and use nonfiction text structures to support their comprehension as they read control a powerful tool for understanding and interpreting text.

→ *Pause and Ponder* ←

Reflect on the resources available to your students to read—resources in both the classroom and school libraries. To what extent are nonfiction texts represented in these resources? How frequently do students opt to read nonfiction instead of fiction? When teaching students about text structures, do you draw their attention to nonfiction materials that are familiar to them? Invite students to describe text structures they have encountered in nonfiction texts that they have enjoyed reading. Through these examples, help students link what they have learned in strategy lessons with what they do with materials they select themselves. ✑

Chapter 10

Monitoring Comprehension: The Ongoing Orchestration of Meaning

"Metacognition is a key to successful learning. Learners with high levels of metacognitive abilities are able to monitor and regulate their learning processes to accomplish the learning goals they set. More importantly, supporting learners in developing self-regulation mechanisms should be an important aspect of metacognitive literacy instruction" (Griffith and Ruan 2005, 16).

Considerations from Research

- Effective readers are metacognitively active as they read.
- Metacognition can be developed through instruction.
- Students need to have control over procedures for monitoring comprehension and in repairing comprehension if they are to become independent, self-sufficient readers.
- Self-questioning is an effective metacognitive strategy.
- Motivation, self-efficacy, and collaboration between and among students, and between students and teachers are important factors in a constructivist view of reading comprehension (Baker and Beall 2009, 379-382).

Many teachers present monitoring comprehension to their students as a reading strategy that successful readers use. However, when teachers ask students to explain the process of monitoring comprehension or describe what it looks like during reading, responses such as these are often given: "Monitoring comprehension is ... well, you monitor, um-m-m, comprehension" or "You ... monitor." When teachers consider the many facets of reading comprehension, such responses are to be expected. As students read and actively process meaning from text, many comprehension strategies come into play, just as in an orchestra where many instruments combine to create a perfect musical composition. During instruction, these strategies are introduced individually and are illuminated through metacognitive language and demonstration of the strategy in context. In this way, students learn to engage with the mental processes of each strategy's use. However, each of these strategies must be integrated into a repertoire of productive behaviors that successful readers use to comprehend text. No single strategy comprises the complete reading comprehension picture. Strategies interact simultaneously in the readers' minds, orchestrated together in a fluid, seamless process to build and sustain meaning during reading (Duke and Pearson 2002).

As students participate in interactive and guided practice for one particular reading-comprehension strategy, they talk about their reading, exploring the modeled procedural language of that strategy and incorporating it into their conversations about text. The students negotiate meaning as they read and interact with group members, freely talking about the ideas of the text, listening to differences in thinking, and discussing ways to clarify any confusion they encounter as they read (Allington 2001). The teacher strives to develop a social context for thoughtful literacy experiences where students, without being prompted, stay cognitively active throughout and converse about the text and the actions of a strategic reader. Even though a single strategy may be the focus of the lesson, the teacher recursively references former strategy instruction and expects students to apply both

> "Metacognition is about readers 'knowing'—knowing when they know, knowing when they don't know, and knowing what to do when they don't know" (Davis 2007, 14).

the new strategy and previously learned strategies to problem solve and monitor comprehension as they read.

When students acquire new reading comprehension strategies through instruction, have authentic discussions about text, and participate in independent practice, those strategies become available as "instruments" for them to "play" in their minds as they monitor their comprehension while reading. Every known comprehension strategy becomes a powerful option for readers to draw upon to establish, clarify, and maintain meaning, as well as to problem solve any of the tricky parts encountered in a text. As students effectively weave together multiple comprehension strategies before, during, and even after reading, they move from the strategic level to the skill level. This transition is marked by increasing automaticity of response and independence in the fluent processing of text meaning. These skilled readers develop an inner control of known reading strategies. As these readers advance through text, their ability to self-regulate the use of those strategies enables them to efficiently repair any miscue or breakdown in understanding.

✦ *Pause and Ponder* ✦

Observe a small group of students as they read an instructional-level text in a guided-practice context. Drop in on different students as they read and note their points of difficulty.

What do the students do to help themselves get "unstuck" when they encounter a tricky part in the text? Do they attempt to figure out the meaning of the text, or do they just continue to read? What strategies do they seem to control as they monitor meaning? What strategies would help them more effectively address their confusions so they regain comprehension? ✦

Learning from a Skilled Reader: The Teacher

The teacher models how readers successfully monitor their own comprehension by integrating previously addressed strategies into their repertoire of responses to establish and maintain meaning. The STAR Model Lesson is constructed in such a way that students observe and respond to the behaviors of a skilled reader as the teacher models a particular strategy. Throughout all phases of this model lesson, the teacher prompts the students to use their reading strategies, providing specific feedback that facilitates and extends their learning. After the lesson, that strategy immediately provides readers with an additional support for problem solving meaning challenges in text, thereby adding to the readers' self-regulating actions to maintain meaning during reading.

Knowing How to Deal with Comprehension Confusion

Each strategy developed in a STAR Model Lesson becomes a fix-up strategy for students, and that strategy is recorded on a STAR Points chart for monitoring comprehension (see examples of STAR Points charts in previous chapters). In my lessons, I present a novel context for conceptualizing the reader's comprehension-monitoring intentions by representing every fix-up strategy on the STAR Points chart as a strategic "bandage" (   ) to help "repair" meaning problems. As strategies are added to the chart, students have access to an increasing number of options to help them correct comprehension confusions.

Teachers can introduce the STAR Points chart to their students by reminding them that reading is a meaning-making process that represents a creative engagement between the reader and the text. However, readers sometimes lose track of the meaning of a text as they read and need to ask, "What can I do to help myself?" To answer this question, students can refer to a STAR Points chart for help. Typically, the teacher and students collaborate to develop the statements that appear in the charts. In this way, students have additional opportunities to focus on the strategies—what they are and how they help readers monitor their comprehension before and during reading.

The STAR Points chart is a cumulative statement of metacognitive strategies students can use to monitor and self-regulate their reading. In the sections that follow, I examine three phases during which students can monitor their reading: dealing with the tricky parts, making connections between self and text, and monitoring comprehension. Three figures—Figure 10.1, Figure 10.2, and Figure 10.3 on the following pages—show the critical steps students should take during each phase. In practice, these attributes are cumulative; the features defined in each of the figures ultimately lead to a single STAR Points chart that students can refer to as they develop proficiency in regulating their own reading behaviors. The entire STAR Points chart typifies the concept that strategies are not isolated learnings; rather, they are tactics to be used in concert to help the reader make meaning.

Dealing with the "Tricky Parts"

Three initial fix-up strategies are designed to provide students with alternatives when they encounter tricky parts in a text—words or expressions that don't seem to make sense and impede comprehension (see Figure 10.1, p. 264). The first strategy, rereading, often helps to re-establish meaning in the mind of the reader. Rereading is used again in the second strategy. However, this time, the confusing part is read aloud; the reading is slower, allowing the reader to pause and think. Hearing the text may alert the reader to other cues to meaning—word pronunciation, intonation, or phrasing. A third fix-up strategy encourages the student to read on a bit further in the text to see if the next part gives any information to relate to the tricky part. The reader also checks to see if what came before the problematic part can provide the reader insight.

> "Reading comprehension is not an isolated process that is activated only after reading, but is a network of in-the-head processes that work together before, during, and after reading" (Cummins, Stewart, and Block 2005, 279).

Figure 10.1 STAR Points Chart: Monitoring Comprehension—Dealing with the "Tricky Parts": Before- and During-Reading Strategies

> ### STAR Points
> ### Monitoring Comprehension—
> ### Dealing with the "Tricky Parts":
> ### Before- and During-Reading Strategies
>
> Reread the tricky part. Does it make sense now?
>
> Reread the tricky part aloud and more slowly. Stop and think. Does it make sense now?
>
> Read on a bit further in the text. Go back to the tricky part. Link the chunk of text that came before the tricky part and the chunk that came right after it to understand the meaning of the tricky part.

Making Connections Between Self and the Text

Monitoring comprehension is a process that readers initiate even before the actual reading of a text. Students begin to construct meaning and monitor their comprehension before they even enter a text. With guidance from the teacher or on their own, students reflect on what they already know about the topic and seek connections between their prior knowledge and the text—its topic, vocabulary, or structure. If students do not have the necessary concepts for reading a nonfiction text with meaning, the teacher can use an array of activities to build background in preparation for reading (see Chapter 4).

Next, readers preview the text organizers to capture any possible big ideas of the text before reading. The Text Walk strategy, described in Chapter 6, is an effective strategy that enables students to systematically preview a text and gain insights that will foster comprehension as they begin reading. During the text walk, students become aware of the organizational pattern of the text and can use that information to make predictions about the author's purpose. In Chapter 9, I described several ways in which authors structure their texts to show relationships among the ideas (for example, description, sequence, cause-and-effect, problem-and-solution, compare-and-contrast) and how readers can use that information to support comprehension. Text features—headings, visuals, design elements—provide additional information that the reader can use to formulate self-to-text connections and determine the main ideas of the text (see Chapter 6).

Students come up with a personal purpose for reading a text to help them stay focused on their goals for reading that text. Before reading, the students also make decisions about how they will read a text based on their purpose: *Will I read the entire text? Will I just read certain sections of this text? Should I just read the parts of the text that interest me? Should I read quickly or slowly?* These intentional moves before reading, now added to the STAR Points chart (see Figure 10.2 below), set readers up to monitor meaning as they prepare to enter a text.

Figure 10.2 STAR Points Chart: Monitoring Comprehension—Self-to-Text Connections: Before-and During-Reading Strategies

---

STAR Points

Monitoring Comprehension—Self-to-Text Connections:

Before- and During-Reading Strategies

Connect what I know to what I am reading now. What do I know about this information? How does the information that I am reading now relate to what I have already read?

Look at the text organizers to determine what they tell me about the main ideas and important details of the text.

Consider the structure or the patterns of the text. How does the author organize the information to help me locate the big ideas and relate those big ideas to one another?

Think about my purpose or goal for reading. Why am I reading this text? What is my plan for how I will read it?

Maintaining Comprehension During Reading

During reading, students adjust their reading to maintain meaning. They vary the speed of their reading, slowing down and being more deliberate when the text becomes more difficult or the ideas become unclear. They break longer text into smaller chunks and take "thinking breaks" to process the text in bits. Reflective readers recognize that when they lose the meaning of the text as a result of an unknown word, a confusing sentence or text chunk, or a difficult concept, they engage in at least one self-regulatory activity to get back on track. Read a Little, Think a Little (see Chapter 6, p. 145) provides an effective framework to demonstrate and practice how readers actively process text as they read. The cue cards provided in the lesson provide concrete prompts for the students to consider as they monitor their comprehension.

As the students participate in the reading-strategy engagements from the other STAR Model Lessons in this book, the teacher continues developing the monitoring-comprehension STAR Points chart by adding corresponding self-monitoring strategies as shown in Figure 10.3 on the following page.

Figure 10.3 STAR Points Chart: Monitoring Comprehension—Making Reading Make Sense: Before- and During-Reading Strategies

STAR Points

Monitoring Comprehension—Making Reading Make Sense:

Before- and During-Reading Strategies

- Summarize in my own words what I have read so far. What is the main idea? What are the most important details?

- Think about the possible meaning of a tricky word. Look in the word for a part or chunk that I know. Look around the word for clues that help me figure out what the word means.

- Ask a question to help me focus on my reading, such as "What are the important ideas of what I am reading?" "Why did the author put this in the text?" "Why did this happen?" "How will what I just read help me understand the next part of the text?"

- Make a prediction based on what I read. Keep on reading to see if I am right or if I need to change my prediction based on new information.

- Make a picture in my mind of what I read. Imagine what the text describes.

- Code the text for the most important details or jot down short notes or sketches about the important information presented in the text.

- Read between the lines to make an inference about the author's meaning.

- Use another source to look up any information that will help clear up what I am reading, such as a dictionary or another reference text.

- Ask for help from a friend, my teacher, or another adult if what I try does not help me solve the tricky part.

Tips for Helping Students Monitor Their Comprehension

- Wording of the fix-up strategies on the STAR Points chart can be simplified for younger readers, and sketches or symbols can be added to illustrate each strategy.

- Frequently remind students that the monitoring strategies in the chart are suggestions for multiple positive moves they can try when they encounter comprehension confusions during reading.

- Create opportunities for students to participate in think alouds that feature examples of how readers might orchestrate several of the ideas on the chart to get their meaning making back on track.

- Name the strategies employed and discuss the effectiveness of specific procedural processes in re-establishing comprehension.

- Drop in on readers during guided and independent reading and use "prompt and praise" comments to promote monitoring and clarifying behaviors.

- Use a variety of responses to support and extend students' self-monitoring behaviors. For example:

  » Why did you stop here? What did you notice or think about when you came to this part in the text?

  » I can see that this was a tricky part of the text for you. What did you try to figure out this part?

  » When you got stuck, I saw you look at the picture beside the text. Then you went back and read the text again. Did that help you fix up your reading? How?

  » When did you notice that this part of the text was not making sense? What can you do to get yourself going again?

  » I see that you went back and reread the text aloud when you experienced confusion. How did this help you as a reader? What do you understand now about what you read?

  » You stopped here because you do not know what that

word means. What can you do to help yourself? What are two things you can do to try to figure out this word?

» During your independent reading, I notice that you have tried our strategy of Pluses, Lines, and Stars to code the text for main ideas and important supporting details. Why did you choose to try this strategy? How did this strategy help you maintain meaning as you read the text? Do you have any questions about the strategy now that you have tried it on your own to monitor your comprehension?

» After you read that text chunk, you stopped and summarized what you just read in your own words. Explain how summarizing this chunk of nonfiction text improved your understanding.

» When you read this part, you stopped and made a quick sketch on a sticky note. Tell me more about what you did and how it helped you make sense of what you read.

» I saw you do some things that good readers do when they get stuck on a tricky part in a text. You searched the text organizers and then you reread the confusing part again. You made a prediction aloud about what you thought that part meant and then you read on for more information. I saw that smile on your face when you realized you had figured out the tricky part. Explain to me how some of the things you tried worked together to help you regain meaning so that you could go on reading the text.

STAR Model Lessons are designed to help students acquire an array of strategies that will enable them to make meaning before, during, and after reading. The STAR Points charts serve to summarize core concepts about strategies that students can draw upon to monitor their comprehension.

→ *Pause and Ponder* ←

Reflect on the prompt-and-praise conversations you had with individual students when you dropped in on their reading. Identify specific actions the student takes to fix up the tricky parts in his or her reading. Provide feedback that names the student's strategic moves, and ask the student how his or her actions helped repair meaning. Then consider how you might prompt that student into further orchestration of monitoring strategies to extend his or her independence in problem-solving text challenges. ∽

Summary

As students take on the strategic language and actions of readers, their ability to monitor their own comprehension increases. Students' processing of meaning as they read becomes more automatic, reflecting all of the multiple strategies they have learned and internalized. When they encounter a tricky part in a text, the students are able to draw from a mental reservoir of effective moves to re-establish meaning and move on in the text.

As teachers, we strive to make the unseen monitoring moves of strong readers visible to students through targeted, specific instruction. Various strategies that readers employ to construct meaning from text and self-correct their confusions are addressed in the STAR Model Lessons provided in this book. As the students orchestrate all these strategies, they are able to monitor their comprehension with increasing efficiency and competence.

→ *Pause and Ponder* ←

"As we consider the reader's individual and unique differences, the characteristics of the context, and the features of the text, we are left to wonder exactly what happens when these three come together" (Prado 2004, 276).

Think about your experiences with teaching for reading comprehension. What makes you "wonder exactly what happens" with your students as a result of the teaching and learning that goes on in your classes?

Teachers often invite their students to create "I Wonder" charts. What would you write on an "I Wonder" chart about teaching for reading comprehension? ⤶

Conclusion

"If we are serious about nurturing active and thoughtful readers, we must also be serious about being active and thoughtful teachers who work from both the outside in and the inside out as we continue to develop deeper understandings of our own reading processes and of what constitutes effective comprehension instruction" (Villaume and Brabham 2002, 675).

Our vision of effective teaching for reading comprehension drives the evolution of our own teaching expertise and fuels the powerful instructional choices we must make to meet the needs of all our students in a classroom community of readers. When we can articulate our personal meaning-making processes to students in clear language that concisely describes the strategies that good readers use to comprehend text, students can adopt those strategies as their own. That skillful teacher language carefully imposed into a gradual release of responsibility framework—modeled, shared, guided, independent use—provides opportunities for students to see, hear, practice, and eventually adopt the many strategies that successful readers employ. Through understanding how students apply various comprehension strategies as they monitor their reading and clarify confusions, we begin to evaluate what each student currently knows. Therefore, we can make significant choices to differentiate both content and process through carefully planned and scaffolded lessons that move students to where they need to go next as readers. As we give students a great deal of actual reading time with authentic texts, including multiple nonfiction genres, we hand them a significant tool for developing flexibility in selecting and applying these strategies to maintain comprehension as they read. These are strategies that we have brought to life through active learning in the classroom and are now putting back into context through real experiences with text. Multiple encounters with a variety of texts provide students with opportunities to weave newly-introduced and more familiar reading strategies together to access meaning. When students interact in productive reading engagements supported by our purposeful conversations about text processing, they have the opportunity to orchestrate all of their known strategies while integrating newly learned strategies into their meaning-making networks.

No perfect set of instructions or formulas exists for what comprises the most effective reading comprehension lessons, but students who engage in explicit, targeted reading instruction can dip into an ever-increasing personal bank of known effective strategies to process meaning. These experiences will enable them to use their current strengths to successfully negotiate new text in productive and meaningful ways. Students are freed up to select and comprehend self-selected texts at their own reading levels. They can set personal goals—determine their stance or objective—for reading a text. Their purpose can be aesthetic—responding to ideas, feelings, and the attitudes reflected through text—or they can read from an efferent stance—reading the text for the information or knowledge it provides (Rosenblatt 1978). Using their internalized structure of comprehension strategies, students can choose simply to read and enjoy a story or read a nonfiction text for new facts they want to learn. These students have that choice because they can effectively construct and maintain meaning as they read.

Knowing what we do as experienced readers serves as a reminder of what we attempt to instill in our students through strategy instruction: "Remember when we read, we use all these strategies at the same time and that our comprehension process is largely unconscious" (Routman 2003, 119). Having multiple differentiated venues for teaching reading comprehension strategies to develop this unconscious comprehension process and meet the strengths and instructional goals of our students requires us, their teachers, to say "it" *better*, not louder. The ideas you found in this book provide you with the rationale, the targeted strategic language, and the active, explicit teaching models to do just that. Thus, all the rich reading experiences students encounter in your classroom become a part of them to carry into a lifetime full of personal engagements with text.

➤ *Pause and Ponder* ⬅

Look back at the various quotations presented in this book—at the beginning of each chapter and interspersed throughout the text. Which of these quotes did you find especially appealing? What were your thoughts initially when you read the quotes? What are your thoughts now as you reread them?

Take some time to review the "Considerations from Research" at the beginning of each chapter. Practice also offers many factors for consideration. What ideas would you contribute to your own "Considerations from Practice" to augment those from research? ✎

Possible Roots for Instruction

Prefix	Meaning	Example
ab-	away, from, away from	absent, abstain
ad-	to, toward, add to	addition, advance
ante-	before	antebellum, antecedent
anti-, ant-	against, opposed	antibody, antonym
auto-	self	autobiography
bi-	two	bicycle, biceps
circum-	around	circumference, circumspective
con-, com-, co-	with, together	contract, commit, collect
contra-	against	contradiction
de-	down, downward, off of, from	deconstruct, deflate
dis-	not	distrust, dislike
ex-, e-	out, out of	exit, expensive
en-, em-	in, on, into	envision, empower
im-, in-, il-	not, in, into, on	ineffective, impossible, illegal
inter-	among, between	international
macro-	big, large	macrobiotics
micro-	small, tiny	microscope
mis-	wrongly	mistake, mislead
multi-	many	multivitamin
non-	not	nonexistent

Prefix	Meaning	Example
over–	beyond, above	overwhelmed
post–	after	postmodern
pre–	prior to, before	preview
pro–	for, in favor of, ahead	pronoun, protect
re–	back, again	redo, reread, renew
sub–	under, below, beneath	submerged
super–	above, over, beyond	supercharged
tele–	far	telephone
trans–	across	transportation
tri–	three	tricycle
un–	not	unhappy
uni–	one, single	unicycle

Suffix	Meaning	Example
-able	able to, can do	capable, adaptable
-ance, -ence	state of, quality of	importance, difference
-ant, -ent	one who, having a quality of	important, participant, opponent
-arium, -orium	place for, room for	aquarium, auditorium
-cracy	rule by	democracy
-ent	one who	resident, president
-er	one who, more	writer, larger
-ess	one who (female)	actress
-est	most	happiest, brightest
-ful	full of	pocketful

Suffix	Meaning	Example
-ion, -tion	state of, characterized by	termination, perfection
-less	without	homeless, powerless
-ly	every, in a particular way/manner	monthly, quietly
-ness	state of being	loneliness
-ologist	expert in, one who studies	biologist
-ology	study of	zoology
-or	one who	actor
-ous, -ious, -ose	full of	gracious, verbose, adventurous
-phobe, -phobia	one who is afraid, fear of	claustrophobia, ailurophobe
-y	state of	breezy, gloomy

Base	Meaning	Example
aero	air, wind	aerodynamics, aerobics
aqu, aqua	water	aquarium, aqueduct
astro	star	astronomy, astronaut
audi	listen, hear	auditory, audition
bi, bio	life, live	biology, biography
cap, capt	take, hold, get	capture, capacity
ceed, ced, cess	yield, go, move	procession, recede, proceed
clam, claim	shout	proclaim, exclamation mark
cred	believe	incredible

Base	Meaning	Example
dent	teeth	dentist
dic, dict	speak, tell	prediction, dictator
flex, flect	bend	reflection, flexible
gen	be born, race, produce	generation, regenerate
geo	earth	geography, geometry
grad, gress	go, step	graduation, progress
graph	draw, write	autograph, graphics
hemi	half	hemisphere
leg, lect, lig	pick, read	collection, legible, calligraphy
liber	free	liberate, liberty
man, manu	hand	manual, manuscript
miss, mit	send	dismiss, permit
mon, mono	alone, one	monologue, monotone
nat	born, produce	natural, prenatal
nov	new	novel, innovation
oct	eight	octopus, October
omni	every, all	omniscient, omnipresent
path	feeling	pathetic, empathy
ped	foot, feet	pedal, pedestrian
phil	friend, love	philanthropist
pol, poli	city	politician, metropolis, interpol
port	carry	transport, import
rupt	break	eruption
sec, sect	cut	section, secede

Base	Meaning	Example
spec, spect	look, watch, see	spectacles, respect, speculate
stru, struct	build	construct, structure, construe
ter, terr	land	terrarium, territory
therm	heat	thermometer, thermal
trac, tract	pull, drag, draw	retract, traction, tractor
vert, vers	turn	reversible, vertigo
vid, vis	see	video, vision, invisible
vit, viv	live, life	revive, vital
volv, volu	roll	revolve, evolution

Source: Rasinski, Padak, Newton, E., and Newton, R. M., 2008

References Cited

Afflerbach, P., P. D. Pearson, and S. C. Paris. 2008. Clarifying differences between reading skills and reading strategies. *The Reading Teacher* 61 (5): 364–373.

Allington, R. L. 2001. *What really matters for struggling readers: Designing research-based programs.* New York: Addison-Wesley Educational Publishers, Inc.

Allington, R. L., and P.H. Johnston. 2002. *Reading to learn: Lessons from exemplary fourth-grade classrooms.* New York: The Guilford Press.

Allington, R. L., and A. McGill-Franzen. 2009. Comprehension difficulties among struggling readers. In *Handbook of research on reading comprehension,* eds. S. E. Israel and G. G. Duffy, 551–568. New York: Routledge.

Au, K. H., J. H. Carroll, and J. A. Scheu. 1997. *Balanced literacy instruction: A teacher's resource book.* Norwood, MA: Christopher-Gordon Publishers, Inc.

Baker, L., and L. C. Beall. 2009. Metacognitive processes and reading comprehension. In *Handbook of research on reading comprehension,* ed. S. E. Israel and G. G. Duffy, 373–388. New York: Routledge.

Baumann, J., E. Kame'enui, and G. Ash. 2002. Research on vocabulary instruction: Voltaire redux. In *Handbook of research on teaching the English language arts, 2nd edition,* ed. J. Flood, D. Lapp, J. Squire, and J. Jensen, 752–785. Mahwah, NJ: Lawrence Erlbaum Associates, Publishers.

Beck, A. S. 2005. A place for critical literacy. *Journal of Adolescent & Adult Literacy* 48 (5): 392–400.

Block, P. 2001. *The answer to how is yes: Acting on what matters.* San Francisco: Berrett-Koehler Publishers Inc.

Bell, N. 1991. Visualizing ad verbalizing: For language comprehension and thinking. Paso Robles, CA: Academy of Reading Publications.

Bodrova, E., and D. Leong. 1996. *Tools of the mind: The Vygotskian approach to early childhood education.* Englewood Cliffs, NJ: Prentice-Hall, Inc.

Bromley, K. 2007. Nine things every teacher should know about words and vocabulary instruction. *Journal of Adolescent & Adult Literacy* 50 (7): 528–537.

Byron, G. G. N. 1818–1823. *Don Juan*, cto. 3, st. 88. Cited in *Book of familiar quotations.* 1970. 209. New York: Award Books.

Cervetti, G., M. J. Pardales, and J. S. Damico. 2001 (April). A tale of differences: Comparing the traditions, perspectives, and educational goals of critical reading and critical literacy. *Reading Online* 4 (9). http://www.readingonline.org/articles/art_index. asp?HREF=/articles/cervetti/index.html

Chapman, C., and R. King. 2005. 11 practical ways to guide teachers toward differentiation (and an evaluation tool). *Journal of Staff Development* 26 (4): 20–25.

Christen, W. L., and T. J. Murphy. 1991. Increasing comprehension by activating prior knowledge. *ERIC Digest.* Bloomington, IN: ERIC Clearinghouse on Reading, English, and Communication.

Clay, M. M. 1991. *Becoming literate: The construction of inner control.* Portsmouth, NH: Heinemann Education.

Clay, M. M. 1993. *An observation survey of early literacy achievement.* Portsmouth, NH: Heinemann Education

Cummins, C., T. Stewart, and C. C. Block. 2005. Teaching several metacognitive strategies together increases students' independent metacognition. In *Metacognition and literacy learning*, eds. S. E. Israel, C. C. Block, K. L. Bauserman, and K. Kinnucan-Welsch, 277–295. Mahwah, NJ: Lawrence Erlbaum Associates, Publishers.

Davis, A. 2007. *Teaching reading comprehension.* Toronto, ON: Thomson Nelson.

Dechant, E. 1991. *Understanding and teaching reading: An interactive model.* Hillsdale, NJ: Lawrence Erlbaum Associates, Inc.

Denton, P. 2007. *The power of our words.* Turners Falls, MA: Northeast Foundation for Children, Inc.

Dodge, J. 2005. *Differentiation in action.* New York: Scholastic, Inc.

Dorn, L. J., and C. Soffos. 2005. *Teaching for deep comprehension: A reading workshop approach.* Portland, ME: Stenhouse Publishers.

Duffy, G. G. 2002. Afterword. In *Reading to learn: Lessons from exemplary fourth-grade classrooms.* R. L. Allington and P. H. Johnston, 229. New York: The Guilford Press.

Duffy, G. G., and L. R. Roehler. 1989. Why strategy instruction is so difficult and what we need to do about it, In *Cognitive strategy research: From basic research to educational application,* eds. C. B. McCormick, G. Miller, and M. Pressley, 133–154. New York: Springer-Verlag.

Duke, N. K., and P. D. Pearson. 2002. Effective practice for developing reading comprehension. In *What research has to say about reading instruction, 3rd edition,* eds. A. E. Farstrup and S. J. Samuels, 205–242. Newark, DE: International Reading Association.

Earl, L. M. 2003. *Assessment as learning: Using classroom assessment to maximize student learning.* Thousand Oaks, CA: Corwin Press.

Flavell, J. H. 1977. *Cognitive development.* Englewood Cliffs, NJ: Prentice-Hall.

Fountas, I. C., and G. S. Pinnell. 1996. *Guided reading: Good first teaching for all children.* Portsmouth, NH: Heinemann.

Frayer, D. A., W. D. Frederick, and J. J. Klausmeier. 1969. A schema for testing the level of concept mastery. *Working Paper No. 16.* Madison, WI: Wisconsin Research and Development Center for Cognitive Learning.

Gardner, H. 1983. *Frames of mind: The theory of multiple intelligences, 2nd ed.* New York: Basic Books.

Goldman, S. R., and J. A. Rakestraw, Jr. 2000. Structural aspects of constructing meaning from text. In *Handbook of reading research, Volume III*, eds. M. L. Kamil, P. B. Mosenthal, P. D. Pearson, and R. Barr, 311-335. Mahwah, NJ: Lawrence Erlbaum Associates, Publishers.

Griffith, P.L. and J. Ruan. 2005. What is metacognition and what should be its role in literacy instruction? In *Metacognition in literacy learning: Theory, assessment, instruction, and professional development.* eds. S. Israel, C.C. Block, K. Bauserman, and K. Kinnucan-Welsch, 16. Mahwah, NJ: Lawrence Erlbaum Associates.

Harvey, S., and A. Goudvis. 2000. *Strategies that work: Teaching comprehension for understanding and engagement.* York, ME: Stenhouse Publishers.

Heacox, D. 2002. *Differentiating instruction in the regular classroom: How to reach and teach all learners, Grades 3—12.* Minneapolis, MN: Free Spirit Publishing.

Herman, P.A., and C.R. Weaver. 1998. *Contextual strategies for learning word meanings: Middle grade students look in and look around.* Paper presented at the Annual Meeting of the National Reading Conference. Tucson, AZ.

Holdaway, D. 1979. *The foundations of literacy.* Sydney, Australia: Ashton Scholastic.

Hoyt, L. 1999. *Revisit, reflect, retell.* Portsmouth, NH: Heinemann.

Hoyt, L. 2002. *Making it real: Strategies for success with informational texts.* Portsmouth, NH: Heinemann.

Jensen, E. P. 2000. *Brain-based learning: The new science of teaching and training.* San Diego, CA: The Brain Store.

Jensen, E. P. 2001. *Arts with the brain in mind.* Alexandria, VA: Association for Supervision and Curriculum Development.

Jensen, E. P., and G. Johnson. 1994. *The learning brain.* San Diego, CA: The Brain Store.

Keene, E. O., and S. Zimmermann. 1997. *Mosaic of thought: Teaching comprehension in a reader's workshop.* Portsmouth, NH: Heinemann.

Kovalik, S. J., and K. D. Olsen. 2001. *Exceeding expectations: A user's guide to implementing brain research in the classroom.* Black Diamond, WA: Books for Educators, Inc.

Littky, D. and S. Grabelle. 2004. *The big picture: Education is everyone's business.* Alexandria, VA: Association for Supervision & Curriculum Development.

Long, S. A., P. N. Winograd, and C. A. Bridges. 1989. The effects of reader and text characteristics on reports of imagery during and after reading. *Reading Research Quarterly* 19: 353–372.

Lyons, C. 2003. *Teaching struggling readers: How to use brain-based research to maximize learning.* Portsmouth, NH: Heinemann.

Macceca, S. 2007. *Reading strategies for social studies.* Huntington Beach, CA: Shell Education.

Marzano, R. J. 2007. *The art and science of teaching: A comprehensive framework for effective instruction.* Alexandria, VA: Association for Supervision & Curriculum Development.

Marzano, R. J., D. J. Pickering, and J. E. Pollock. 2001. *Classroom instruction that works: Research-based strategies for increasing student achievement.* Alexandria, VA: Association for Supervision and Curriculum Development.

McGee, M. G., and D. W. Wilson. 1984. *Psychology: Science and education.* New York: West.

Moore, D. W., and S. A. Moore. 1986. Possible sentences. In *Reading in the content areas: Improving classroom instruction, 2nd edition*, eds. E.K. Dishner, T. W. Bean, J. E. Readence, and D. W. Moore. Dubuque, IA: Kendall/Hunt.

Ogle, D. M. 1986. K-W-L: A teaching model that develops active reading of expository text. *The Reading Teacher* 39: 564–570.

Palincsar, A. S., and A. L. Brown. 1985. Reciprocal teaching: Activities to promote reading with your mind. In *Thinking and concept development: Strategies for the classroom*, eds. T. L. Harris and E. J. Cooper. New York: The College Board.

Pearson, P.D. and L. Fielding. 1991. Comprehension instruction. In *Handbook of reading research, Volume Two*, eds. R. Barr, M. L. Kamil, P. Mosenthal, and P.D. Pearson, 815–860. White Plains, NY: Longman.

Pearson, P. D., and M. C. Gallager. 1983. The instruction of reading comprehension. *Contemporary Educational Psychology* 8: 317–44.

Perkins, D. 1995. *Smart schools: Better thinking and learning for every child*. New York: Free Press.

Prado, L. S. 2004. What every teacher needs to know about comprehension. *The Reading Teacher* 58 (3), 272–280.

Pressley, M. 2002a. Metacognition and self-regulated comprehension. In *What research has to say about reading instruction, 3rd ed*, ed. A. E. Farstrup and S. J. Samuels, 291–309. Newark, DE: International Reading Association.

Pressley, M. 2002b. *Reading instruction that works: The case for balanced teaching, 2nd ed.* New York: The Guilford Press.

Pressley, M. 2005. Final reflections: Metacognition in literacy learning: Then, now, and in the future. In *Metacognition in literacy learning: Theory, assessment, instruction, and professional development*, eds. S.E. Israel, C. C. Block, K. L. Bauserman, and K. Kinnucan-Welsch, 391–411. Mahwah. NJ: Lawrence Erlbaum Associates, Publishers.

Rasinski, T., and N. Padak. 2004. *Effective reading strategies, 3rd ed.* Upper Saddle River, NJ: Pearson/Merrill Prentice-Hall.

Rasinski, T., N. Padak, R. M. Newton, and E. Newton. 2008. *Greek and Latin roots: Keys to building vocabulary.* Huntington Beach, CA: Shell Education.

Rosenblatt, L. 1978. *The reader, the text, the poem: The transactional theory of literacy work.* Carbondale, IL: Southern Illinois University Press.

Routman, R. 2003. *Reading essentials.* Portsmouth, NH: Heinemann.

Ryder, R. J., and M. F. Graves. 2003. *Reading and learning in content areas, 3rd ed.* New York: John Wiley and Sons, Inc.

Sadoski, M. 1983. An exploratory study of the relationship between reported imagery and the comprehension and recall of a story. *Reading Research Quarterly* 19 (1): 110–123.

Short, K. G., J. C. Harste, and C. Burke. 1996. *Creating classrooms for authors and inquirers.* Portsmouth, NH: Heinemann.

Spencer, B. H. 2003. Text maps: Helping students navigate informational texts. *The Reading Teacher* 56 (8): 752–756.

Sprenger, M. 1999. *Learning and memory: The brain in action.* Alexandria, VA: Association for Supervision & Curriculum Development.

Stauffer, R. 1980. *The language experience approach to the teaching of reading, 2nd ed.* New York: Harper and Row.

Stead, T. 2005. *Reality checks: Teaching reading comprehension with nonfiction, K-5.* Portland, MA: Stenhouse Publishers, 75.

Stone, M.L. 2002. *Giant pandas: Early bird nature book.* Minneapolis, MN: Lerner Publications.

Sutton, R. 1995. *Assessment for learning.* Salford, UK: RS Publications.

Taba, H. 1967. *Teacher's handbook for elementary social studies.* Palo Alto, CA: Addison-Wesley.

Tate, M. 2003. *Worksheets don't grow dendrites: 20 instructional strategies that engage the brain.* Thousand Oaks, CA: Corwin Press.

Tennyson, A. L. 1842. *Ulysses.* I.6. line 13. Cited in *The Oxford University Press Dictionary of Quotations, second edition.* 1985. ed. B. Darwin, 540. New York: Crescent Books.

Tharp, R. G., and R. Gallimore. 1988. *Rousing minds to life: Teaching, learning, and schooling in social context.* New York: Cambridge University Press.

Tomlinson, C. A. 2001. *How to differentiate instruction in mixed-ability classrooms, 2nd ed.* Alexandria, VA: Association for Supervision & Curriculum Development.

Villaume, S. K., and Brabham, E. G. 2002. Comprehension instruction: Beyond strategies. *The Reading Teacher* 55 (7): 672-675.

Vygotsky, L. S. 1962 (original published in 1934). *Thought and language.* Cambridge, MA: MIT Press.

Wilhelm, J. D. 2001. *Improving comprehension with think-aloud strategies: Modeling what good readers do.* New York: Scholastic.

————2004. *Reading is seeing: Learning to visualize scenes, characters, ideas, and text worlds to improve comprehension and reflective reading.* New York: Scholastic.

Wolf, M. 2007. *Proust and the squid: The story and science of the reading brain.* New York: Harper/Collins.

Wolfe, P. 2001. *Brain matters: Translating research into classroom practice.* Alexandria, VA: Association for Supervision & Curriculum Development .

Wood, D., J. C. Bruner, and G. Ross. 1976. The role of tutoring in problem solving. *Journal of Child Psychology and Psychiatry* 17: 89-100.

Zimmermann, S., and C. Hutchins. 2003. *7 keys to comprehension: How to help your kids read it and get it.* New York: Three Rivers Press.

Instructional Resources and Children's Literature

Armour, C. 2004. *Tornadoes and hurricanes. Time for kids. Nonfiction readers. Early fluent level.* Huntington Beach, CA: Teacher Created Materials, Inc.

————2004. *Volcanoes. Time for kids. Nonfiction readers. Early fluent level.* Huntington Beach, CA: Teacher Created Materials, Inc.

Day, A. 1997. *Good dog, Carl.* New York: Aladdin.

Lockyer, J. 2009. Life in the abyss zone. *Life in the ocean layers. Math readers—measurement.* Huntington Beach, CA: Teacher Created Materials, Inc.

Mulhall, J. K. 2005. *Causes of the Revolution. Primary source readers for social studies.* Huntington Beach, CA: Teacher Created Materials, Inc.

Noonan, D. 2009. *Natural disasters. Mathematics readers—estimating.* Huntington Beach, CA: Teacher Created Materials, Inc.

Parker, C. 2009. *Abraham Lincoln. Primary source readers for social studies.* Huntington Beach, CA: Teacher Created Materials, Inc.

Rice, D. H. 2003. *Water. Time for kids. Nonfiction readers. Emergent level.* Huntington Beach, CA: Teacher Created Materials, Inc.

————2003. *Workers. Time for kids. Nonfiction readers. Emergent level.* Huntington Beach, CA: Teacher Created Materials, Inc.

Rice, D. M. 2004. *A visit to an automobile factory. Nonfiction readers. Early fluent level.* Huntington Beach, CA: Teacher Created Materials, Inc.

Rice, William B. 2009. *Leveled text for science: Earth and space science.* Huntington Beach, CA: Shell Education.

————2004. *A visit to a publisher. Time for kids. Nonfiction readers. Early fluent level.* Huntington Beach, CA: Teacher Created Materials, Inc.

Rice, William B. 2007. *The world of rocks and minerals.* Huntington Beach, CA: Teacher Created Materials, Inc.

Spielman, M. 2004. How is chocolate made? *All about chocolate. Time for kids. Nonfiction readers. Early fluent level.* Huntington Beach, CA: Teacher Created Materials, Inc.

Stone, M. L. 2002. *Giant pandas: Early bird nature book.* Minneapolis, MN: Lerner Publications.

Teacher resource CD in *Primary source readers: Expanding and preserving the Union.* Huntington Beach, CA: Teacher Created Materials, Inc.

Time For Kids. 2008. Cell phone agreement. *Exploring nonfiction. Language arts, level 6.* Huntington Beach, CA: Teacher Created Materials, Inc.

————2008. A big chunk of ice. *Exploring nonfiction. Science, level 3.* Huntington Beach, CA: Teacher Created Materials, Inc.

———— 2003. *Pandas. Nonfiction readers. Early fluent level.* Huntington Beach, CA: Teacher Created Materials, Inc.

————2008. A killer quake in Asia. *Exploring nonfiction. Science, level 4.* Huntington Beach, CA: Teacher Created Materials, Inc.

————2008. Adaptation in living things. *Exploring nonfiction. Science, level 5.* Huntington Beach, CA: Teacher Created Materials, Inc.

————2008. A trip to the hospital. *Exploring nonfiction. Social studies, level 1.* Huntington Beach, CA: Teacher Created Materials, Inc.

Weir, J. 2007. States of matter. *Inside the world of matter. Physical science readers.* Huntington Beach, CA: Teacher Created Materials, Inc.

Wiesner, D. 1991. *Tuesday.* New York: Clarion Books.

Zamosky, L. 2007. *Fishers then and now. My community then and now. Primary source readers.* Huntington Beach, CA: Teacher Created Materials, Inc.